The British Ethical Societies

The British Ethical Societies

I. D. MacKillop

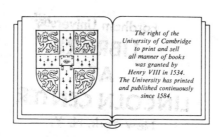

The right of the
University of Cambridge
to print and sell
all manner of books
was granted by
Henry VIII in 1534.
The University has printed
and published continuously
since 1584.

Cambridge University Press

Cambridge

London   New York   New Rochelle

Melbourne   Sydney

Published by the Press Syndicate of the University of Cambridge
The Pitt Building, Trumpington Street, Cambridge CB2 1RP
32 East 57th Street, New York, NY 10022, USA
10 Stamford Road, Oakleigh, Melbourne 3166, Australia

First published 1986

Printed in Great Britain at
the University Press, Cambridge

British Library cataloguing in publication data
MacKillop, I. D.
The British ethical societies.
1. Vice control − Great Britain − History − 19th century
2. Vice control − Great Britain − History − 20th century
3. Great Britain − moral conditions
I. Title
170   HN400.M6

Library of Congress cataloguing in publication data
MacKillop, I. D. (Ian Duncan)
The British ethical societies.
Bibliography; p.
Includes index.
1. Ethics, English − History. 2. Ethics, English − Societies, etc.
− History. I. Title.
BJ602.M33   1986   170'.6'041   85-10978

ISBN 0 521 26672 6

GG

Contents

Preface

The origin of *The British Ethical Societies* goes back to the chance purchase of a collection of books in a south London furniture auction. They had belonged to an author and former London County Council inspector of schools, Frank H. Hayward (1872–1954). The tea-chests contained an annotated set of his own works (twenty-nine in all). An interest in Hayward's books led me back to the history of moral education in Britain and of relations between social class and the teaching profession, and thence to the societies which flourished at the turn of the century and were preoccupied with these things and many others. Frank H. Hayward did not, however, play a direct part in the life of the British ethical societies, and so with great regret I excluded him from this book. I shall be returning elsewhere to pay tribute to the career which disappointed him.

There are other exclusions of which I am acutely aware. Two major figures are neglected, F. H. Bradley and J. A. Hobson. I know that others are better qualified to protect their interests, so it is perhaps enough that I have indicated that the first was continuously inspiring to the Idealist wing of the ethical movement, and that the second was active through a long life in several of its groups. There are several lesser figures to whom I would have liked to give some or greater presence, notably Mrs. Stephen Winkworth and Joseph McCabe. There are several regions, in my view adjacent to the movement, which go uncharted in this book: the largest is the history of organised British humanism and the smallest, in its degree of specialisation, is the history of the celebrated chamber music concerts at South Place Ethical Society. As to the ethical societies themselves, I have concentrated on three major groups in the metropolis, at the expense of provincial societies, for the sake of clarity, and in order to make a modest contribution to the history of London.

This book itself will have to show whether its contents legitimise the omissions. Its aim is to define the 'unformulated content' of the ethical movement, its 'active social conscience, always in contact with "progressive" social action', to quote phrases by Harold J. Blackham, from a review in *The Ethical Record* (April 1968), used to characterise what a study of ethicism should aim for. Especially, I have tried to show what individuals were like.

As to the individuals who have helped me, I would like to specify the following who looked things up or shared their expertise with me: Harold J. Blackham, Susan Budd, John Burrows, Peter Cadogan, John D'Entremont, Jeff Fiedorowicz, Kathleen Flynn, Sir Gilbert and Lady Virginia Flemming, Kenneth Furness, Sabine Hotho, David Joseph, Alan J. Lee, Ray Lovecy, David E. Muspratt, Athene Seyler (Hannan), Gillian Tindall, and Al and Martha Vogeler. I would also like to thank Sebastian Gardner and the staff of Cambridge University Press who provided inestimable help; and also Mrs Iris Walkland, who helped with the index.

I wish to thank the universities of Birmingham and Newcastle for allowing me to reproduce material in their care and especially the manuscript librarians of these universities, and the librarian of the Greater London History Library. I am indebted to the Research Fund Committee of Sheffield University.

The British Ethical Societies would not have been started without the example of two graduates of Downing College, Cambridge: Emeritus Professor W. H. G. Armytage and Morris Shapira. My greatest debts are to my mother, Mrs D. E. MacKillop, who unstintingly supported my research in London, and to my wife, Jane Rawlingson MacKillop, who has blessed me for a decade with her professional knowledge of what writing is.

Ian Duncan MacKillop

Prologue

On 8 July 1899 a paragraph appeared in a modest London weekly called
The Ethical World:

That Detestable Term – Ethicist

We believe that Mr. Frederic Harrison may claim the honour and responsibility
of the parentage of the word *ethicist*. He is its father. He did not mean to describe
only members of Ethical Societies, but all persons whose supreme interest is in
ethical truth as distinct from metaphysical theory about it. But, although the term
applies to others, it will inevitably be attached foremost to members of Ethical
Societies as a convenient label. Especially the unsympathetic critics will delight
in dubbing us with such an ugly, lisping, hissing combination of syllables. In
America the members of Ethical Societies have escaped without a label, although
in Philadelphia a member, we believe, is sometimes called – humorously, we
hope – an 'ethic'. In England the phrase, 'an ethical', was becoming somewhat in
vogue among us, until Mr. Harrison – by the weight, no doubt, of his literary
pre-eminence – introduced *ethicist*.

The paragraph was undoubtedly written by the editor of the paper, Stanton Coit, who (we shall see) was responsible for the foundation of
ethical societies in Britain. So it was well informed, more so than the
following paragraph which is nonetheless worth attention. It is taken
from a novel, *The Legends of Smokeover* (1921), by a Unitarian writer,
L. P. Jacks. Jacks describes a provincial English club, supposedly a
branch of 'The Society of Ethical Culture'.

In one of the local directories it appeared under the head of 'Places of Worship';
in another under the head of 'Clubs and Societies'. The members of the Branch
were divided among themselves as to which of the two was the correct caption for
their 'movement'; but the discussion of the matter had proved so acrimonious and
absorbed so much of the intellectual energy needed for greater things, that finally
the question was dropped by common consent and the two directories left to have
it their own way. It was a peculiarity of the Ethical Society, at least of its
Smokeover Branch, that members could never agree as to whether their cult was
'a religion' or something else. The Smokeover Ethical Society was active and
enlightened; but it was small, and obstinately refused to grow larger. A Society
more up-to-date in the programme it offered the public you could not imagine;
the last thing out in science, politics, philosophy and social reform was always its
theme. The members were the most excellent people, with a leaning towards the
iconoclastic side; several professors of the local university were among them;

1

there was the headmistress of a leading school; the Warden of a Women's Settlement; a radical lawyer; a dentist; a banker's clerk; a male designer of women's frocks; several spiritualists; two labour agitators; three or four argumentative working men; and last, but not least, a beaming champion of the Simple Life, who lived in a caravan, and nourished himself on crushed oats which he ate out of a nose-bag, like a horse, thereby avoiding the use of crockery. His name was Whistlefield.

Purge this passage of its prejudices (including a tacit 'Pshaw!' following the 'male designer') and it remains a fairly truthful account of at least the appearance of the ethical societies which opened doors in Britain predominantly for two decades from 1890. Jacks was not wrong to point up uncertainty of purpose in the societies but wrong to satirise it, because lack of definition was what many ethicists valued: the clubs gave them space; often, advantageously, they were *un*societies.

If the ethicists could be excused for being uncertain in their aims, so can Jacks for making some mistakes about the appearance of the societies. There was never, for instance, *the* Ethical Society with *branches*, nor was there in Britain a Society *for* Ethical Culture. Nor was there even a London organisation called the 'Ethical Culture Society', as T. S. Eliot would have it in 'Second Thoughts on Humanism', written in 1929, when there had been for years an established Ethical Church in Bayswater. Whatever the societies were called, Jacks and Eliot could not be expected to approve of them. A. J. P. Taylor, on the other hand, was much in sympathy with some ethicist habits of mind, yet still refers to J. A. Hobson's life-long affiliation to 'South Place Ethical Church' in *The Trouble Makers: Dissent over Foreign Policy, 1792–1939* (1957), written twenty-five years after South Place Ethical Society moved into its custom-built Conway Hall, one of the best known public meeting-halls in London. There must have been more than one member who winced at having the society called a church.[1]

British ethicists were not the same as American Ethical Culturalists; nor were they all like each other. We shall hear them and see how they differed from each other in the coming chapters.

Chapter 1

Ethical Epoch

The real and the good, 1876–1903

There was a time when the word 'ethics' possessed popular resonance. In the late nineteenth century it could appear on title-pages or advertisements as intelligibly and invitingly as 'ecology' in the 1970s. The heyday of the word can be dated to several events in the 1870s. In 1874 Henry Sidgwick published *The Methods of Ethics* in which utilitarianism was taken to a new level of sophistication. In 1876 F. H. Bradley's elegant attack on utilitarianism, *Ethical Studies*, was published. Just over a year later T. H. Green delivered in Oxford the lectures which were to be posthumously published as *Prolegomena to Ethics* (1883). In 1876 the first British journal of philosophy commenced publication, that is, *Mind: A Quarterly Review of Psychology and Philosophy*. It was in the October 1903 issue of *Mind* that an article appeared which proved to be a cold chisel into the masonry of the ethical epoch, G. E. Moore's 'The Refutation of Idealism'. Moore had graduated into the epoch from Cambridge, where he wrote a fellowship dissertation on Kant (an almost inevitable choice) between 1896 and 1898. In the winter of 1898 he lectured for one of the ethical societies, then known as the London School of Ethics and Social Philosophy. He worked under the ethicist J. S. Mackenzie on the review section of the *International Journal of Ethics* while he wrote his 'Refutation' and in 1903 published the epoch-breaking *Principia Ethica* which showed to many the end of an era. It delighted, for example, Lytton Strachey for whom it slammed the door on 'that indiscriminate heap of shattered rubbish among which one spies the utterly mangled remains of Aristotle, Jesus, Mr. Bradley, Kant, Herbert Spencer, Sidgwick and McTaggart! Plato seems the only person who comes out tolerably well. Poor Mill has, simply, gone.' Moore enabled Strachey to relegate to history the sombre and eminent Victorian debaters, among which he was perhaps right to include Christ and Plato, the first having been cast into a contemporary mould by J. R. Seeley in *Ecce Homo* (1865), and the second captured in Balliol by the translations of Benjamin Jowett (*Dialogues*, 1871 and *Republic*, 1888).

Merely in its Latin (and Newtonian) title Moore distinguished his

Principia Ethica from the sober volumes produced under the imprint of Bloomsbury progressive, William Swan Sonnenschein, whose 'Ethical Library' included Sidgwick's *Practical Ethics*, Leslie Stephen's *Social Rights and Duties* and Sophia Bryant's *The Teaching of Morality in the Family and the School*. Moore offered an exhilaratingly fresh view of the moral life. Strachey reacted frivolously, in a letter to Leonard Woolf, about the mental baggage that could be discarded; one of his near-contemporaries, Hugh Dalton, later to be the Labour politician, express-ed more clearly what was felt to be the gain. At Cambridge from 1907 to 1910, 'I cared', he remembered, 'much more about what was good than what was real.'[1]

Moore separated the 'good' from the 'real', or from the 'real' as it had formerly been understood. It was the way he kept 'goodness' close to another kind of 'reality' which made him attractive to Dalton, Strachey and many others. He dissociated a sense of the good from a sense of authority, separating 'is' from 'ought', for which he became known as a casuist to the seniors of the epoch, like J. S. Mackenzie. In 1883 Macken-zie published a *Manual of Ethics*, which became required reading in several ethical societies. When he revised it in 1929 he looked around in dismay at a world seemingly conquered by Moore in which it appeared that 'the object of Ethics is to provide us with a complete system of Casuistry'. For Mackenzie a genuine problem of conscience was not a puzzle over how *exemption* could be granted from a moral law. It was one in which 'we must fall back upon the supreme commandment, and ask ourselves: Is the course that we think we are pursuing the one that is most conducive to the realisation of the rule of reason in the world and of all the values that that rule implies?' Moore, on the other side, set a wedge bet-ween a person's consciousness of right and wrong and the attitudes assembled outside the person towards what is thought to be right and wrong. Whatever right or wrong may mean, 'it is not identical with any assertion whatever about either the feelings or the thoughts of *men*'. 'To predicate of an action that it is right or wrong is to predicate of it something quite different from the mere fact that any man or set of men have any particular feeling, or opinion, about it.' Rightness can therefore exist apart from the feelings and opinions that other people have about it, and apart, as well, from the exercise of the will of others in imperative or prohibitive ways. Moore rejects the idea of right as indistinguishable from ought, or as an order from some thing or body (most obviously, from God), or even as an order from a 'faculty' within a human being (that is, from *part* of a person rather than from an actual man or woman). Equally he rejects right as an order from an abstract source, which may be called 'Reason', or one called 'The Practical Reason', or one called

4

Ethical Epoch

'The Pure Will', or one called 'The Universal Will', or one called 'The True Self'. Or one called, in Mackenzie's terminology, 'the supreme commandment'. These are the authorities of the ethical epoch, Kantian, Comtian, or Arnoldian, coolly observed by Moore. He thinks it unlikely that any such commanding voices really exist, 'neither a God, nor any being such as philosophers have called by the names I have mentioned'. What is interesting is less Moore's agnosticism than how little he believed he was *obliged* to say about it (enacting, as it were, his position). He claims that he is not required to justify his doubts about the existence of the famous authorities: all he is after is consolidation of the view that 'ought' means something different from, and more than, the recognised presence of an exercised coercive force. In the ethical epoch it was not so easy to pass by the existence of God, or cut the cord to a sustaining ethical placenta.[2]

In the ethical epoch the 'names' (like the Reason or the True Self) referred to voices which were commanding because they were real. This is illustrated in T. H. Green's *Prolegomena to Ethics* (1883) at the point at which the genuine problem of conscience is discussed (as opposed to 'a conceit which it is pleasant to air'). Towards the end of his course of lectures Green considered how and when a theory of good can be relevant to daily practical life, attempting at the same time to distinguish the rôle of the philosopher from that of the preacher. He believed that it was no part of the work of a philosopher to excuse people from the pressure of external commandments or what he calls 'imponents' (things imposed) of duty. These commandments, he argues, are not *merely* external to a person: their authority is the same as 'the individual's presentation to himself of a true good, at once his own and the good of others, which it is his business to pursue'. When this good is pursued, the person is looking to an end, that is not imposed upon him, but 'in which he is interested on his own account'. Or he may have been *got* interested in it by training, growth of instinct, or philosophy, so discovering what the felt 'imponential' authority means (to employ Green's home-made adjective). Such an authority may be much less vague than Moore's scorned airy ethical somethings or 'names': it may be the authority of a Church, or that of scripture, or that of the state. For Green the genuine problem of conscience is not that which arises against these authorities and the wishes and needs of the individual person; it is that which arises *among* such authorities when the authorities are acknowledged, understood and (in modern terms) internalised. As an example Green considers the conflict between laws of family and state epitomised in the story of Antigone. More vividly, he adduces the contemporary problem of the soldier who is ordered to put down a revolutionary rising which he nonetheless believes

5

to be for the cause of 'God and the People'. Green's treatment of this issue shows how the 'good' and the 'real' cannot be separated:

If [a] private opinion is more than a conceit which it is pleasant to air; if it is a source of really conscientious opposition to an authority which equally appeals to the conscience; if, in other words, it is an expression which the ideal of human good gives to itself in the mind of the man who entertains it; then it too rests on the basis of social authority. *No individual can make a conscience for himself.* He always needs a society to make it for him. A conscientious 'heresy', religious or political, always represents some gradually maturing conviction as to the social good, already implicitly involved in the ideas on which the accepted rules of conduct rest, though it may conflict with the formulae in which those ideas have been authoritatively expressed, and may lead to the overthrow of institutions which have previously contributed to their realisation. (My italics.)

Here 'conscience', 'ideal' and 'authority' are stations on a line which leads to 'society'. The real is in society, or in the 'gradually maturing convictions' of numerous people. A conscientious objection is only worthy of the name when the objector is speaking on behalf of such convictions, even if they be inarticulate ones. One function of the philosopher (as opposed to the preacher) is to show people to the places in which the maturing process is fermenting.

The function of the philosopher was described in fairly similar terms by Henry Sidgwick in a presidential address to the London Ethical Society. He should 'assist in constructing a Theory or Science of Right, which, starting with the reality and validity of moral distinctions, shall explain their mental and social origin, and connect them in a logical system of thought'. Sidgwick was not an affable speaker. He promised no easy reading to the members of this society, a warning which illustrates another aspect of the ethical epoch. Even if the members agreed with his definition of the work of a philosopher, it could probably be done only 'by experts – *i.e.* by persons who have gone through a thorough training in psychology, sociology, and logic – in short, philosophers', not by members of an ethical society, 'thoughtful persons' though they may be. Sidgwick delivered this address on 23 April 1893 and said what Carlyle, Arnold or Mill would have never done – that serious enquiry had to be carried out by *experts*, even though these experts should still study 'with reverent and patient care the Morality of Common Sense'. Sidgwick's candour about the difficulty of philosophy showed that the subject had become professionalised, which was even illustrated by the fact that his paper could be published six months later in *The International Journal of Ethics*, founded only in 1890 and run with strong ethicist and ethical culturalist affiliations.

A growth of professionalism in philosophy and consciousness of a need for professionalism were features of the ethical epoch. But the issues of the epoch were capable of being popular, even glamorous, as is illustrated in material of a coarser kind than the reflections of Green and Sidgwick. Mrs. Mary Ward's novel *Robert Elsmere* (1888), both in what it is and what it says, illustrates some of the conditions (even geographical ones) which brought people to the platforms and benches of ethical societies. It also tells us something about ethicists because it was a book which on occasion they wanted to deride.[3]

Views from Westminster Bridge and Russell Square

Problems of conscience were all the rage in the spring of 1888:

The excitement among the reading public was very great. It penetrated even to the streets, for one of us overheard a panting lady, hugging a copy of the *Nineteenth Century*, saying to her companion as she fought her way into an omnibus, 'Oh, my dear, have you read Weg on Bobbie?'

That is, W. E. Gladstone on the hero of Mrs. Ward's *Robert Elsmere*, published on 24 February 1888, about which the Grand Old Man had contributed an essay to the May issue of *The Nineteenth Century*. (The spy on the omnibus was one of Mrs. Ward's daughters.) *Robert Elsmere* illustrates some of the circumstances in which ethical societies were started in what it shows (as a work of history), and what it is (as an historical document). One moment in 'Bobbie's' story is particularly significant. Although it is not dated in the novel it is easy to ascribe it to year and season.

Not long before Christmas of 1883 Robert paused in Parliament Square, arrested by an exceptionally beautiful sunset. He stood in solemn mood, by the statue of Sir Robert Peel, remembering that a German friend had once told him he thought the Houses of Parliament were more symbolically thrilling than the Roman Forum. He said that the British, alone, had freedom in the true sense, and religion, and that 'I would give a year of life to know what you have made of your freedom and your religion two hundred years hence.' Musing on this, Robert set off home for Bloomsbury where he had recently settled with his family. At Westminster Bridge he paused to look down river to the smoke-shrouds of dockland. There, he thought, was the challenge to the freedom and democracy of a transitional England. He strolled along the Embankment, a river walk not more than ten years old, and branched off at the even more recently built Northumberland Avenue, near which was excavation in progress for the underground railway which would create rapid transit from Westminster to the East End. The new thoroughfares, north to Bloomsbury and east to dockland, stimulated Robert's sense of mission. He was, like many Bloomsbury dwellers, an immigrant of sorts. Until lately he had been a Surrey clergyman: he resigned his living because he could not intellectually equate pulpit Christianity with his highly developed historical sense. He had formerly been taught at Oxford by T. H. Green who had impressed upon Robert a formula for daily living: be the king of your world for one half of the day and in the other half make yourself slave to something out of your world, in the life of thought, of man as a whole, of the universe. Green's injunctions and his personal example set many on to the path of public service − 'a stream of ex-pupils who carried with them the conviction that philosophy and in particular the philosophy they had learned at Oxford, was an important thing, and that their vocation was to put it into practice', as noted R. G. Collingwood; and the philosophy was not necessarily that of Green's Idealism. When Robert was still a clergyman his pastoral duties took him 'out of his world'. For the part of the world in which he was king he had History, which increasingly he related to modern England. In Final Schools he studied the decline of the Roman Empire, fascinated by the 'fierce incoherence' of its decay and by the presence of Rome as a backcloth to the beginnings of modern European civilisation in Gaul. When he looked east from Westminster the atheism of the massed working class made him imagine a new Gaul.

Robert Elsmere's rejection of conventional Anglicanism in the early 1880s was hastened by his contact with the local squire, a brilliant and aggressive sceptic. Squire Wendover was engaged on a comprehensive study of historical testimony, 'to get at the conditions, physical and mental, which govern the greater or lesser correspondence between human witness and the fact it reports'. His research overwhelmed Robert's orthodox view of the verbal inspiration of scripture. Desperately unhappy, he paid a visit back to Green in Oxford who tried to console him by saying that Robert's doubts were a kind of education by God Himself: 'The leading strings of the past are dropping from you: they are dropping from the world, not wantonly, or by chance, but in the providence of God. Learn the lesson of your own pain − learn to seek God, not in any single event of past history, but in your own soul, in the constant verifications of experience, in the life of Christian love.' Robert resigned the living and moved to London with this difficult conception to work on. In his own eyes he was still a Christian, but he found the familiar structure of Anglicanism an impediment to genuine faith, inhibiting (so he dramatised his predicament) as the decaying fabric of Rome had been during the early history of Europe. He wanted to propagate a new kind of Christianity. In London he found a way to do so, having made friends with a Cambridge man, Murray Edwardes, a Unitarian minister in Rotherhithe. Edwardes mustered a small Unitarian revival in this area, his congregation mostly having come on the rebound from a nearby Puseyite church, which, though passionately devoted to social good works, was losing its congregation to dissent and rewarded for its Romish excesses by being pelted with rotten eggs and dead cats. The more thoughful protesters attended Edwardes's chapel, which Robert used as a training ground for his own mission. He became close to dissenters for the first time, as well as Positivists, rationalists and secularists. He started his personal campaign as a result of a brush with militant atheists. Outside a working-man's club, a poster shouted –

Read FAITH AND FOOLS! Enormous Success!! Our COMIC LIFE OF CHRIST now nearly completed. Woodcut this week: TRANSFIGURATION.

Robert angrily took up the gauntlet and offered the club a lecture for Easter on the life of Christ. It was accepted and against the odds he received an ovation worthy of the best-seller that bore his name. He became a popular lecturer, even to the ungodly. His scholarship appealed to sceptics: he stood up to questioning from a watchmaker, Lestrange; he interested a pottery designer, MacDonald. The latter disliked the intuitionism of Reid and those who thought that 'a babby's got as mooch mind as Mr. Gladstone'. He approved of Robert's argument that centuries were necessary for men to learn a historical sense – which in the late nineteenth century was indispensable for an understanding of Christ. Robert explained or (in his expression) 'reconceived' the historical Christ as a spiritual leader, creating a demand for the kind of history which had formerly occupied one half of his day. A helper would hang up drawings of Nazareth, Robert using all his powers of story-telling to coax into life 'the majestic figure' of Christ in his natural background.

Robert's charisma impressed the prosperous serious-minded. He raised contributions for a community centre or 'settlement' for working people, by means of which he wanted to implant 'a fresh social bond', which would replace conflicts of egoism: the rich would devote themselves to the poor and the poor would 'bear with' the rich. Robert, unfortunately, did not live to see his plan bear fruit: he developed pulmonary consumption and the 'New Brotherhood' had to carry on without him.

Mrs. Ward's novel is faithful to contemporary trends in several ways. T. H. Green (as 'Mr. Grey') speaks many of his own lines. Commentators agree that Squire Wendover is a partial portrait of another Oxford figure, Mark Pattison. The East End clubs and missionaries are plausible. The New Brotherhood is a romanticised amalgam of St. Jude's and Toynbee Hall, both run by the Reverend Samuel Barnett, the latter named after Arnold Toynbee who died, partly from Elsmerean overwork, in March 1883. If Mrs. Ward's delineation of Robert is romantic, so were men like him. *Robert Elsmere* is an observant piece of semi-reportage, but it possesses two flaws which make the reader conscious that it is a historical document (when he should be under its spell); though the 'flaws' could simply be called features of consciousness in the period of the novel's composition, features which are part of the history in which ethical societies were founded. One flaw (or feature) relates to the theme of the book and the kind of Christian movement sponsored by Robert. The other relates to novel's characterisation and the novelist's attitude to the ungodly denizens of heretical London.

The theme of *Robert Elsmere* is Doubt and the rediscovery of Faith. In execution it shows Doubt poorly and the rediscovery of something other than Faith; but what it does show is so interesting that it is perhaps harsh to speak of a flaw in the handling of the theme. The novel shows that the overt purpose of a mission, such as Robert's, may conceal an inner purpose of greater vitality, which may or may not be recognised by the missionary himself. Robert's ostensible purpose is to propagate a new Christianity. In his East End lecture he told the working men that history is good, but religion better: which is meant to be the message of the novel. The novel may be described as reversing this formula: for its portrayal of religion is good (or quite good), but its portrayal of the historical sense, and how it can excite, is better. The novelist identifies more intensely with Robert the historian than with Robert the progressive Anglican. And this is not surprising when it is remembered that Mrs. Ward was a historian: in two of the years covered by the novel (1880–2) she contributed more than two hundred articles to the *Dictionary of Christian Biography*. Robert is an historian's hero.

In an obvious sense *Robert Elsmere* is about a conflict over Christian faith, but this conflict is seldom credible, either because Robert's peers do not test him sufficiently, or because he is already almost of their persuasion. This was recognised by Mrs. Ward's friend, Mandell Creighton, later Bishop of Peterborough and himself an historian, who wrote to her that he never believed Robert *was* a Christian. Structurally the central conflict of the novel is supposed to be the struggle, almost to the death of faith, between the youthful Anglican intellectual and the old sceptical Squire who melodramatically inhabits a mansion of historical and heretical treasures. On one occasion Robert warns the tempter to back off, declaring that a minister may not debate the reliability of the scriptures: 'I believe in an Incarnation, a Resurrection, a Revelation', he declares, staking out the regions forbidden to argument. But he did not stay so resolved and it was 'Bobbie's' consideration of the taboo that made the novel talked-of on the omnibus, his 'whole new picture' of divinity that was independent of miracle. But Robert's conversion was not really generated by Squire Wendover. The novelist keeps him physically away from the presence of the squire by skilful fictive devices, including stout declarations (like the one just quoted) which set up an illusion of distance between the two men. The reader soon realises, however, that they are of one mind. The minute the squire reveals the scale of his researches the historian in Robert responds and his reservations evaporate: intellectually he was always of the squire's party. He never stops believing that Christ is glorious, but his sense of this glory ultimately derives its warmth from an enthusiasm for history. His adoration of this Christ derives from his delight at having pushed back the stone of legend and found a human figure behind it. The concluding chapters of *Robert Elsmere* glory in the human Christ, but more winningly they glorify history, whether being researched at the level of the squire and progressive parson, taught in Sunday school or to adults in lectures with titles like 'The History of the Moral Life of Man'. As history fills the consciousness of the novelist, it emerges that the New Brotherhood is an educational mission rather than a spiritual one. (And that is what, in real life, it became, in the hall for residents, named after Mrs. Ward, which was founded on a crest of enthusiasm driven by *Robert Elsmere*: the warden of this settlement, Philip H. Wicksteed, was aware that his position was contradictory.)

The consequence of a spiritual discovery is often (always?) educational. Is it, then, fair to claim that Robert's mission was 'really' an educational rather than spiritual one? If Robert had existed as a live person the claim would be legitimate if it were argued that his spiritual discoveries were cued to and by secular discoveries and movements of a diffused kind. So a real Robert could have been taught about his Christ by the prevailing problems of what Mrs. Ward called 'this transitional England'. Turning from Robert to the novel, it is certainly legitimate to claim on literary critical grounds that it is really about education rather than religion. We are entitled to say that it shows evidence that history, education, and social sympathies were what Mrs. Ward clearly knew about, and that on religious experience she was at a loss. This was shown when, in audience with Gladstone and flattered by his essay in the *Nineteenth Century*, she tried to rally the old man into sprightly debate on miracle and the 'religious problem'. He opposed her reformism with an awesome urbanity: 'The great traditions are what attract me. I believe in a degeneracy of man, in the Fall − in *sin* − in the intensity and virulence of sin.' According to the shaken Mrs. Ward, he said this 'smiling'.[4]

If *Robert Elsmere* is a novel of education rather than a novel of doubt, the same may be said of the ethical societies which began to grow soon after it was written − which is not to say that ethicists liked it: they were especially aware of its second flaw, to which we now come.

The second flaw (or feature) of *Robert Elsmere* relates to the world out-

11

side the fiction in a way different from the first. It is a flaw of characterisation. Mrs. Ward peoples her East End with the right denominations, from Tractarian to Unitarian and on to atheist, but her portrayal tends to quaintness. Her heretics are solitaries, unsustained by peers, tradition, or ancestors. While she is undoubtedly curious about them, and sympathetic, she does not avoid condescension. In actuality the equivalents of Unitarian Murray Edwardes and his fellows would never have been so easily impressed by Robert. This weakness in the novel was caused by the author's distance from some of the material. It is an instructive one because it points to the great space between the official and unofficial intellectual classes (or between enlightened establishment and intelligentsia). It was this space which made ethicists foreigners in their own land. This fact was noticed by the sometime leader of South Place Religious (later Ethical) Society, Moncure Daniel Conway. In his autobiography he describes the gap between enlightened establishment and intelligentsia in terms of a time-lag, while assessing *Robert Elsmere*:

If ever there was a cockcrow over yesterday's sunrise, it was Mrs. Humphry Ward's *Robert Elsmere*. The plot is interesting enough, but even that sadly provincial; and as for the religious statements, with their air of paradox, they are the commonplaces of two generations before her romance was born.

Conway knew that heterodoxy had roots, traditions, and even its own establishment. Robert would have found in London of the 1880s more formidable figures than he encountered in fiction. Let us consider some of them: they were soon to be accompanied by ethicists.

Robert walked back from his Westminster meditation to the house in Bloomsbury in which Mrs. Ward herself lived from the summer of 1881, when she came up from Oxford to join her husband, Thomas Humphry Ward, who had settled into his post as leader-writer for *The Times*. *Robert Elsmere* was written from 1885 to January 1888. Mrs. Ward noticed enough of the metropolis to give her book colour; she had some personal contact with a slightly more elevated sector of the working class than that of Limehouse, having visited her father-in-law's parish in Finsbury. But her knowledge of London heterodoxy was limited, and she brought much of her material with her from Oxford (Green and Pattison), from her reading (Amiel) and from the Arnold family, especially Uncle Matthew, who in the 1870s she felt had been 'a Modernist long before his time' in *Literature and Dogma*, even though he was unsympathetic to Anglicans who 'went out', as the current phrase had it. While Mrs. Ward worked on her novel, in an improvised writing-room at the back of Number 61, Russell Square, the present site of the Hotel Russell, she was surrounded by people who were well and truly 'out'. (Unfortunately, acquaintance was delayed until the published novel became her calling-card.) To the west of the Square, in Gower Street, there was University College, a centre of heresy, of which J. R. Seeley was able to remark, apropos of his period there as professor of Latin from 1861, that 'I have lived for many years in the intimate society of people to whom Christianity in all its forms seemed as ridiculous as any religion professed by barbarians.' At University College there were thriving alternatives to Anglicanism, both in Seeley's time as professor and in Mrs. Ward's as author. Positivism could be found there, not in the form of the down-at-heel lawyer in *Robert Elsmere*, but represented by Edward S. Beesly, co-translator of Comte's *System of Positive Polity* (1875–7), known to *Punch* as 'Professor Beastly' for his courageous claim that all trade unions should not be judged as adversely as if they were the saw-grinders at the time of the Sheffield Outrages. Beesly followed Richard Congreve as president of the Positivist Society in 1868. There were two camps of Positivism in London, both near Russell Square. In Chapel Street, off Lamb's Conduit Street, there was the Positivist School, run by Congreve and later known as the Church of Humanity when he seceded from the 'official' Parisian Positivism of Pierre Lafitte. Those who remained loyal to it formed the second group, which established itself in Newton Hall at the bottom of Fetter Lane near its junction with Fleet Street; it was so called because it abutted a house purchased in 1710 by Sir Isaac Newton for the Royal Society, honourable heritage for a religion of science. This group was led by Frederic Harrison.

Still near the Square, Unitarianism flourished alongside Positivism. Besides being Positivist and professor of history, Beesly was also for a time warden of an unusual student residence, University Hall, to which he could repair from his neo-classic college by means of a footpath leading to the back entrance of this Hall on Gordon Square. It stands out today as one of the earliest pieces of British academic redbrick in the Tudor idiom, housing Dr. Williams's Library and the Royal Institute of Philosophy. This building was erected in 1848 to commemorate the Dissenters' Chapels Act, from which year it was inhabited by young dissenters studying for London degrees, receiving some tuition on the premises. From 1853 it had a second function, when the long-established Unitarian academy, Manchester New College, moved down from the north. Neither Hall nor College ever worked as well as the founders, wardens or principals wanted, but the building on Gordon Square was still a major metropolitan base for Unitarians, and provided a uniquely exploratory approach to religion for its students, as we shall see when we come to the career of J. H. Muirhead and the London Ethical Society (which incidentally was founded in the Hall). At University Hall the professors were definitely 'out'. 'The Church won't want you when you come out of that place', a young man was told by his schoolmaster, when he naively expressed an ambition to study there, and then go on to an Anglican living, having been inspired to modernism by Arnold's *Literature and Dogma*.

During this period, James Martineau was principal of Manchester New College: he retired in 1885. Formerly, when a teacher in the college, he had been minister at the Unitarian Little Portland Street chapel to the west of Gordon Square near the present site of Broadcasting House. There he was succeeded by Philip H. Wicksteed; and nearer to the Square there was, at Bedford Place chapel, Stopford Brooke who 'went out' in 1880 and who had a fashionable following. Brooke differed from Wicksteed in that he was sympathetic but not attached to Unitarianism. Nonetheless, it was his chapel which Martineau attended on Sundays, rather than Little Portland Street where he found too shocking Wicksteed's pulpit mixture of mystical Dantean theology, Henry Georgeite economics, and even Ibsen. Martineau still had on occasion to reprove Stopford Brooke for his all-enveloping conception of the Love of God. Considerably more advanced, there was South Place chapel, further east in Finsbury, originally Unitarian, though it was disowned in 1835 by the Unitarian Association, for not wholly doctrinal reasons, as we shall see in Chapter 2. In Mrs. Ward's early London years its minister was Moncure Conway, whom we have heard complaining of the 'provinciality' of *Robert Elsmere*. His position was not greatly different from that of the novel's Squire Wendover, whose wicked book, 'Idols of the Market-Place' at least resembles in its title Conway's *Idol and Ideals: With an Essay on Christianity* (1877), which concluded that if a tree is to be judged by its fruit then Christianity 'though not altogether evil, [is] preponderantly evil'.

Closer to the world of *Robert Elsmere*, there were those who attended the Working Men's College, situated in the early 1880s east of Russell Square in Great Ormond Street. The godless workers with whom Robert contended could be found to the west at the secular hall in Cleveland Street, running parallel to Tottenham Court Road on its far side. When Frederic Harrison tired of teaching at the Working Men's College ('parasites of the middle classes, not really working men . . . ordinary *literary* trifling'), he lectured at the Freethought Hall:

The delivery was rather an effort. The nauseous entourage of the 'low infidel hall' came full upon me, and one was made rather a part of a serio-comic entertainment in the introductory platform addresses in the large hall. But a class of twenty contained some excellent fellows quite of the right sort.

The distasteful trappings (music, choral singing, readings, facetiousness and solemnity from the chair) were common at public debates or lectures in the period – and when we later find them at ethicist meetings we must not mistake this behaviour for churchiness.

At its southern end Cleveland Street is crossed by Goodge Street and on the other side becomes Newman Street. There stood St. Andrew's Hall in which two lectures of great significance were given in January 1883. The speaker was Arnold Toynbee, a Londoner with a similar educational history to that of Robert Elsmere, having been a disciple of Green at Oxford. He had worked at St. Jude's with Samuel Barnett. He lectured critically on Henry George's theory of land nationalisation, following the London publication of his *Progress and Poverty* (1881). Toynbee was sick: he was to die some six weeks later, five months before his thirty-second birthday. In St. Andrew's Hall he spoke without notes, hurrying exhaustedly to a peroration to working men, expressing the emotional drive that possessed some of the first ethicists:

You have – I say it clearly and advisedly – you have to forgive, for we have wronged you; we have sinned against you grievously – not knowing always, but still we have sinned, and let us confess it; if you will but forgive us – nay, whether you will forgive us or not – we will serve you, we will devote our lives to your service, and we cannot do more.

Toynbee was commemorated in the naming of the university settlement in Whitechapel run by the Barnetts to initiate young people into a sense of this type of service. Toynbee Hall was designed in manorial style, with implications of a collegiate new start. In a very few years the mood at this Hall moved further towards socialism than would have been suspected from the change-of-heart reformism of Toynbee himself. In the late 1860s Barnett had been at the centre of the Charity Organisation Society (through which he met Henrietta), but once working at Toynbee Hall he began to support measures that dissociated the settlement from the basic doctrine of the C.O.S., that charity should be strictly controlled, lest the will of the needy be corrupted. Barnett became progressively less convinced that the needy were responsible for their condition, as he learned more of the powers of capital and landlordism. When, in 1886, he repudiated C.O.S. doctrine Beatrice Webb reported that a thrill ran round philanthropic London. 'I do not want many alterations in the law,' observed Barnett, with characteristic innocence, 'but I would like the best things made free.'

The growing political consciousness of settlement-attenders is illustrated in a more obscure novel than *Robert Elsmere*. In the following passage Angus, a settlement leader, thinks about his work in the context of the events leading up to the defeat of Gladstone's Home Rule Bill in June 1886:

The city might be ruined, but his clubs would do nothing to avert the danger; the slums where he was so well known were perhaps more dead since he came than before he came. So with fear and trembling one morning, when everyone read the political columns of the newspaper first, because there were storms in Parliament and a likelihood of a dissolution, he resolved that the time was come for the application of the great test of the value of his labours. The dissolution came, he put himself in communication with the Radical Committee and he began his 'stock-taking' work.

The test was to make the settlement committed to political action: 'There was to be less religion in sentiment and more religion in work.' Spiritual exhortations, whether from Angus himself or visiting Italian politicians, were to be discontinued under the new régime. 'We are to have a people's church, we are to be more robust in our thoughts and words: we are more in line with you socialists now.' The Pall Mall riot in February 1886 and 'Bloody Sunday' in November fuelled such convictions – which could be illustrated from countless sources, but the piece of reporting-in-fiction just quoted has a special interest because it is taken from an unpublished novel by the young embryo ethicist, J. Ramsay MacDonald.

Toynbee Hall was geographically furthest from the cluster of heterodox halls, chapels and colleges near Mrs. Ward's writing-room in Russell Square. Before her novel was finished it became more accessible to the concerned middle class, looking anxiously to outcast London in the East End. Only months after Barnett published his blueprint for a settlement in the *Nineteenth Century* it became possible to reach Whitechapel easily from Bloomsbury and the West End by means of a new underground railway. On 6 October 1884 the Inner Circle Line was completed, making access easy from Bloomsbury (served by Gower Street station) to Toynbee Hall (served by Aldgate East). The ethical movement began between Toynbee Hall and Bloomsbury. Societies were formed by those who were 'out', on the fringes of Positivism, Unitarianism and socialism. The idea of an ethical society appealed to several kinds of people who had settled in London: from places to people, and their arrivals in London, we shall now turn.[5]

Arrivals: Frederick James Gould and Harry Snell

The ethical movement was created (not quite coincidentally) by a group of non-Londoners who settled in the metropolis in the late 1880s. Their leader was Stanton Coit, though many, sooner or later, shook themselves free of his influence. His adventures will be traced in Chapters 2 and 4; in this section and the next we shall consider the early experience of four people who became prominent in the ethical societies.

F. J. Gould (1855–1938) and Harry Snell (1865–1944) were non-graduates in the quartet. Neither founded ethical societies, but they were always in demand on ethicist platforms, Gould from November 1889, when he helped with the East London Ethical Society, and Snell from 1898, when Coit offered him £150 per annum for three years to act as an ethicist lecturer and organiser. At the turn of the century both were especially concerned with campaigns for non-religious moral instruction in schools, through the ethicist Moral Instruction League, discussed in Chapter 5 on 'The Ethical Movement'. Both worked hard to educate themselves, and for both contact with Charles Bradlaugh was pivotal.

Frederick Gould's father had a regular trade as a London metal-worker, but he preferred to try to live off his musical talents in the opera chorus. At home he mended cheap jewellery, carpentered at the toy theatre which accompanied the family on theatrical tours, and flits from lodgings. He taught Frederick to sing so well that his mother was able to place him as a chorister at St. George's Chapel, Windsor, where he spent two years soaking up ecclesiastical glamour and an excellent knowledge of scripture. He sang at the wedding of Princess Helena to Prince Christian, remembering the Prince's Germanic 'I *vill*', the Queen's tiny crown and the jewelled turbans of the imperial guests. One wet, birdless dawn he sang 'Hark, hark, the lark!' on the east terrace for the birthday of a princess.

Harry Snell's childhood lacked this kind of magic, spent in the fields around the Trent in Nottinghamshire in a labourer's household. His mother was as resourceful as Gould's: the domestic compliment was that she could spread a pound of butter over the churchyard and have enough left to do both sides of the gravestones. From the age of eight Snell worked the fields, learning his numbers and alphabet at the village school in off-seasons; at ten he was a day-lad at a farm two miles from home, which meant scaring journeys on foot through the dusk when the Trent was in flood. When he was twelve the boy was hired as an indoor farm servant at Newark Michaelmas Fair. He took a similar post a year later at Hazelford Ferry and was able to save enough to get to Nottingham where he found work at a succession of taverns, mostly used by market-traders and gamblers (as well as whores).

From the age of twelve Gould lived away from home, but in comparative security. At Windsor a benign canon, Lord Wriothesley Russell, took a liking to the boy and installed him in his rectory at Chenies, near Rickmansworth in Hertfordshire, a rural backwater. There was no organ in the church: the local schoolmaster sounded the key for hymns from a pocket box of metal pipes. Gould stayed in Chenies for nine years, going from pupil to teacher in the church school. In spite of his secure material condition he was no stranger to mental agony. While Harry Snell was frightened by the brutal life of market-square hostelries, Frederick Gould had to contend with religious horrors. The kindly canon was nonetheless an evangelical of the strictest sort. He encouraged Frederick's sense of sin and the devout fury with which he devoured all the theology he could find. The adolescent particularly favoured works of eighteenth-century religiosity, such as James Hervey's *Meditations among the Tombs* (1745–7) which continued to retain currency among 'serious' Victorians, or earlier devotional works, such as those of the Puritan Stephen Charnock, from whom Gould never forgot this devastating morsel: 'What is this life but a wallowing in a sink, a converse in the dregs of the creation, in an earth polluted by the sin of man, wherein we every day behold fresh affronts to God and find motions in us dishonourable to ourselves?' Such, reflected Gould later, was the nourishment supplied to youth by the evangelical school of Charles Simeon, Bickersteth and Wilberforce in the age of Chartism, trade unions and (almost) Karl Marx.[6]

Harry Snell was more simply and tranquilly devout in his teens, the problems of want and work troubling him most. Before leaving the parental home he listened attentively each Sunday to Canon Hole, learning to believe in the literal truth of scripture words and a sense of faith as supplication. He believed that a Christian had to pray and pray until God relented and took sin upon Himself. Faith was thus both desperate and passive, almost a kind of spiritual nagging. It was not until Snell heard some heretical outdoor preachers in Nottingham (as so often with Unitarian connections) did he learn that faith need not be so expectant, that people could and should be effective in shaping their own destinies. It dawned on Snell that God could be 'honoured', by regarding oneself 'as in some infinitesimal degree, associated with God the Creator in the tremendous business of running the universe . . . I began half-unconsciously [sic] to think about religion as progressive in meaning and purpose, rather than as an unchangeable revelation of an age long past.' Strangely enough, this fresh idea of religion was confirmed by Snell's experience of the atheist Charles Bradlaugh, whom he heard at the Alhambra Music Hall in Nottingham in 1881. He thought Bradlaugh 'cyclonic', 'built on a bigger plan than any other man I have ever known'. Snell forthwith joined the local branch of the National Secular Society, to participate in the fight Bradlaugh was waging to be allowed to take his elected seat in Parliament without religious commitment. It was characteristic of the ethical epoch that contact with secularism led to a renewed interest in the Bible, 'as a precious record of a phase of human development'. Gould was equally impressed by Bradlaugh. He had heard him two years earlier in October 1879, when he first came to London, witnessing at first-hand Bradlaugh's efforts to claim a right to affirm instead of swear an oath on the Bible. He later watched Bradlaugh's attempts to enter the House in August 1881.

As a boy Snell got no further than thinking that people waited on God's mercy. From Bradlaugh the possibility was opened that God needed human beings as much as they needed Him. This discovery was exciting when a similar independence or progressiveness was seen expressed in the person of Bradlaugh. Both Snell and Gould began to sense what might be meant by progress, a feeling that they wished to incorporate into a personal philosophy and a career. There were plenty of barriers in their ways – including the 'Silas Marner Syndrome', betrayal by a formerly protective institution. Such betrayals occur so frequently in the biographies of those struggling for self-command in this period that it is tempting to conclude that they were an effective factor in the creation of ethical societies. Because other societies were so tyrannical, the ethical society had to be systematically pluralist.

Snell was betrayed after he became acquainted with members of the High Pavement Unitarian chapel which ran Sunday classes that provided him with the beginnings of his secondary education. Unfortunately word came through from the chapel authorities that he was not an acceptable visitor – for no reason he could discover other than that he had favoured Byron against Coleridge in formal debate with a chapel senior. He was declared unwelcome and fell into a period of unemployment, from which he was rescued by a friendly superintendent from the Sunday school who helped Snell into a clerical post with the Midland Institution for the Blind. He attended some classes at the local University College, and of course his secularist meetings. He began to take the step from radicalism to socialism, a grave one considering that his early sense of the progressive derived from Bradlaugh, who opposed socialism:

Only very slowly did I discard the hesitations and misgivings which the neo-Darwinians and Malthusian economists had implanted in my mind . . . It was only after I had made a careful study of the debates between Bradlaugh and Henry Mayers Hyndman.

He joined Hyndman's Social Democratic Federation, helping to secure the return of John Burns to Parliament from West Nottingham in 1885. At the age of twenty Snell was chairing meetings addressed by the candidate. He soon met a Toynbeeite, the Reverend C. H. Grinling, formerly of Nottingham, who was secretary of a London (Woolwich) branch of the Charity Organisation Society. Grinling invited Snell to follow him as a secretary and investigator, which he did, by bicycle, at Easter 1890. Four years later he found a post as secretary to W. A. S. Hewins, the first director of the London School of Economics and Political Science. At the same time he was studying and travelling up and down the country to lecture for the Fabian Society. In 1898 Stanton Coit persuaded Snell to change his allegiance from Fabian to ethicist lecturing, but he was burned out. Coit sent him abroad, to recover and study in Germany. Coit also rescued Frederick Gould.

Having proceeded from pupil to teacher at Chenies, Gould became in 1877, then in his early twenties, head teacher to the church school in Great Missenden. He wrote in his journal – 'I read the *Jewish World*, the *National Reformer*, the *Catholic Opinion*. Each claims the truth. What is Truth? Thou, O Christ!' – but the exclamation could have been a question. He worried over infant baptism, on the subject of which he wrote a paper which he presented to his mentor the canon. He read the deist lectures of Ben Charles Jones, and went infrequently to communion. Eventually the vicar challenged him on whether he believed in the atonement and he gave such a hesitantly affirmative answer that he knew he would have to resign. He did so in 1879, finding a post in London in the East End. He soon converted to secularism and began to write for secularist publications: in 1882 he began a lifetime's friendship with Charles A. Watts, the rationalist publisher. In the winter of 1887–8 Gould published some satirical paragraphs in *The Secular Review*, in one of which he facetiously noted that a photograph was currently on sale of Queen Victoria smiling: 'Extremely interesting, of course; but how much more so if we could obtain a similar representation of the royal grin adverted to by the Psalmist: "The Lord shall laugh" (*Ps.* xxxii, 13).' His superiors in the London School Board were not amused: he was carpeted for teaching the Bible at school and making fun of it outside. A reproof for indiscretion does not amount to betrayal, but Gould's case was complicated by being a 'raging and tearing' (his words) radical *and* having a deep desire to teach the Bible 'as a human poem'. This was why he had not exercised his right to seek exemption from Bible classes. The School Board censured him, required him to be exempt from religious teaching, and moved him from Turin Street to Northey Street school in a much rougher district, in Limehouse. To no avail Gould persisted in trying to get permission to teach the Bible and his predicament even reached the House of Commons. For eight months at Northey Street he had to leave his class-room a few minutes after nine o'clock and return at nine forty-five, when the head teacher, who replaced him for the statutory lesson, would solemnly close the Bible. 'I was an alien, unable to utter a Bible shibboleth . . . I was *in* the school, but not *of* it.' In his Limehouse years Gould learned more about teaching, wrote several books (including a four-volume *Concise History of Religion*) and continued to work for rationalists and ethicists. In 1893 he and Charles A. Watts changed their secular propagandist committee into a more specifically publishing body, which was to become the Rationalist Press Association in 1899 and to produce its celebrated 'Thinkers' Library' series. The change shows a small movement in the index of transition from the epoch of verbal debate (often elaborately staged) in all kinds of lecture halls to that of printed controversy. In 1896 Gould was delivered from his anomalous position in Limehouse by Coit, who invited him to give up Board School teaching and become ethicist lecturer and journalist. As with Harry Snell a painful apprenticeship came to an end.[7]

Arrivals: John Henry Muirhead and John Atkinson Hobson

J. H. Muirhead and J. A. Hobson came to London in 1885 and 1887. Unlike Snell and Gould they had the most complete education that Britain could afford and were to acquire a greater national reputation as intellectuals. They were pillars of the ethical movement because Muirhead was progenitor and main organiser of the London Ethical Society, and Hobson was successively associated with that society, the West London Ethical Society, and with South Place for nearly forty years, which he described as 'a liberal platform . . . of great help to me in clarifying my thought and enlarging my range of interests in matters of social conduct'. Muirhead was a philosophical Idealist and an academic, who built up a department of philosophy at the University of Birmingham. He was a liberal. Hobson was an author, journalist and lecturer, and liberal of a different cast as indicated in a remark by David Caute about Harold Laski, whose 'mind rested on the nineteenth-century tradition of Benthamite radical rationalism (though he also admired Disraeli), but he extrapolated that tradition further to the Left than any other British thinker except J. A. Hobson'. Hobson was respected by R. H. Tawney, H. N. Brailsford and G. D. H. Cole.

Coming after Snell and Gould, Muirhead and Hobson look at first glance more like Robert Elsmere than his disciples, especially Muirhead who was taught by T. H. Green for whom he had a lifetime's admiration. Both Muirhead and Hobson graduated from Oxford in the 1880s; both turned unwillingly to teaching the Classics, Muirhead as Senior Assistant at the University of Glasgow and Hobson in schools in Kent and Devon. In 1887 Hobson went to London to make a living from writing and lecturing. Muirhead had arrived there in 1885, to study religion in University Hall, across the Square from Mrs. Ward's writing-room, as an enrolled student of Manchester New College.

Hobson was head boy at Derby School where he was cynically coached up to Oxford scholarship level by a former don appointed for this purpose. Once at Lincoln College he did not distinguish himself. He occasionally sprinted for the university, but was not awarded a Blue. He went down in 1880 with a Third in Greats, about which course of study he expressed no more enthusiasm in his autobiography than to say that 'some humanity may be got out of the study of *Literae Humaniores*'. In Muirhead's case there were closer traditional ties between his school (Glasgow Academy) and Glasgow University which he entered in 1870. There was also a connection between the university and Balliol College, to which he advanced for a second undergraduate degree: there was regular traffic from Glasgow to Oxford by means of a tied scholarship, the Snell Exhibition. This path had been taken by Edward Caird, Muirhead's professor of moral philosophy at Glasgow, who became Master of Balliol in 1893. With five years at Glasgow and three at Oxford, Muirhead's education was exceptionally long and disjointed by disappointments. He first went to university a year early to avoid a contest over prizes with his brother and once there missed the Latin prize that was expected of him. Having begun early he decided to stay the course for five years, saving philosophy for the end of it, but his weakness in classics and mathematics nearly lost him the Snell Exhibition, though fortunately when his time came he was favoured by the availability of an extra award. At Oxford he missed the First in Greats that would have led to a fellowship. There was therefore a fifteen-year prelude to his discovery of the profession of philosophy on which he was intending to embark when he moved to London from Glasgow in 1885.

Hobson's family was well known in Derby. His father was part-proprietor of *The Derbyshire Advertiser*. He was a churchwarden whose 'moderate puritanism' was outraged when the vicar, following a ritualist trend in the 1860s, changed his black gown for a white surplice. Hobson himself was pious until his faith was terminally given pause by reflection on the atonement and on everlasting punishment: from his second year at Oxford he was permitted to absent himself from chapel. Muirhead was brought up by his mother (and a brace of aunts) in Hamilton, Lanarkshire, his father having died when he was two years old. His relatives on his mother's side were evangelicals of the Presbyterian Church of the kind who had joined in the forming of the Free Church of Scotland in the 1840s. He experienced among them the austerities of sabbatarianism in which weekday business, like railway journeys, could not be mentioned, let alone dispatched. At home there was characteristically Scottish active supervision of school-work by a mother who indefatigably heard the boys' lessons. There were frequent west-coast holidays of which the best loved were on the Isle of Arran on the shores of which, before the age of iron piers, children would be handed down from a wherry to a waiting farm-cart. The Muirhead boys wandered and messed about in boats at Invercloy, Corrie Gills, Glen Sherraig, Glen Rosa, Glen Sannox, Corrie, Loch Ranza and Blackwaterfoot. The family moved to Hillhead in Glasgow when Muirhead was eleven in 1866, so he could attend the Academy. Later he was to holiday at the family home of his German teacher in the pine-forests between Berlin and Dresden, where Schiller, Goethe and Kant dominated the school curriculum, as well as Goldsmith's *The Vicar of Wakefield*.[8]

In 1987 Muirhead joined the students in their scarlet gowns who milled about the new Glasgow university buildings designed by Sir Gilbert Scott. At university he found that students were exposed to powerful persuasions which could penetrate the influence of family religious environment. Henry Jones, later a fellow-philosopher and originally a Calvinist Methodist who won a scholarship to Glasgow, wrote that he was born in Wales and in 1876 born again in Edward Caird's class-room. At Glasgow Muirhead encountered a philosophical problem pitched across two sides of the new quadrangle. On the north side there was the Logic class-room of John Veitch, on the south the Moral Philosophy class-room in which Caird delivered his series of lectures on thought from Socrates to Kant and in which (according to Muirhead) a sensitive student could be 'taking his religious faith in his hands'. In less personal terms, it was Veitch who represented

the tradition of Reid's Philosophy of Common Sense [which] was still strong in Scotland. Its particular strength lay in the appeal, as against the subjective Idealism of Berkeley and the Scepticism of Hume, that was founded upon it, to the fundamental judgment or reference to reality involved in all knowledge, perceptual or other. So interpreted, it could be claimed for it, not only that it anticipated Kant's insistence on this logical element in apprehension, but that it went beyond Kant in refusing to be denuded of its significance by interpreting the 'judgment' as referring after all to *mere* appearance.

So far so good; but another element from Kant had been brought in to temper Reid's 'wholesome faith in the objective validity of Science' by Sir William Hamilton, whose *Lectures* were co-edited by John Veitch, the consequence of which was to put the object of religious faith in

a transcendental world beyond rational experience, in which the doctrines of *orthodox* religion might freely expand themselves, as they did in the writings of Dean Mansel. Unfortunately, robbed of this support, as it was by Herbert Spencer, it could be made the basis of thoroughgoing Agnosticism. It was the confusion that was thus introduced into the national [i.e. Scottish] philosophy that drove Carlyle, and with him many of the more alert minds of the time both in Scotland and England, to put themselves to school in the literature and philosophy of Germany.

23

Henry Longueville Mansel was Veitch's collaborator on an edition of Hamilton's lectures. The key role of this little-remembered figure was clearly described by Leslie Stephen in his entry on the metaphysician in the *Dictionary of National Biography*:

Mansel's theory was a development of that first stated by Sir William Hamilton in his article on 'The Philosophy of the Unconditioned'. He aimed at proving that the 'unconditioned' is 'incognisable and inconceivable', in order to meet the criticisms of deists upon the conceptions of divine morality embodied in some Jewish and Christian doctrines. His antagonists urged that the argument this directed against 'deism' really held against all theism, or was virtually 'agnostic'. Mr. Herbert Spencer, in the 'prospectus' of his philosophical writings (issued March 1860), said that he was 'carrying a step further the doctrine put into shape by Hamilton and Mansel'.

The Scottish school, therefore, seemed to deliver students into either the hands of religious orthodoxy or into those of agnosticism. Edward Caird offered a way out of both, a route back to the spiritual, or (in Muirhead's words) an explication of human ideals as 'the underlying reality of the world in which we live', not something away in the heavens.

Muirhead was not suddenly 'born again'. In his undergraduate period he approached Kant through J. M. D. Meiklejohn's translation of the *Critique of Pure Reason* (1852), John Hutchinson Stirling's *Secret of Hegel: Being the Hegelian System in Origin, Principle, Form and Matter* (1865), and F. C. A. Schwegeler's *Handbook of the History of Philosophy* (1867), translated and annotated by Stirling. As he was studying in Glasgow, in Oxford Green was publishing his introductions (1874) to Hume's *Treatise*. When Muirhead became his pupil he heard in person Green's celebrated lay-sermon on 'Faith' delivered in a room in the first quadrangle of Balliol (which was attended in imagination by Mrs. Ward through her surrogate, Robert Elsmere). It was this sermon and its companion, published together as *The Witness of God, and Faith: Two Lay Sermons* (1883, an edition prepared by Arnold Toynbee), along with the final chapter, 'Concluding Remarks', of F. H. Bradley's *Ethical Studies* that encapsulated the Idealist reply to agnosticism – a mere fifty pages, but, he decided years later in retirement, containing 'the gist of everything that has since been said in this field by idealistic writers, and the best that has been said by any writers on the essential nature of religion, whether Christian or not'. It was not, however, until he returned, somewhat disconsolately, to teach in Glasgow, that he experienced a full, emotional reaction to Idealism. The occasion was a meeting of a discussion group, the Witagemote. Caird was the honoured guest but he was snowed under by Oxford examination scripts and so instead of offering a paper of his own he read out an extract from Green's yet-to-be-published *Prolegomena to Ethics*. The extract came from Chapter 5 of the published text, on 'The Greek and Modern Conceptions of Virtue', about temperance and self-denial. Green re-stated the Kantian maxim that people should always be treated as ends, never as means, an insight and proposition which was, he argued, alien to Greek culture, which (he could have added) fashioned upper-class British ideology. As he listened to Caird, and through him Green, Muirhead was brought 'nearer to what in the language of the time was called "conversion" than anything else I have ever experienced'. He became even more anxious to leave the world of the Classics in which he was entrenching a career. To the displeasure of his Free Church relatives he thought of entering the Church of Scotland, and to this end spent some experimental months in the university Theological Faculty, only to discover that it was out of touch with 'the new spirit' and 'an effort in which some of us combined to get the terms of subscription to the Westminster Confession relaxed as an ease to our troubled consciences came to nothing'. So he took a daring step 'out'. He decided to become a Unitarian minister and embarked on the last stage of his long education: he enrolled at Manchester New College in University Hall and James Martineau welcomed the troubled Scotsman to London.[9]

Muirhead did not know yet what his career would be – that he would be both a philosopher, and a popularist of philosophy and Idealism. Late in life he wrote an explanatory book on Idealism, which he planned to call 'Where Goodness Dwells: An Essay on the Metaphysics of Value'. It lucidly sets out some of the attractions of Idealism which were felt in Muirhead's group in the coming ethical movement, a group which other ethicists sometimes found intellectually rarefied, but which was as well (for the intellectuality cannot be denied) intensely emotional. Its strain of feeling is illustrated in a passage of 'Where Goodness Dwells' about what 'reality' means to the Idealist:

What cannot be kept too deliberately in mind is the meaning to be assigned to the distinction between 'appearance' and 'reality' and the relation in which they stand to each other. The distinction is not between 'seeming' and 'being', but between manifestation in a time series and that fullness and wholeness of being which cannot be contained in any such series, and so as far as time is concerned lies beyond it: *a 'something more' that is necessary for the verification of what appearance claims to be* [my italics]. Only when apart from such a verification a fragment is taken for the whole reality, Macbeth's vision of the dagger, is it 'mere' appearance – in other words when the discrepancy of what-is-actually-given and the idea is healed (as it would have been if the dagger had been touched) – do we have a sense of reality as in a non-discrepant whole. Idealism maintains that there is nothing in the whole range of finite temporal experience which if merely taken by itself, without leaving room for supplementation from an ideal beyond it, does not have the seeds of error in it, and, if taken as the full reality, will not in the end betray us.

This world-view was very different from those of Gould and Snell.[10] It was certainly different from that of the materialist, J. A. Hobson. Hobson went to London early in 1887. He resided in Shepherd's Bush and Holland Park until the mid-1890s, when he moved to Limpsfield in north Surrey, a favourite place for progressives, and less expensive than the plutocratic pastures of Sussex which Hobson was to revile in his *Imperialism: A Study* (1902). Having been a classics master in Kent and in Exeter, he decided to live by his pen and was given a start by his father who offered him a 'London Letter' column in the *Derbyshire Advertiser* from October 1887. At this stage of his life he did not have the private income on which he later ruefully prospered. He took some classes on literature organised by the London and Oxford university extension delegacies. His career was not assisted by the publication of his first book, written with a friend of the Exeter days, Alfred Frederick Mummery, called *The Physiology of Industry: Being an Exposure of Certain Fallacies in Existing Theories of Economics* (1889). This was Hobson's debut as a writer on social theory and economics – the subjects on which he wanted to lecture in the growing field of adult education in London. His interest had been fired by Mummery, and also undoubtedly by Florence Edgar whom he had met and married in Exeter, a vigorous proponent of women's rights. However, the *Physiology of Industry* prevented him from lecturing on economics for six years. He was first turned down by the London Society for the Extension of University Teaching because of a 'want of knowledge'; and in 1892 his application was blocked again, this time by James Bonar, a founder of the London Ethical Society. Hobson took the rap because A. F. Mummery (1855–95) had no academic ambitions. He was a business man, son of a mayor of Dover in Kent and part-owner of his father's tanning factory. A well-known mountaineer, he was to disappear in the Himalayas when attempting Nanga Parbat in 1895. Reputedly he was cold-shouldered by the climbing establishment, blackballed by the Alpine Club which suspected that the family tannery was a boot-shop. This confusion of manufacturing with retailing is of interest when we come to one of the theories proposed in the *Physiology*.

Although the *Physiology* was jointly written, and although he later played down some of its ideas, the *Physiology* can legitimately be regarded as a foundation stone of Hobson's life's work. For it J. M. Keynes hailed him as a pioneer, and to it Hobson adverted in the title of his autobiography (if such it should be called), *Confessions of an Economic Heretic* (1938).

Hobson and Mummery did not invent their heresy. It was 'underconsumptionism', the theory which attacks over-saving and over-supply (indiscriminate investment and re-investment), advocating the defeat of economic depression by increased consumption and fiscal control over industry. It says that while the individual may excusably save to his pocket's content, whole communities should not because in so doing they heap up 'new material forms of capital, but the real *effective* capital will be absolutely limited by the actual extent of their future consumption'. The 'fallacy of saving' — the title of a book by J. M. Robertson, friend of Hobson and fellow under-consumptionist — had been demonstrated by earlier economic dissenters, including Sismondi, Lauderdale, Malthus, Rodbertus and Marx. Whether or not advocacy of the theory showed 'a want of knowledge' it flew in the face of both Victorian domestic values and of the doctrinaire policy of controlled charity exercised by the Charity Organisation Society, whose sympathisers in the London Ethical Society were well known to Hobson. A presumption of the C. O. S. was that the poor should thriftily help themselves. Hobson and Mummery claimed that poverty was established beyond the reach of the individual will, created in structures of making and selling which destroyed the opportunity for a prosperity worthy of the name. They recognised that there was a paradox in saying that spending, not saving, produced prosperity,

but unlike most paradoxes which gain credence for a falsehood by tickling the ear with a pointed antithesis, it contains a truth which will bear the closest scrutiny. As the community can only increase its consumption by increasing its saving, it cannot increase its consumption without a proportionate increase to its saving fund. So long as there still exists any portion of Over-Supply, this increase of saving is not required, but the moment Supply is once more brought to the normal relation with quantity demanded, any increase in the latter requires a corresponding increase in the former, and every increase in the former requires more Saving. But Saving is the result of the operation of motives on individuals. If people are bent on increasing as fast as possible their standard of consumption, how will they be induced to save more. In the following way . . .

which we shall not pursue, but in preference remain with one element in the *Physiology*'s analysis of what ailed Britain and accepted economic theory (the defect and the fallacy). This element shows clearly the kind of views which Hobson put on offer on London lecture platforms.

The defect in the economic system was a lack of cooperation between the manufacturing and selling (both wholesale and retail) sides of production. The fallacy was the tendency of current economic theory to separate out the making and selling processes, if, indeed, it took any note of the selling process at all. (We saw that the manufacturing–sale, or production–trade, distinction proved important when Mummery applied for membership of the Alpine Club: is there a connection between his betrayal – sporting ostracism – and his economic theory?) Hobson's *The Social Problem: Life and Work* (1901), collecting essays first published in the *Ethical World*, showed the application of the abstract theory. Hobson attacked current economics for its obsession with production and myopia over distribution, both in its quantitative and qualitative aspects. Even Jevons, he thought, went no further than platitudes, offering no 'organic' theory of distribution. 'Organic' has two implications: it refers to the human value of goods (the kind of benefit they may bestow, the human qualities employed in their production) and, besides human needs, it refers to the system of production within which goods are made and sold, to the health and effectiveness of that system. *In*effectiveness is what Hobson saw about him, in the form of dis- or un-employment, 'stagnant pools of adult labour' rotting in the bodies of the owners because they could not get access to the material of production. Hobson's indignation, he articulated sharply, was not fed by what he called, at about the same time, 'the crude humanitarianism of pity'. He wished to offer a 'rational humanitarianism' that showed the inefficiency of wasting labour, offering a unified conception of production and distribution which exposed both the inhumanity and the incoherence of the existing structures.

In the *Physiology* Hobson and Mummery attempted this. Their view was 'unified' because they saw distribution as part of the production process, defining a 'commodity' as only that which lies in the hands of a purchaser, not something awaiting collection in a factory loading bay. Making, wholesaling and distributing are described as movements in a single system, movements which were proceeding out of harmony. The major historical event for the authors of the *Physiology of Industry* was the Franco-German war on which they looked back with the perspective of fifteen years, seeing an industrial system running through the repertoire of boom and slump. With the war came hyper-production and investment to meet the needs of the nations at war. In this phase over-supply was prevented. After the war the industrial plant remained and investment shifted from industry to banks, at which began over-saving and under-consumption. Prices then fell, but at the wholesale stage and not proportionately at the retail stage, for numerous reasons, one of which was that the number of retailers claiming a price actually increased as makers moved from ineffective manufacturing to trade. Trade for the sake of the trading community, rather than for the sake of production or the consumer, became the order of the day, and, as the point is made in *The Social Problem*,

the social waste involved by the growing proportion of energy put into competition, the effort to get work, orders, markets, is the unique feature of present industry. It is testified in every civilised community by the alarming growth in the proportion engaged in work of distribution, the number of agents, canvassers, touts, and other persons 'pushing' trade, the energy put into advertising, shopdressing, and other arts of selling . . . This is not a denial of the social gain from competition, but simply a recognition of the waste involved by keeping twelve instead of two competing grocers in one street.

Hobson wrote over fifty books and had many interests. Any short list of them must include his recognition of *waste* by means of what he called intelligible organic theory which, drawing strict biological parallels, allowed him to define a conception of the parasite. For him parasitism extended into many regions, even to the sporting mania of his contemporaries:

Considered as an organised and regular pursuit – and, as such, distinguished from 'play', which in all animal life is the wholesome expenditure of superfluous vitality in unorganised displays [perhaps sprinting came close?] – Sport is a device to avoid the natural law by substituting voluntary, useless, physical exertion for useful labour directed to the social good. It is practised alike by the upper class of 'unemployed', and by specialised brain-workers.

(Curiously, the concept of 'game' is not distinguished from that of 'sport'.) Hobson observed parasites obstruct culture and the life of the mind, favouring (for example) only a literature endowed with a class-life, and preventing experiment with new subjects and methods in education. In the period of his essays on the 'social problem' he remarked about the Classics that

compulsory Greek still struggles successfully to retain our universities in the old form, as aristocratic literary preserves; those who have put their intellectual capital into these stocks fight selfishly against any reform which shall depreciate their value. Perhaps the worst effect is the sterilisation of those studies which come under the head of 'the humanities'; the almost total neglect of our great English literature, and the complete subordination of the studies of social and moral philosophy to the mechanical drill of language and mathematics still remain a fatal distinction of our English universities.

The universities were not necessarily administered by the leisure class, but parasite preferences created the climate in which barbarian subjects (language and literature taught as mere accomplishments) had undue prestige, and useful subjects awkwardly combined with them, fashioning bastard curricula.

He may have learned something of the way in which contemporary universities grew from what Muirhead could have told him about the evolution of Mason College, Birmingham, into a civic university from 1896. To qualify for university status the college council decided to establish new chairs of philosophy and of brewing. When the viability of a chair of brewing was questioned some defenders argued that its usefulness was counterbalanced by the uselessness of philosophy. Not that the council's interest in philosophy was disinterested. The government (specifically, the Treasury) had the final word as to whether the college qualified and it recommended that there should be in its attached teacher training department some elementary psychology, a term thought by the coucil to be undignified, so the nobler word 'philosophy' was selected, and, to show that the new university would not have its head in the clouds, 'political economy' was sewn to it. Hobson did not have to look to Birmingham for philistinism or conventionality of thought about the nature of academe: he could see to hand in London the problems of establishing schools of economics and social science. But he would have considered the Birmingham exercise in curriculum cobbling as distinctly inorganic.

At the end of the introductory chapter of *The Social Problem* Hobson quotes with approval a sentence from D. G. Ritchie: 'The history of progress is the record of a gradual diminution of Waste.' Ritchie was an idealist of the Green school, like Muirhead, and was distant from Hobson in several ways, the number of which was increased at the time of the Boer War — in 1900 he dissociated himself from most of the contents of the volume of ethicists' essays called *Ethical Democracy*. But on Waste they were in agreement, and the concept of Organism was one which Hobson shared, in a different form, with the Idealists. For a time they had the outline of the conception common. In this moment the ethical movement flourished.[11]

Mentors: Henry Sidgwick, John Robert Seeley, Felix Adler

Gould, Snell, Muirhead and Hobson fostered ethical societies: they were exemplary figures and people joined to have contact with them. They looked to examples of their own, seniors who did not play an active part in society life (they gave the occasional presidential address), but who were respected presences to whom the rank and file could point as to the founders of a movement. Three in particular call for consideration, three different kinds of university teacher; two were Cambridge professors, of philosophy and of history, and one an American professor of oriental studies.

Henry Sidgwick (1838–1900) was appointed Knightsbridge Professor of Moral Philosophy in 1883. Despite *The Methods of Ethics* (1874) he was probably best known to the ordinary ethicist for his sophisticated primer, *Outlines of the History of Ethics for English Readers* (1886), the title showing its stress on British thought as well as hinting at an anticipated readership of non-classicists. To ethicists he would have been celebrated for the way in which he 'went out' by resigning his fellowship at Trinity College in 1869 because he was conscientiously unable to subscribe to the Thirty-nine Articles. The second professor was J. R. Seeley (1834–95), appointed to his chair in 1869. Although he remained in Cambridge until his death in 1895, and although he was almost equally active for university reform, he was not so specifically a Cambridge figure as Sidgwick. We have already encountered him as professor of Latin at University College, London, where his peers thought Christianity as ridiculous as any barbarism. He travelled more widely than Sidgwick, to lecture, and differed in that he was author of two virtual best sellers, *Ecce Homo* (1865) and *The Expansion of England* (1882). His most quoted book at ethical society meetings was *Natural Religion* (1882), especially if Stanton Coit was on the dais. Thirdly among the mentors was Felix Adler (1851–1933) whose role in one respect was more significant: without him there would have been no ethical societies at all because as the founder of the New York Society for Ethical Culture he inspired Stanton Coit into agitating the London societies into being. Adler was, however, an ethical culturalist rather than an ethicist and, though active in America, only an occasional visitor to the British societies, some of which he disliked. The views of the mentors can be conveniently ascertained from their contributions to a collection of essays, mostly presidential addresses, *Ethics and Religion* (1900). Most of the essays were written or delivered as papers ten years before the year of publication, unlike those in the companion collection called *Ethical Democracy: Essays in Social Dynamics* (1900). Both volumes, published by the Society of Ethical Propagandists, a ginger group organised by Stanton Coit, provide a good general survey of ethicist assumptions, though *Ethical Democracy* shows some of the fractures which led to the collapse of the movement: in its preface two contributors, Muirhead and D. G. Ritchie, dissociated themselves from the volume's majority line on imperialism.

Sidgwick published one book that relates directly to his experience of ethicists, *Practical Ethics: A Collection of Addresses and Essays* (1898). In one of these called 'The Pursuit of Culture' he drily rejects Matthew Arnold's approach to the pursuit of truth as belonging to a pre-scientific epoch: 'Intellectual culture at the end of the nineteenth century must include as its most essential element a scientific habit of mind; and a scientific habit of mind can only be acquired by the methodical study of some part of what the human race has come scientifically to know.' His version of 'culture' possesses the ardour of scientific curiosity, 'driving us continually to absorb new facts and ideas'. The ethicists appreciated Sidgwick's 'ardour of curiosity', his patient disentanglement of problems in what he calls 'our complicated modern life'. He is aware that casuistry is 'unedifying', but

> though certain casuists have been reasonably suspected of . . . misapplication of their knowledge and ingenuity, the proper task of casuistry has always been quite different; the question with which it has been properly concerned is how far, in the particular circumstances of certain classes of persons, the common good demands a special interpretation or modification of some generally accepted moral rule. This, at any rate, is the kind of casuistical problem that I have now in view.

In his essays for ethical societies Sidgwick addresses himself to the problem of specialist values, cases in which the standards of sections of the community diverge from the recognised values of the whole community. In a paper for the newly founded Cambridge Ethical Society, delivered in May 1888, he discusses this matter in general terms, remarking how many such deviations there are, 'even omitting those obviously unfit for public oral discussion'. Hindsight may find this passing comment ominous for assessment of the later development of the ethical movement, which too rarely acknowledged the importance of the unmentionable, and hardly ever, indeed, treating the very issue broached by Sidgwick himself in the same paper, that of the collision between accepted moral standards and those of artists who 'may deliberately disregard the claims of sexual purity'. The implication is that this disregard extended into artists' lives. Philosophers were not ostriches in the 1890s. When Havelock Ellis's *Studies in the Psychology of Sex*, on 'sexual inversion', appeared it was reviewed in the July 1898 issue of *Mind*, but the moral implications of the work were studiously ignored by a reviewer who supplied only summary. However, it was to the credit of a leading member of the London Ethical Society, Mrs. Mary Sophia Gilliland Husband, that she dealt sympathetically, if patronisingly, with Edward Carpenter's *Love's Coming of Age* in a review in the *International Journal of Ethics* in April 1897.

In his essays Sidgwick brings forward cases for subtle consideration of both the claims of individuals and groups. In 'The Morality of Strife' he notes that war is often created by a collision (very much a Sidgwick word) between not passions but states convinced by a sense of legitimate interest, states which cannot be expected to resort to arbitration when there seems insuperable difficulty in finding an arbiter whose impartiality can be relied upon. In 'The Ethics of Religious Conformity' he notes that a doubter is not obliged to excommunicate himself from his or her church, 'for the mere presence at a religious service – by a clear common understanding – does not imply more than a general sympathy with its drift and aims; it does not necessarily imply a belief in any particular statement made in the course of it, as an ordinary member of the congregation is not obliged to join in any such statement unless he likes'. In numerous such cases Sidgwick copes with the problems of particularity, allowing for extenuations that could be brought to the bar of morality and for the range of attitudes that might be adopted towards 'divergences', including in 'Public Morality' indulgence ('an alteration in the weight of censure attached to a breach of [a] rule'). So 'public opinion is indulgent to the amorous escapades of gallant soldiers and sailors, though it would condemn similar conduct in schoolmasters'. Sidgwick's oft-remarked 'delightful hesitancy' in speech can almost be heard here.[12]

In his attempts to exercise a legitimate casuistry Sidgwick pays more attention to the happiness of individuals (persons, or individual professions, classes, even nations) than might be expected from a utilitarian who holds that ethics must be determined by reference to a 'universal end'. In *Practical Ethics* there are drives which appear to work against the author's utilitarianism, or against his statement in the address to the Cambridge Ethical Society that 'each of us wants to do what is best for the larger whole of which he is a part, and that it is not our business [as ethicists] to supply him with egoistic reasons for doing it'. But Sidgwick is not indifferent to egoistic reasons, in spite of a powerful quotation from J. S. Mill on men's obligations to the 'larger whole' and the happiness of the greatest number:

'I do not attempt to stimulate you with the prospect of direct rewards, either earthly or heavenly; the less we think about being rewarded in either way the better for us,' I think . . . is a hard saying, too hard for human nature. The demand that happiness shall be connected with virtue cannot be finally quelled in this way; *but* for the purposes of our Society I am ready to adopt, and should prefer to adopt, Mill's position. (My italics.)

In *Utilitarianism* (1863) Mill had argued that people desire virtue not for reward but for itself: it is 'a psychological fact' that the individual may pursue virtue as 'a good in itself, without looking to any beyond it'. In spite of directing the Cambridge ethicists to Mill an improvement on his utilitarianism had after all been attempted by Sidgwick in *Methods of Ethics*. Mill said that 'the greatest amount of happiness altogether' is the end of human action because if each desires his happiness (the 'psychological fact'), then the general happiness must be a good to the aggregate of persons. Sidgwick responded to this in the thirteenth chapter of Book Three. While Mill may show that the happiness of the many is desirable, he does not show that the few actually want that happiness to be created, and – more damaging – even if there were such wishes (or even such sets of wishes possessed by the whole community) an aggregate of actual desires, 'each directed towards *a different part* of the general happiness in any individual', does not constitute 'an actual desire for the general happiness in any individual'. So there is in Mill a gap between the individual and the happiness of the greatest number: its well-being cannot be joined up, as Mill wanted, to individual human wishes. Sidgwick wanted to bridge this gap by saying that the ideal of the greatest happiness need not be related to individuals' senses of happiness for themselves, but related to intuitions of what is good for all, especially an intuition of rational benevolence.[13]

In the ethical movement critics of Sidgwick and of utilitarianism after Mill were not satisfied with the way in which he closed the gap between the needs of individuals and the universal end of the greatest happiness. J. H. Muirhead thought that Sidgwick's position did 'not entirely escape the reproach of eclecticism'. This did not discredit him as mentor, the 'idealist Pharisee' (Muirhead) admiring the 'utilitarian Publican' (Sidgwick). In spite of seeming contradictions, Sidgwick impressed ethicists by his general recognition of 'the habit of devotion to the good life', and recognised, too, the modern conception of society as organism. In *Reflections* Muirhead quotes enthusiastically Sidgwick's address to the Cambridge Ethical Society in which he says that the rules and sentiments of any particular class must be condemned if they threaten the social organism. Nonetheless, Sidgwick devoted much energy to explaining the problems of particular classes, scrupulously 'placing himself at the point of' so-and-so, or 'looking at the opponent's case from the inside', and more often than not finding the individual claim not culpably 'esoteric'. His work for ethical societies is characterised by an investigative or (as he would call it) 'scientific' spirit. Perhaps he found congenial the idea of a thinkers' club in which much could be taken for granted, certainly that 'each of us wants to do what is best for the larger whole': why else join it? In these circumstances there was enough agreement for some matters of theory to be shelved: with ethicists it was safe to consider exceptions.[14]

The second mentor and significant contributor to *Ethics and Religion* was J. R. Seeley. His *Natural Religion* was made by Stanton Coit a primer for ethicists. He thus planted a Coleridgean growth within the movement, for Seeley's conception of church and state expressed in a simplified, aggressive and practical form some of the ideas in Coleridge's *On the Constitution of Church and State* (1829). A key concept in that book which Seeley popularised was that of the intelligentsia as 'clerisy'.[15]

For Coleridge the clerisy was a class of 'learned men, whether poets, or philosophers or scholars', which stands in relation to the actual clergy as does the actual Church to what Coleridge called the 'National Church'. This National Church represents civilisation or the soul of the nation.

The clerisy are its agents as the clergy are the agents of the actual Church. Coleridge compares the actual Church to an olive tree and the National Church to a vine. The olive fertilises surrounding soil and improves the strength and flavour of the vine's grapes and wine. Coleridge had meditated on this concept earlier than *Church and State* in *Biographia Literaria* (1817), when he took issue with Wordsworth on what appears at first glance to be a purely literary matter – what imparts vitality or poetic quality to a language. In Wordsworth's view 'the best part of language' is formed by people's direct experience of familiar objects. Coleridge contested this, claiming it to derive from 'reflections on the acts of the mind itself' and that even uneducated people were capable of such reflections. How? 'By imitation and passive remembrance of what they hear from their religious instructors and other superiors, the most uneducated share in the harvest which they neither sowed nor reaped.' These instructors and other superiors are the same as the clerisy of *Church and State*, which there comprises the 'learned of all denominations' who are masters of the two major sciences, mathematical and theological. Coleridge defines these sciences very broadly. Mathematics covers natural science and liberal arts, including law, jurisprudence, medicine, physiology, music and architecture. Theology embraces 'the doctrine and discipline of ideas', including 'interpretation of language, conservation and tradition of past events, the momentous epochs, and revolutions of the race and nation, the continuation of the records, logic, ethics and the determination of ethical science, in application to the rights and duties of men in their various relations'. Theology, in this sense, comprised the curriculum of the ethical movement.[16]

In *Church and State* three social classes are defined, on whose relationship Coleridge claims the health of a community to depend. Besides the *clerisy* there is a *landowning* class (maintaining permanence) and a *mercantile* class (promoting progression). Ideally, permanence and progression are held in equipoise to form the state. By 'state' Coleridge meant two things, which may be distinguished by a capital letter, though Coleridge himself did not do so. The state is the balance of the secular forces of permanence and progression; the State is the total structure (or organism) to which all three classes belong. The state becomes the State by the addition of the clerisy, the civilising or cultivating force. Coleridge is scornful of *mere* cultivation – varnish, not polish, he calls it. Real cultivation fosters harmonious development of the faculties that are supposed to characterise our humanity. Only a State can be said to have a constitution, and the constitution is the basic subject in which the clerisy is 'learned'. The constitution is a community's idea of itself, 'an idea arising out of the idea of a state'.

This schema exposes some of the main terms in *Church and State*, but omits some and should not be understood to imply that Coleridge describes real social forces in any detail. He offers meditation on ideas and their relationships rather than sociology. His treatise is itself 'a reflection on the acts of the mind itself', those acts which underlie social systems. Coleridge considers at length the two words in his title, but also another which is equally important, which is *nation*. His idea of nationhood was taken up by Seeley from whom it was publicised for the ethical societies by Stanton Coit.

In *Church and State* Coleridge tries to define the idea of a nation in terms of its ultimate purpose or end. Here and elsewhere in his work an ultimate end may be for Coleridge something quite different from an ostensible or self-confessed end. The ostensible end of the Christian Church, for example, is the worship of God. According to Coleridge its ultimate end is cultural or educational. When such an end is seen, or such an inner purpose discerned concealed within the idea of an institution, fresh relationships with other institutions can be discovered. But to find the idea is difficult. When Coleridge's literary executor summarised the passage about ideas and ultimate ends in *Church and State* he glossed the words of the original with an addition: the philosopher seeks to know 'and sense' (the addition) ultimate ends. The explanation is appropriate because for Coleridge the idea of an institution cannot be simply observed by looking. Men, he said, tend to be possessed by ideas, directed by they know not what. So the idea of an institution can only be deduced or glimpsed. To discover the idea of a nation is especially hard because nationhood tends to be characterised by its own lack of definition. In the state (small 's') the forces of permanence and progression flow along marked channels, but the force of a nation is latent or dormant. The whole point of the concept of nation, says Coleridge, is that its power is 'left obscure . . . suffered to remain in an Idea, unevolved and only acknowledged as an existing, yet indeterminable Right'. Nationhood may be only defined in retrospect by an historian who becomes conscious that a nation has been 'in travail'. He hears 'that Voice of the People which is the Voice of God'. As if to admit that this power appears to baffle observation, Coleridge breaks away from this phrasing to remark (semi-humorously?) that his theme 'might seem to many fitter matter for verse than sober argument'. He concludes this phase of his lucubrations with a verse quotation from George Wither's *Vox Pacifica* (1645), rewriting it to include the words 'a deeper life', to point to a life beyond state and secular authority.[17]

In Seeley's *Natural Religion* nation and religion are brought together, but more plainly:

To us it would be startling if the name of England were introduced in our hymns or sung in churches. What should we think then if its name and its glories formed the staple of our religious worship, if our church-goers sang – 'Oh, pray for the peace of England – they shall prosper that love thee . . .' But it may be answered by one party that Jerusalem really was a sacred place but that England is not, and by an opposite school that the Jews were fanatics whose devotion to their own institutions caused their own ruin and misled the world.

Seeley parries these thrusts by citing Athens, surely a sacred place? Might not modern people improve their idea of religious society by reference to the model of Judaism, and realise that the current model – a secular society within which dwells organs of theology of 'an essentially personal and private character' – needs to be replaced? Like T. H. Green in his lay sermon on faith, Seeley attacks secularism: he wishes to define society as sacred. Thus he can write perfectly seriously in an early essay of 'the ministry of journalism'. If the Church is only interested in questions of personal salvation, then inevitably it remains sectional within secular society. But it could get back its confidence and society at large could be dignified, even sanctified, if the community recognised the presence of what Seeley calls the 'unconscious' church, the 'communion of all those who have been inspired by culture and civilisation'. He has to be as careful with 'culture' as Coleridge was with 'cultivation', cautiously explaining that he means something different from 'training, art-schools, academies, universities', relevant to more than 'the favoured few'. His culture, he argues, is modern and came to England from Germany through the agency of Carlyle. It asserts 'the religious dignity of Art and Science'. Goethe and Schiller may have been anti-clerical, but they rebelled only against an orthodox church which did not have absolute validity, if seen in the longest perspective, one which includes Attic and Judaic religion. Art and Science joined the Coleridgean viticulturalists because they were unwelcome in the olive grove. They should return because their opposition to religious orthodoxy was actually religious.

But how is all this to be squared with the subject as opposed to the style of religion, with 'the truths of religion'? Seeley disposes of this question with austere satire:

To most of us the English state seems to exist as necessarily as the sun and moon, and an Englishman does not ask himself what discoveries historical research is making about our early kings, or whether he *agrees* with Hengist and Horsa.

Seeley was aware of the practical difficulties of being a religious reformer in a secular era. He tells the story of the 'theo-philanthropist' who confided to Talleyrand that his scheme for an improved Christianity was faltering. 'I should recommend', came the reply, 'you to be crucified and rise again on the third day.' But Seeley has a premise which relieved him of this ultimate responsibility: that a modern revival need not be based on a theology 'of an essentially personal and private character'. He shifted the problem from individual salvation, turning attention (and, he hoped faith) to the state, the sacred state, recognition of which he believed was a desperate necessity:

The people have long ceased to understand or follow their own development. In England the ideas of the multitude are perilously divergent from those of the thinking class. No sufficient pains have been taken to diffuse everywhere the real religion of the age. Accordingly a large section of the people adhere to the limited religion of the past as it was in the last age of the real efficiency of ecclesiastical organisations, and another large section have abandoned this and gained no other religion in its place. No adequate doctrine of civilisation is taught among us. Science only penetrates either in the form of useful information or else in that of a negative doctrine opposed to religion, as the grand revelation of God in these later times supplementing rather than superseding the older revelations, it remains almost as much unknown as in the dark ages. Still less known perhaps is that doctrine of the gradual development of human society which alone can explain to us the present state of affairs, give us the clue to history, save us from political aberrations and point out the direction of progress.

Patriotism, then, becomes an understanding of 'the gradual development of human society', making its culture an object of worship. It was a necessary part of Seeley's argument to persuade his readers that the relationship between religion and the state in ancient society was the normal one, and urge them to abandon the familiar Christian model of their view of religion and state. They should learn more of church and state from Judaism.[18]

Seeley appealed to the Jewish model of state religion. This interested Stanton Coit who had direct experience of Reform Judaism in New York, before he settled in Britain, though he was not Jewish himself. This experience derived from knowledge of the third mentor, Felix Adler, without whose New York Society for Ethical Culture there would have been no ethical societies in Britain. Adler's family was at the centre of the New York Jewish community. Felix himself was born in Alzei in southern Germany. His father, Samuel, was a distinguished rabbi who in 1857 was appointed for the Temple Emanu-el, the synagogue for one of the wealthiest Jewish groups in New York, indeed in America. He was an enlightened advocate of Reform Judaism, but in modernism he was exceeded by his son. Felix Adler was educated at Columbia Grammar School and Columbia University, after which he went to Germany where he studied in Berlin and Vienna, taking a doctorate in Heidelberg in 1873. He returned to New York, expected to succeed his father as rabbi, but in the autumn of 1873 he delivered a radical sabbath address on 'The Judaism of the Future' whose message was not consistent with an orthodox career. He argued that the masses had lost respect for *all* ministers of religion. To meet this crisis Judaism should do as it had always claimed to do, adhere not to creed but to deed. The slogan 'Deed, not Creed' stuck to Adler henceforth. He impressed many of the members of the synagogue, including its president, the banker Joseph Seligman. His admirers were won over by Adler's youthful mixture of Kantian idealism, Emersonian transcendentalism, and a traditional Jewish emphasis on action, or even 'conduct' in a sense of which Matthew Arnold would have approved. He was encouraged to lecture and drew large audiences, which led to the foundation of a Society for Ethical Culture in 1876, which Adler ran while pursuing the career on which he embarked in 1874 as professor of oriental and Hebrew literature at Cornell. The aim of the society was to find 'common ground' on which believers and unbelievers could meet 'for purposes in themselves lofty and unquestioned as any'. These purposes were the exploration and affirmation of the Kantian maxim that 'every human being is an end *per se*, worthwhile on his own account'. Adler began by understanding this as a protective concept: he was perhaps less interested in how people could realise themselves than in protecting them from exploitation. This early view he called 'non-violation ethics', which he frankly confessed to have derived psychological urgency from his experience of adolescent sex. Desire should be inhibited, 'out of reverence for the personality of women': ethical culturalists were taught that honouring women was of cardinal importance, and were even sworn to chastity. His other major preoccupation was with the desperate mass population of New York. This 'second arrow in my quiver', as he called it (in fact it inspired most of his daily work), he learned in Germany, principally from Friedrich Albert Lange and his book on the labour question, *Die Arbeiterfrage* (1865), to which he had been introduced by his Berlin professor, Hermann Cohen, who told him that 'if there is to be anything like religion in the world hereafter, Socialism must be the expression of it'. Adler himself stopped well short of socialism, but the 'wide and tragic prospect' of Lange stirred him to an emotional social concern 'not of the creed, but of the deed', the deed being first to arouse a sense of guilt among wealthy New Yorkers at their violation of the minds and bodies of the labour force.

Adler applied what he learned from Lange and Cohen to the social problems of New York caused by the notoriously great influx of immigrants. Between 1880 and 1900 nine million people settled in America, as many as had entered it in the six preceding decades. The Society for Ethical Culture aimed to educate older citizens in responsibility and to find methods of care and education for the new citizens. In 1877 the society founded a District Nursing Department and tried to set up a small printing shop to work on co-operative principles. In 1878 it opened the first free kindergarten school east of the Mississippi that taught on Froebelian lines. Adler's lectures inspired the formation of the Tenement House Building Society whose first dwellings went up in 1887. He was himself a conscientious social investigator, playing an important part in the Tenement House Commission hearings of 1884.[19]

The story of the ethical culture societies of America has been told elsewhere. Seen against the British societies they can provoke melancholy reflections because the original societies across the Atlantic had at least two major advantages never enjoyed by the British ethicists: they were created in a wealthy environment and they systematically avoided creed and the appearance of religion, so members of all churches could participate in their work without personal compromise. Ethical culture, unlike ethicism, was to be prosperous, able to make a clean start without the knotted ramifications of church and dissent amidst which the British societies had to grow.

We have seen something of the early lives of four ethicist stalwarts and a little of three ethicist mentors. To the societies themselves we now turn.

Chapter 2

South Place in Finsbury and Holborn

An open door, 1793–1853

The society of South Place takes its name from the London street in Finsbury next to which it purchased land in 1823 to erect a chapel. But the congregation was first established as an unorthodox Baptist group at a chapel in Parliament Court, Bishopsgate, in 1783. It was one of the many new foundations in an era of social, doctrinal and administrative change on the map of British dissent. For the theology of the Parliament Court chapel we can look back earlier in the eighteenth century to a Welsh preacher, James Relly, who died in 1778. Relly, 'an ungovernable youth of great bodily strength', was converted by Whitefield, became a Methodist, but broke away and propagated his own doctrine of universal salvation in several London chapels. His Universalism did not immediately catch on in Britain, but Relly made one convert, John Murray, who took the idea to America in 1770, preaching it in Massachusetts, New York, New Jersey and Pennsylvania. In Pennsylvania he met the man who was to found South Place, Elhanan Winchester (1751–97). Winchester had been a Particular Baptist, a convert to strict Calvinism, believing that only the elect are spared torment in the after life. He preached this doctrine with great success to the largest Baptist congregation in Philadelphia. He was converted from it by an accidental meeting with a young woman in a stage-coach, whose gentle advice apparently convinced him of 'an ultimate fullness in Christ for All the world'. He joined with Murray's Universalism, which he preached as dynamically as before, but in college halls rather than in chapels. Murray travelled to build up a Universalist denomination, settling in Gloucester, Massachusetts. In 1787 Winchester went to spread the word in London, in a number of Baptist pulpits. In 1793 he gathered a church in Parliament Court, calling it 'Philadelphian' after one of the seven churches addressed by St. John in the Book of Revelation: 'Behold, I have set before thee an open door, and no man can shut it' (3: 8). Perhaps the name reminded him of home. The original chapel still stands, near London's Liverpool Street railway terminus; it is now a synagogue.[1]

With the settling of the congregation William Vidler (1758–1816) enters the story. Vidler was a minister of a struggling Baptist chapel in Battle, Sussex. Like Winchester he was the son of an artisan. In 1791 he toured England to raise funds for his chapel. He met some Universalists, possibly Winchester himself, and also some Arminian Baptists whose five articles of Remonstrance had signified departure from strict Calvinism. The second of these, stating that the Atonement is in intention universal, would have won favour with a Universalist. Excited by these liberating ideas Vidler hurried back to preach them to his rural flock, to the displeasure of the local Baptist association. The congregation divided, those remaining with Vidler disowned by means of a form of nonconformist excommunication to be found later in the history of South Place chapel. Winchester then invited Vidler to join him at Parliament Court chapel, which he did in February 1794, though still travelling back regularly to the loyal remnant in the country. Within months, however, Winchester, pressed by family problems, returned to America, leaving the Philadelphia chapel in Vidler's charge. He settled to it, supplementing his stipend by bookselling in partnership with a member of the congregation, Nathaniel Scarlett, with whom he collaborated on a version of the New Testament in dramatic form. In 1787 Vidler founded a journal, *The Universalist's Miscellany; or Philanthropist's Museum*, to publish propaganda against 'the Antichristian Doctrine of Endless Misery'. Lacking the commercial experience of many dissenters he was not a successful editor, but the *Miscellany* started a tradition of journalist-ministers in this congregation. Some of the issues broached in it, such as those of womens' rights, were later important in the congregation.

Vidler's conversion to Universalism had been clinched by Winchester's *The Universal Restoration* (1788), a series of dialogues contesting the doctrine of endless misery. Vidler contributed a note to the third edition of 1799, remarking that Winchester's position had never been conclusively disputed, in spite of an attempt by Dan Taylor in *The Eternity of Future Punishment* (1789). Taylor had been instrumental in founding the General Baptist New Connexion, representing those congregations which resisted a trend towards questioning the divinity of Christ, to be found among an increasing number of Baptists in the south of England. This trend to Unitarianism influenced Vidler, through the agency of Richard Wright who heard of Vidler and Parliament Court from a Baptist congregation of Universalist sympathies in Lincoln. Wright contributed a series of papers to Vidler's *Miscellany* and in the end converted Vidler to Unitarianism. Once again he endured convulsions and secessions within his congregation, and again a group stayed faithful to the minister. By 1802 he was a confirmed Unitarian. Wright was active in the cause and helped him set up a Unitarian Fund in 1806. He acquired help with the *Miscellany* from the young Robert Aspland, who came from long-established dissenting stock. Aspland was a favourite son of dissent until 'unsoundness' became outrageously evident and he was excised from the register of the prosperous London chapel in which he was baptised. He quitted college for an artists' colours shop in St. Martin's Lane, continuing to preach at the Baptist chapels in which Unitarianism was indulged. In 1806 he bought out the *Miscellany* from Vidler, changing it and re-naming it *The Monthly Repository*. It became the leading Unitarian journal. Aspland became minister at Gravel Pit chapel in Hackney, which catered for a congregation similar to that which was growing at Parliament Court. Vidler died at the age of fifty-eight; in 1816 his funeral at Gravel Pit chapel was of some scale, deservedly: he had established a congregation as an institution having struggled across social and doctrinal divides, having neither the money nor the educational sophistication of many dissenters before him.[2]

His successor at Parliament Court had more of these advantages. William Johnson Fox (1786–1864) was a Norfolk man whose father left farming after a dispute about trespass and poaching to become a weaver. Fox was no Aspland, but he was able to attend an Independent chapel school, and then received a broad education at Homerton, the dissenting academy in Hackney. Fox completed the six-year course in half that time. At home he was brought up in an atmosphere of religious and political non-conformity in the traditionally radical city of Norwich. After college he became an Independent minister, though he was increasingly doubtful about the validity of the Trinity. He converted to Unitarianism in 1812, when he preached for the Southern Unitarian Society in Portsmouth and Chichester. He threw himself into administration, helping to found the Unitarian Domestic Mission, and was made responsible for Unitarian missionary work abroad. In 1817 he was invited to become minister at Parliament Court chapel. Fox accepted, but at the outset enunciated terms: he was to be committed to no doctrine whatever and would stand merely as a Christian, with faith in religious liberty and freedom of enquiry. The candour was characteristic.

William Johnson Fox, to whom the congregation owed its meaning for many years, and who is still spoken of respectfully at South Place, was a short man with a coppery complexion and bright eyes. His spoken delivery was beautiful but not theatrical or gesturing. 'It is only by the movement of his lips', said an observer, 'that you perceive he is speaking.' He was a challenging minister. In October 1819 he reproved the congregation for not publicly defending deists, as, he said, charity prompted, after the prosecution of Richard Carlile for selling Paine's *Age of Reason*.

The chapel liked being bullied and thrived, attracting more members, who brought welcome pew-rents. In 1823 the site for a new chapel in Finsbury was purchased and the building was completed on 1 February 1824. The structure was neatly set in a terrace of some elegance, to the frontage width of about four houses, its shallow pediment rising not much higher than the chimneys of the adjacent houses. This pediment was supported by four Ionic columns, framing three doors or windows on ground and gallery level. The style was typical of the period in which the British Museum was designed (begun 1823). Indeed, Finsbury in those years is sometimes compared to Victorian Bloomsbury.

Fox declared that the chapel was to be dedicated 'to the standard of religious liberty'. According to the Trust Deed the chapel was to be

used and enjoyed by the Society or Congregation of Protestant Dissenters now assembling therein whereof the Reverend William Johnson Fox is the present minister and by the future members for the time being of the said Society, as a place for the public religious worship of ONE GOD even the Father and for instruction in the Christian Religion as professed by the said Society at such times according to such forms and under such regulations as are now adopted or shall from time to time be adopted by the said Society.

Finsbury was well-to-do and the chapel was attended by thoughtful dissenters. Several official Unitarian events were mounted there, including the celebration of the sixth anniversary of the Unitarian Association in 1826. Fox became known as a writer, through the *Monthly Repository*, and also through *The Westminster Review*, whose first issue in 1824 opened with Fox's account of 'Men and Things in 1823'. He became a friend of a respected radical, Benjamin Flower, who had carried the South Place ideal of religious liberty into the squalor of Newgate for six months in 1799 for libelling Bishop Watson. Flower settled in east London in 1820 as a widower with two daughters, Eliza and Sarah, who frequented the chapel. Robert Browning admired them: he would walk across the fields from Camberwell to mix with them and the other Finsbury progressives. It was in conversation with the still-adolescent Browning that Sarah Flower discovered she could not set scepticism to rout by 'a firm belief in the genuineness of the Scriptures'. Her sister Eliza was probably the inspiration of Browning's *Pauline: A Fragment of a Confession* (1833). Fox reviewed this poem in the *Monthly Repository* in terms that show his growing suspicion of theology. He invokes the American Unitarian, W. E. Channing:

Rightly has Dr. Channing told us . . . that 'the great revelation which man now needs is a revelation of man to himself'; and that 'the mystery within ourselves, the mystery of our spiritual, accountable, immortal nature, it behoves us to explore, – happy are they who have begun to penetrate it'. With sorrow and shame we say it, that little is there to be expected from professional theologians in this great service. Here and there, amongst philosophers and poets, we find a true hierophant.

In Fox's eyes Browning, aged only twenty-one, was a true hierophant.[3]

Before this review appeared, Fox had purchased the *Repository* from the Unitarian Association, in the autumn of 1831. By that time he had severed its connections with Unitarianism, having converted it into a general, radical journal. The Unitarians were disturbed by Fox's way of pursuing the 'revelation of man to himself', and especially by an article on the condition of women in England in 1833 advocating divorce. No longer could the *Repository* be 'fearlessly left on the side-board or work-table'. The issue of divorce had personal resonance for the unhappily married Fox. In 1829 Benjamin Flower died and his daughters, Eliza and Sarah, became Fox's wards. A close friendship grew up between the progressive minister and the beautiful, intelligent Eliza. Mrs. Fox distrusted such a help-meet: by 1832 matters were difficult enough for her to resort to complaining to her husband by letter, which she distributed among the congregation. Fox replied in an honourably awkward fashion, proposing that henceforth they should become as 'independent beings' in the same house. This did not satisfy Mrs. Fox who had the sympathy of a section of the congregation which wanted the minister to resign. He did so, but was reinstated after some congregational brawling, after which 46 of the pew-holders (representing 120 members) seceded; but 113 backed Fox. The chapel was then formally disowned by London Unitarian ministers and excluded from the Unitarian Association. However, as well as in the loyal party, Fox was encouraged in some Unitarian quarters. James Martineau wrote to him in 1835 urging him against disillusion with Unitarianism because only in it was there 'any hope of raising up a class of fearless investigators and earnest reformers in morals and religion'. This was support worth having, especially when Martineau regarded Fox's specific views on marriage as obnoxious and on ethics mischievous.

Fox and his wife did agree to live apart. The husband moved to Bayswater, taking Eliza as a chaste housekeeper. Later he moved to Queen Square, Westminster, to be near his journalist contacts and the theatres, as he now regularly reviewed plays. Eliza Flower was a good musician.With Fox she compiled a song-book for South Place whose services had hitherto employed only a simple psalmody led by a precentor. The first in this five-part collection, 'Adoration', appeared in *Hymns and Anthems, the words chiefly from Holy Scripture and the writings of the poets* (1841). The other sections, 'Aspiration', 'Belief', and 'Heaven upon Earth' followed in 1846. Only a few songs were prepared for the final section, 'Life in Death'.

In *Hymns and Anthems* Eliza included a setting of a poem by Sarah which became one of the most celebrated hymns of the nineteenth century, beginning

> Nearer, my God, to Thee,
> Nearer to Thee;
> E'en though it be a cross
> That raiseth me;
> Still all my song shall be
> Nearer, my God, to Thee,
> Nearer to Thee.

The implications of 'E'en though it be a cross' were, probably, less well understood outside the theologically doubting congregation for which the verses were composed. Next to this hymn should be put a letter from Sarah Flower to Fox, written on 23 November 1827 before the death of her father. It shows how problems were experienced at South Place.

I have a firm belief in a resurrection – at least I think I have – but my mind is in a sad state; and before that goes, I must endeavour to build up my decaying faith. How is it to be done? I want to read a good ecclesiastical history . . . My life has been like a set of gems on a string of gold – a succession of bright and beautiful things, without a dark thread to dim their lustre. But it will not always be thus. It is not now and some resources I must have against the evil time which is beginning to set in.

Sarah married William Bridge Adams, who wrote on the woman question in the *Repository*, in 1834. She died in 1846, two years after Eliza. By that time a strong musical tradition was established in South Place. Services would begin with a hymn, followed by a long reading, often from a recently published book, running to about half the length of the discourse that concluded the service and was directly related to the reading. After the reading there were two more hymns and a prayer (such as for 'the progress of rational beings throughout the ages of eternity'), after which came another hymn and the discourse, which was given by the minister, his assistant, or sometimes a visitor.[4]

After the crisis of 1832 the chapel discourses and articles published in the *Repository* were often controversial. In pulpit and journal there were, for example, pioneering studies of German thought in Henry Crabb Robinson's essays on Goethe (in the *Repository* of 1832 and 1833) and in Philip Harwood's discourses as assistant minister in the chapel in 1841 on D. F. Strauss's *Das Leben Jesu* (1835). Miss Brabant, a member of the congregation, planned to translate this book, but the task was taken over by George Eliot, then Mary Ann Evans. South Place had another indirect connection with the novelist in her youth: George Henry Lewes delivered lectures in the chapel which were published as his *Biographical History of Philosophy* (1845–46). Fox gave several series of lectures on socio-political themes, on 'Morality, as modified by the various classes into which society is divided' and on 'National Education' between 1835 and 1840.

Once connections with the Unitarian Association were severed the congregation was responsible only unto itself for the management of its affairs. From April 1837 it was run by a six-man committee and two auditors. The minister was entitled to a place on the committee, but Fox sensibly avoided these meetings. Dissenting congregations did not like the minister to be administratively dominant. When one of Fox's successors insisted on taking his seat on the committee, the rules were changed and he had to resign. Fox did not interfere and wanted to be busy outside the chapel. The congregation approved, naturally wanting a well-known minister who would attract members (and pew-rents). But it still wanted the best attentions of the minister and began to want more of Fox. He was an anti-Corn Law speaker and in July 1847 he was returned to the House of Commons as M.P. for Oldham, which seat he held with one interruption until his death in 1864. In 1850 he was responsible for a parliamentary bill which embodied one of the main concerns of his chapel discourses, national education. But, as Moncure Conway noted later, 'Mr. Fox's Bill was defeated by a combination of Anglicans, Roman Catholics, Wesleyans, Presbyterians and Independents – because in his Bill, while admitting ways for all denominations to train the children of their faith, the government grants were to be given only in respect of the secular education.' Fox anticipated some of the provisions of the Elementary Education Act of 1870. In presenting it he encountered difficulties that were to arise even after 1902.

Parliamentary work gave Fox less time and perhaps inclination for the chapel, so new assistants were appointed in 1849 and 1851. Fox delivered his last discourse in February 1852 and finally retired from South Place (or 'Finsbury Chapel', as he always called it) on 29 January 1853.

What kind of believer was this minister? What did he understand, in Channing's reverberating phrase, by 'the mystery within ourselves'? Fox's position was clearly presented in a series of discourses delivered at South Place in 1849 entitled 'The Religious Ideas'. The following passage from Lecture XI, called 'The Religion of Humanity', illustrates what warmed his spirits and those of the congregation.

If the views which have been advanced are sound, it is plain that there is a Religion of Humanity, a religion which belongs to human nature; which is not the religion of the western world or of the eastern world, or exclusively of this world at all: but it may be of all worlds, – a religion which does not descend to have an earthly metropolis, whether it be Rome, Jerusalem, or Mecca, be it the Veds, the Koran, or the Bible, – a religion which is not the property of the white race or of the black race, not the religion of Europe or of Hindustan, of Greece or of Persia, of Palestine or of Egypt, and has existed since Luther reformed that of Europe, – a religion which is not subordinated to the influences of climate; which does not rise or disappear with the attainment by mankind of a different stage, – a more advanced stage, of civilisation; which is the same permanently; continues as human nature continues; which is to be found whenever man is found; common as sense and reason, thought and feeling, mind and heart; and which, as it refers back to the earliest ages of history, so it will not grow dim with age, nor fade in years through the coming generations . . . These great moral and religious ideas prove themselves by their very existence and nature; they grow and shine as suns grow and shine, by their condensation of the great nebulae. They shed their light upon surrounding worlds, making them luminous with reflected lustre; they prepare humanity for a different world of existence, a spiritual world, unfolded to us by the inward sense, as the external world is created anew to every human being by the influence of the outward senses. They live and reign in the mind; and as I have said, they alone deserve the name of revelation.[5]

Iconoclastic adventures, 1853–1891

After the departure of Fox the chapel had difficulty in finding a comparably eloquent successor. This may be surprising. In the late 1840s there seem, in retrospect, to have been suitable candidates, young men like Froude or Clough who, having rejected the idea of taking orders, might have wished to lead the 'fearless investigators' of Finsbury. Clough, indeed, did take the post of Warden at University Hall, the new Unitarian hall of residence. But it must be remembered that Unitarians were 'everywhere spoken against', and renegade ones were no exception. After Fox the chapel showed a strange preference for a man in orders. In 1853 it made two wrong choices. First came the Reverend Henry Ierson, who was pushy in the administration of the chapel. He was succeeded by the Reverend Henry H. Barnett, who stayed from 1858 to 1863. Barnett brought a whiff of the evangelical to South Place. He had a rough ride, shown vividly in his indignant farewell sermon, which he took pains to have printed to advertise his resentment at what the chapel had grown to need:

I am told that I make a great deal too much of the Saviour for your taste. It is urged against me that I preach all about Christ and never about Socrates; that I glorify Paul and say nothing about Pythagoras; that I bore you with the Bible, and never read in our worship from other books . . . I am reverential and devout – you like criticism and rhetoric. I seek to build up a church; it is your mission to denounce and destroy the churches. I seek, however humbly, to reconcile your sinning and sorrowing souls to the Lord Almighty; you are intent instead on a career of iconoclastic adventures and exploits. The chapel did not deny it. The committee explained that under Barnett

the daily heroisms of our own time, the martyrdoms of old, the great spirits of all countries and of all climes, have ceased to be called in to our assistance; and from our pulpit the rocks and heavens no longer sing their grand hymn of devotion and praise.

Barnett departed and the iconoclasts were fortunate to find an American much more suited to their needs.[6]

Moncure Daniel Conway (1832–1907) was a well-to-do Virginian, formerly a Unitarian minister in Cincinnati for a congregation which had rejected him as a 'frivolous and reckless boy, whose life is a libel upon even the Western standard of clerical propriety, and whose judgment and logic are too feeble to command respect'. He was an abolitionist who came to Britain in 1863 to publicise the arguments against slavery. He discovered that the intelligentsia did not comprehend the issues, not understanding that Lincoln's Union was far from decisive about emancipation. Encouraged by Robert Browning, Conway communicated recklessly with the official envoy from the Southern states in London, but his attempt at diplomacy was maladroit and he found himself in a position which would have made his return to America embarrassing to abolitionists and their opponents alike. Fortunately South Place provided a niche for him. He had spoken there and had met one of its leading supporters, Peter A. Taylor, radical M.P. for Leicester and treasurer of the London Emancipation Party. In 1863 South Place was wondering what to do about the then 'comparatively empty chapel'. Conway's guest appearance had aroused interest among the old radicals of the Fox era. When his name was advanced it was agreed to invite him to become minister for a trial period early in 1864. Conway accepted and the appointment was confirmed for January 1866. His annual stipend was £150 from 1864, but its size hardly mattered because the post provided Conway with a professional base in Europe from which he could take advantage of the opportunities afforded by London for a journalist and newsman. It was curious and altogether characteristic of South Place that one of its favourite ministers was also a war-correspondent. Conway relished London life and soon knew everyone. He stayed because he had been a maladroit diplomat, but there was no such clumsiness in his new role as literary entrepreneur, acting as agent for Hawthorne and Emerson, even securing British publication of *The Adventures of Tom Sawyer*.[7]

In the pulpit Conway broke with tradition by declining to wear Fox's black ministerial gown, an act which was as symbolically encouraging to the congregation as Fox's gesture of long ago in asserting that he was simply a Christian, nothing more. Conway had moved on from Unitarianism to a position close to that of his new flock. When he left the Cincinnati congregation in 1858 he wrote that if the Unitarian movement had any meaning at all, 'it was to satisfy the *sceptical* class . . . it was for those who were alienated, by the unreasonable dogmas of the church'. In 1869 he led the Finsbury sceptics a further stage on their journey. After 'two most valuable lectures on Prayers and Meditation', he persuaded them to abandon petitionary prayer, but to retain periods of meditation. Increasingly the meditations were directed towards non-Christian sacred texts. Conway had been interested in oriental religion since 1853, when he had transcribed a series of passages from books in Emerson's library at Concord. These formed the core of his publication of 1874, *The Sacred Anthology (Oriental): A Book of Ethnical Scriptures* which was devised to open up study of 'the archaeology of the heart of man', in effect a form of research into what Fox described as the 'religious ideas'. Conway came to England as a theist. He continued to refer to 'God', but, notes his biographer, only 'because he felt it expressed better than any other word something universal . . . which all people sensed'. It was not, however, universal order which had evolved from the primal ooze, but humanity, so humanity alone deserved worship. Thus 'the only meaningful religious study was comparative religion, and its value lay in what it taught us about the universality of human aspiration'. This view is expressed in *Idols and Ideals: With an Essay on Christianity* (1877), a work which well illustrates the burly humanistic rhetoric enjoyed at South Place in the 1870s, when the congregation could number about 400. Conway asks whether pains should be taken to protect the faith of the naively pious, as Tennyson enjoined:

> Leave thou thy sister, when she prays,
> Her early heaven, her happy views,
> Nor thou with shadow'd hint confuse
> A life that leads melodious days.

These verses (expostulates Conway) are nearly the only ones which the poet and his friends might wish obliterated from his fair pages, as representing (one must believe) his first timorous and unsteady step on a path which we may hope has since led to heights that shame their faithless fears. Passing their undertone of contempt for the female intellect, of which the poet was probably unconscious, let us consider what our duty is to that prating sister, or brother either, whose illusions we are called upon to spare. If our sister is praying in earnest, if doubt has not crept into her heart – we must not call it her intellect, I suppose – then her faith does not merely include

> Her early heaven, her happy views,

but also her early hell, and some most unhappy views. If her prayer be
not a mere attitude, she is probably imploring an angry God not to send her
children, brothers, or friends into everlasting anguish and despair. If that be her
creed, she can hardly be leading such melodious days that it should be cruel to
hint that her apprehensions may be unfounded.

Conway did not spare pious innocents, even including the old lady who
once said to him that the doctrine of total depravity was very good doctrine if only it was lived up to. South Place relished the satire, and also
found in their minister an emotional adequacy. He could express what it
was like to live without the protections of orthodoxy. His emotional adequacy is displayed in the short lament he published in the chapel
magazine in 1897 on the occasion of the death of his wife, Ellen Dana
Conway, in New York:

On Christmas Day, in a city gay with birthday celebrations of one said to have
healed the sick and raised the dead, I sat beside my dead wife, and recalled the
words ascribed to Martha, 'Lord, if thou hadst been here, my brother had not
died.' But I said, 'If thou hadst been Lord, this women had not died.' I shall not
ascribe any providential purpose to the diseases and griefs that desolate mankind,
and of *themselves* work no moral benefit at all, but tend to sap the mind, lower
courage, and embitter the heart.

Conway's kindliness and openness to experience recreated the sense of
community that South Place had lost in the decade after Fox's departure.
A newly confident body was in the late 1870s a vigorously self-educating
one.[8]

In the summer of 1878 Conway and the mathematician W. K. Clifford
mounted an ambitious Conference of Liberal Thinkers in the chapel,
primarily for 'the scientific study of religious phenomena'. In 1879 there
was an important development for the chapel: an Institute was founded,
which held courses on Sunday afternoons, beginning with ones on *Faust*
and on perception. In subsequent years the Institute had a near-collegiate
function. It offered thorough surveys, with a variety of participating lecturers, on industry, and on the life and thought of different nations as
observed from the socialist point of view, a series organised jointly with
the Fabians. A chapel Library was started because one member had been
so invigorated by the publication of Samuel Laing's *Modern Science and
Modern Thought* (1885) he wanted to make it the founding volume of a
collection for the congregation. Laing's book, a popularisation of Darwin
and Huxley and a best seller (21,000 by the spring of 1894) was agnostic
though it displayed an impatient affection for Christianity, so long as it
placed itself 'in thorough accordance with freedom of thought, and the

whole body of other truths discovered, respecting man and the universe'. South Place was then committed to freedom of thought and to investigation of the whole body of 'other truths'.

Conway by now had been twenty years at South Place and was in his fifties: he was thinking of retirement from the chapel. At the Conference of Liberal Thinkers he had a taste of scholarly internationalism, which had also been stimulated by contact with his friend Max Müller. In the summer of 1883 he returned to America, sailed to Australia, and thence to India, but there much of his enthusiasm for eastern religion waned. Hindu ritual disgusted him: 'I had studied Kali, but how little I had realised what Kali meant to her worshippers!' The spectacle of slaughtered animals, snake-worship and squalor increased Conway's disillusion with religion in general, and he became uneasy even at the thought of the quasi-ministerial role he occupied at South Place. His desire to resign was compounded, and he considered settling in America. He was planning to write on the life of Tom Paine, perhaps as an antidote to his passage to India, where he had been as shocked as E. M. Forster's Mrs. Moore. For a life of Paine Conway needed to work on American archives, so after a series of farewell discourses and celebrations at the chapel he departed for America in the summer of 1885.

Conway's period as minister of South Place had lasted twenty-one years (and he was to return). Before him Fox had served for thirty-seven years. These ministers shaped the identity of the chapel and did so, to the great satisfaction of its congregation, because they were centrifugal figures. They respected the dissenting tradition of congregational autonomy. They provided intellectual authority, but the pew-holders never felt they were meddling in the affairs of the chapel. They kept the chapel in touch with the world of affairs, with 'the daily heroisms of our own time, the great spirits of all countries', as the committee had stated its need in 1863. Both ministers were busy journalists who knew the leading figures of their times. Besides the *Westminster Review* and his own *Repository*, Fox wrote for the *Morning Chronicle*, *The Sunday Times* and the *True Sun*, whose circulation he pushed up from 2,000 to 15,000. He spent some months working with John Forster and Charles Dickens on the *Daily News*. Conway was a news reporter, as well as a man of letters: in 1870 he corresponded from the French front for the *Daily News* and for the *New York World*. Both ministers knew the leading writers: Fox was friendly with Mill, Dickens, Carlyle and, of course, Browning. Conway knew and promoted the works of Twain, Whitman and Hawthorne. Both ministers were public campaigners, Conway as an abolitionist, and Fox for Richard Carlile even before the congregation moved to South Place chapel, and later for reform in 1831, as an anti-

Corn Law publicist in the 1840s, and for a system of national education in the 1850s. Between them Fox and Conway established a special relationship between minister and congregation and made South Place a well-known centre of progressive thought – not the least of its achievements was to make the new ideas available to women. Its place in London intellectual life in the period of Conway's retirement is well illustrated in a cartoon of the period by the secularist, G. J. Holyoake, called 'Our National Church'. Conway himself describes it in his memoirs:

I am in a little tent marked 'Conway's Free and Airy Tabernacle', having a white flag inscribed 'We move on.' Above all is a bust of Darwin, beneath being a stairway of geologic strata on which a gorilla is climbing, and drawing by his tail Huxley and Tyndall. The text connected with Darwin and *Gen.* XXVIII, 'Behold my brother is a hairy man, and I am a smooth man.'

However, there was a hairy man who was on his way to South Place.[9]

In the summer of 1885 Conway departed for New York. For two seasons South Place had no minister. Several candidates were considered, including James Allanson Picton, the radical secularist who 'went out' from the Congregational ministry in 1879. Picton had started classes for working men in Hackney, and his views resembled those of Conway's original sponsor, Peter A. Taylor, to whose parliamentary seat in Leicester Picton had succeeded in 1884. In 1888 he publicised in the House of Commons the deplorable demotion of F. J. Gould by the London School Board. An invitation to South Place was also extended to an American visitor to the chapel, John Graham Brooks, from Harvard Divinity School, who came to Europe to pursue his interests in the politics of labour. But neither Picton nor Brooks could be tempted. In September 1887 another American, Stanton Coit, visited South Place, to deliver four addresses on Shakespeare, on Socrates, and on his experience in New York of 'Ethical Culture as a Religion of the People'. Coit was a willing candidate for the post of minister, and he was backed by the strongest of referees, Conway himself, who had probably heard of him through Adler in New York, or possibly met him in November 1886 when he moved away from Brooklyn to Manhattan. Coit was then becoming known for founding his Neighbourhood Guild. He had visited London, from which he took the conception of the Toynbee settlement to New York. He wanted to come to South Place, but he bluntly stated a condition, that South Place should henceforth be known as an *ethical society*, then 'No longer would persons . . . be asking as you once told me many do – what does South Place stand for?' This demand was sent on 23 November 1887, along with a letter of recommendation from Conway at his most fulsome, rhapsodising that Coit was to the ethical movement what Channing had been to Unitarianism, Fox to rationalism and Emer-

son to transcendentalism, forgetting that the chapel had shown no interest hitherto in an ethical movement. However, 'the Ethical Cause is
Coit's young bride, they are on their very honeymoon', wrote Conway,
and perhaps overwhelmed the committee which agreed on 21 December
that ethical society it was to be and Coit the minister. He could not come
immediately, so they had to wait nine months for the bride to be carried
over the threshold.[10]

'Dr. Coit is almost uniformly persuasive', wrote a clergyman when
some of his lectures were published as pamphlets, 'and we had almost
written "gentlemanly" but he can suddenly blaze up in volcanic fashion.'
His platform manner could be gentlemanly – he valued, as we shall see,
a reassuring quality in the address of an ethical lecturer, but the thirty-
year-old, red-headed American was quite unlike the fatherly Conway and
could indeed blaze up. His lectures had volcanic moments, as in the
following passage from one of his earliest discourses, on Mrs. Ward's
Robert Elsmere:

I once watched a clergyman as he listened to a rough man addressing a crowd. The
speaker was running over with low jests and coarse suggestions; the clergyman
smiled with kindly pity; but when the man quoted in some flippant sense a
beautiful saying of Jesus, the clergyman's face grew ashen white, and from that
moment he sat like one dead. But is Jesus the only person to be held inviolable like
this? Are our own crucified ones not sacred? Are wives and daughters and sons to
be counted cheap? May they be besmutted with foul talk, and we sit by with never
a protest? Is Christ the only person we need to reconceive? Is he the first we need
to attend to? No! Every man and woman of to-day needs, first and foremost, to
reconceive – to get a correct idea of – himself and herself and of those we daily
meet.

This egalitarianism may have intrigued but not excited the congregation.
It would have been more impressed by a moment in which Coit attacked
the quaintness with which heterodoxy is depicted in *Robert Elsmere*.
Unbelievers do not resemble, he claimed, these freaks:

I have no doubt there are among unbelievers in real life just such degraded and
monstrous specimens of human beings as those in *Robert Elsmere*. But, surely, the
earnest unbelievers whom I have known personally – and I have been with such
all my life – are as far removed from such abominations of character and such im-
piety as are the saintliest Christians.

The fictional characters were allowed decency up to a certain level of
heterodoxy, beyond which they were shown as stupid or bad, 'and no
more subtle attack can be made upon [heterodox ideas] and upon those
holding them than to intimate that somehow a deterioration of character
goes along with them'. Coit's frank indignation rose to effective literary
criticism. From then on he lectured regularly at the chapel, giving an
average of nearly fifty Sunday addresses a year until the end of 1891.

New activities sprang up at South Place – a Sunday School and Ethical Class, a Girls' Club and a Junior Ethical Union. But all was not well between Coit and the congregation. He was sensitive: 'I will not be dined out', he once snapped. Unlike Conway he was not occupied with scholarly pursuits, or with intercourse with the leading men and women of the time. He had no sociable domestic life, like Conway's in Hammersmith or in his Norman Shaw house in Chiswick. Much of Coit's spare time appeared to be spent in some kind of social work in the brick wastes of Kentish Town. More particularly there were two reasons for conflict between leader and congregation, first in Coit's poor understanding of some taboos that operated in the administration of dissenting chapels; and second because he had to deal with a substantial group of members who were out of sympathy with his position.[11]

From the platform Coit faced a generation which had been fashioned by Conway, who had re-lit the flame of Fox. Essentially these people were not really social missionaries, but free-thinkers and eclectics. In Coit's day there were still members attending whose experience went back fifty years. John Raftery, a wholesale lace merchant with commercial interests in tea and French flavouring oil, was such a one. He heard Fox on 9 July 1843 and Graham Wallas (on 'The Old Poor Law and the New') on 4 March 1894. When South Place was closed in the summer, Raftery would sample other pulpits à la carte, going from the Free Christian Church in Camden Town (where Conway sometimes preached and he heard Annie Besant), to Westminster Abbey for Dean Stanley, and to Stopford Brooke's Bedford Street Chapel, where he could hear a plea for a Sunday opening of picture galleries (much to his approval as a regular attender of the meetings of the National Sunday League). Raftery was a characteristic individual, but there were also several whole families at present below the dais whom Conway had sustained and who were disappointed by Coit. There were the Seylers. Clarence H. Seyler sent his children to Coombe Hill, the progressive Surrey co-educational school which possessed a South Placian dislike of petitionary prayer, and whose advanced biology classes read Darwin. The headmistress banned the ubiquitous 'school-map' from the walls, favouring pictures alone. Seyler's daughter, Athene, later a celebrated actress, took part in a demonstration against blood sports at the school during which the pupils captured the fox from the local hunt. Athene Seyler was active at South Place in the 1920s. Years before, her father ran a class for the study of Herbert Spencer and frequently contributed to the South Place magazine on rationalist matters. He wrote a treatise on birth control which he had circulated privately among his family. Like many of the members he had medical interests. He was secretary of the Royal Free Hospital and a director of the Rationalist Press Association. His father-in-law, Conrad Thies, another leading member, founded the British Hospitals Association and from 1904 was President of the Incorporated Association of Hospital Officers. As we saw earlier the chapel Library was founded by a member who was impressed by Laing's *Modern Science and Modern Thought*. The librarian married one of the longest serving members, Caroline Fletcher-Smith, secretary to the general committee from 1882 until she was disabled by an accident in 1928, just before the opening of Conway Hall. She had studied and nearly qualified at the Ladies' Medical College in Fitzroy Square, alongside Dr. Garrett Anderson and Dr. Alice Vickery, who maried the neo-Malthusian doctor, C. R. Drysdale. Alice Vickery's brother, J. L. Vickery, left a large bequest to South Place in 1929. A concern for the medical education of women was shown in the career of Robert Hampson, who was for twenty-seven years a member of the council of the Pharmaceutical Society to which he secured admission for women. Even such apparently non-ideological activities as rambling were actually related to the chapel's — or rather, on Coit's insistence, *society*'s — scientism. The rambling group started in 1887 was designed to provide women with instruction in natural history.[12]

Some families of the Conway generation (and earlier) continued into the twentieth century. In 1980, when the society argued its case for recognition as a charity in Chancery, its appellant was C. E. Barralet. In the 1860s the Barralet brothers, William and Thomas, went courting with Charles Bradlaugh in Hackney. They were prominent freethinkers, close to the radical publisher, Henry Hetherington who was imprisoned in 1841 for publishing Haslam's *Letters to the Clergy of all Denominations* which attacked numerous Old Testament cruelties. He was also responsible for the indictment of Moxon, Shelley's publisher, to test whether the courts would bring a blasphemy conviction against a gentleman. William Barralet's daughter, Harriet, was to marry Edward Snelling, a City watchmaker, who was in Coit's time chairman of the Walthamstow branch of the National Secular Society. Mrs. Snelling was a suffragist, Co-operative worker and a secretary of the Hackney branch of the Liberal Association. The Barralets and the Snellings were pillars of South Place. Among other members of this free-thinking and scientifically minded cadre were William Crowder, consulting analytical chemist and initiator of the South Place Institute, and W. J. Reynolds, editor of *South Place Magazine*, who enjoyed sarcasm at the expense of those who rejected the theology of Christianity but found its ethics beautiful: 'What can we make in the ethical sense of hell-fire, or the blood-sacrifice?'

Coit had little in common with these people. In one of his addresses he said that 'religion is not agnostic, but gnostic. It is not the worship of our ignorance, but of our knowledge.' However, the members were less concerned with worshipping knowledge than acquiring it, and Coit himself was perhaps more interested in moral autonomy than in knowledge. He was not preoccupied with scientific method, nor with Conway's favourite subject, ethnology. He did not attract such distinguished scientists to the society as A. H. Pitt-Rivers (Lane Fox) who founded the Oxford Anthropologist Museum. When J. M. Robertson delivered a memorial address on Conway he said that he had preached a 'creedless and dogmaless Rationalism which you all know so well'. True, but not of all members, for some of whom the chapel was a decompression chamber. However, the members recognised this rationalism even if not all shared it and they knew they could learn from it. Coit did not supply an education; and even though he and Conway were Emersonians, Conway was also 'a typical inheritor of the principles and social attitudes of the philosophic radicals of the early Victorian years', as J. A. Hobson accurately described him.

The differences between the elder Conway and the young Coit should not show too much discredit on the latter. Funeral tributes are not delivered on oath and the testimonies of those who found kindly company during a crisis of faith must lack objectivity. Conway's beliefs may have been vague (though his attitudes sympathetic) and Coit's definiteness may have been irritating. Most of his real deficiencies from the point of the society were political, in several senses. For some he was too much of a socialist, or activist: members did not care to hear themselves called (though not from the platform) 'a set of talkers and aesthetics who would never act'. He had ambitions to work in an international ethical movement, wanting the society the affiliate with the transatlantic Union of Ethical Societies, but it declined, apparently uninterested in ethical culture. Coit made some good moves: he acted in the Finsbury tradition when he asked for the title of minister, with its 'odour of sanctity', to be dropped. Fox had done something similar when he told the Parliament Court congregation that he wanted to be known as a 'preaching brother', not as a priest. But Coit made some disastrous demands, for example, that as leader he should be *ex officio* a member of all the society committees. He would not have pressed this had he studied Ierson's resignation in 1857: the congregation did not like its leader (or minister) enmeshed in its administrative affairs and history repeated itself in 1891. Ominously Coit began to set store by general meetings, and some members recognised the autocratic ploy of appealing over the heads of established committees, not surprisingly for several were professional administrators. The anti-Coit party published 'An Appeal to Members of the South Place Ethical Society' signed by fifty-eight members, including half the general committee of twenty and five of the thirteen trustees. It swung opinion against Coit, who resigned. Much of the opposition came from the rationalist and educationalist wing of the society, from the Institute led by Reynolds, William Sheowring and Clarence Seyler. Coit retired to lick his wounds in the Kentish Town communitarian dwelling which had mystified some members of the society and we shall follow him there in Chapter 4. From 1 January 1892 South Place needed a leader again, and an answer to Coit's question, 'What does South Place stand for?'[13]

Aims, principles and Appointed Lecturers, 1891–1912

In December 1885 Annie Besant wrote to Mrs. Conway, saying how much her husband was missed at the chapel: 'The fact is that many of the older and more orthodox there could put up with his heresy, because they had grown into it, but they shrink from anyone as advanced and less familiar; while the more heretical ones don't approve of the theistic leanings which suit the first class.' She was stating Coit's question of what the society stood for in a different way. Fortunately it was able to postpone an answer because Conway agreed to return temporarily in October 1892 so he could preside over the centenary celebrations planned for 1893. At them he delivered four lectures on the society's history. Possibly this retrospect helped to concentrate the mind of the society because not long after it found itself able to say what it did stand for, and to solve the problem of leadership.

The committee moved cautiously. In 1894 it reported that stating the society's beliefs was 'fraught with no ordinary difficulty'. Only in spring 1896 did it come up with a statement that was to be ratified by the whole society (with the exception, in the original form, of the phrase in square brackets below):

The object of the society is the cultivation of a rational religious sentiment, the study of ethical principles [and the promotion of human welfare] in harmony with existing knowledge.

In June 1897 this was inserted into the society's rules and became the official credo for years. This insertion had no legal authority (relating to the tenure of the property) because the society did not immediately make a change in its trust deed which in 1897 was still framed in its original Unitarian terms. The statement was to enter the legal constitution by stages: in 1907 the original Unitarian aims were cancelled by an amending deed, which nonetheless did not actually include the new credo, only a reference to its presence in the rules. In 1930 was it written into a fresh deed.

The credo of 1897 was a remarkably successful answer to the problem of being precise about the imprecisions of the society. This 'object' was produced by Edward Dallow, a member of the Seyler and Reynolds group. One of the early drafts of the credo shows how some of the terms in the 'object' should be interpreted. This brief draft of May 1896, headed 'Aims and Principles', makes plain what is meant by 'rational religious sentiment' in the 'object'. The phrase was meant to be a protest against Calvinist theology, specifically against 'the cruel and degrading fantasy of eternal tortures after death'. 'Ethical' in the 'object' is seen to be a provisional substitute for 'theological', conveying the society's wish to 'to transfer man's aspirations from God to Man' and to endorse individual freedom – which is said to be 'the fundamental principle of ethical religion'. We must stay longer with 'ethical religion' to grasp what this phrase meant in South Place.

The key sentences in the draft called 'Aims and Principles' are, first, 'We may . . . confidently depend on reflecting minds to recognise in this very absence of any ethical formula an affirmation of the principle of ethical religion – individual freedom', and, second, '[The Society] wishes for a peaceful and rational religious revolution, aiming to transfer man's aspirations from God to Man.' What is at issue is whether a new kind of religion was being proposed, or whether the society was essentially concerned with dissociating itself from the ills of religion as it had been understood. The latter interpretation is surely the correct one: the society was not offering *an* ethical religion.

In the key sentences one concept (God) is held in suspense against another (Man). Or one concept (religion) is held in suspense against a cluster of others (individual freedom, ethics). It could be argued that there is no tension between the opposing sets of concepts, that in the sentences there is an affirmation about something called ethical religion. But this is not plausible because they are unashamedly tentative. The statement says that 'the name ethical may be replaced', meaning that it is being used for the time being as a suitable replacement for 'theological'. The statement refers to the experience of 'those who know the emancipation from such views [of eternal damnation] in imperfect phases of opinion'. The reference is quite consistent with the wish expressed in the 'object' that the society should keep abreast of current knowledge. The society shows itself to be committed to exploration: its faith in the evolution of opinion shows that no clear belief in an ethical religion is being avowed. The concepts actually *are* being held in suspense. When the society says that it wishes for a 'religious revolution' it is not casting itself in the rôle of a revolutionary. It is merely welcoming a revolution *in* religion. When ethical religion is mentioned the society is referring to that part of religion which is not barbaric, the part to which assent may be given. If there is any bridge between the concepts held in suspense it is in the near-concluding word 'aspirations'. In the last sentence it is, indeed, almost stated that religion is aspiration.

'Aims and Principles' delicately maintains an interest in religion, but it does not declare the society to be religious. The 'object' left plenty of room for variations in spoken emphasis which could generate variations in meaning. A member could understand that the object of the society was the cultivation of a rational *religious* sentiment, not too far from theism. Another member could understand that the object of the society was the cultivation of a *rational-religious* sentiment, and find in this hyphenated expression a direct allusion to George Jacob Holyoake's secularist periodical *The Reasoner* (1845–61) which took a stand on 'Rational Religion'.[14]

At last South Place had managed to state what it stood for. It dealt with the problem of finding a new minister with equal flair – by finally discarding the ministerial rôle.

In the summer of 1897 Mrs. Conway fell seriously ill, so her husband returned to New York. By April 1899 the society solved its problem by deciding that the inclusiveness and provisionality of the recent 'Aims and Principles' and the 'object' should be mirrored in new leadership arrangements. It resolved once and for all to abandon leaders, quasi-ministers, and to have a panel of 'lecturers' instead, who would divide up the task of delivering Sunday discourses. It decided that there should begin in 1900 a series of discourses reviewing the achievement of the past century. The speakers or 'Appointed Lecturers' were to be J. A. Hobson, J. M. Robertson and Herbert Burrows.

Initially this plan faltered because of the South African war, in which an intense interest was taken by the predominantly pro-Boer society. When S. C. Cronwright-Schreiner came to Britain 'to tell the truth about the war', one of his first speaking engagements was at South Place. Despite fear of riot the invitation was honoured, though Cronwright-Schreiner was dismayed to see a crowd of working men thronging the entrance. He was told they were 'free speech men' come to see him through. The audience was advised that applause was not customary in a religious building. The war delayed the Appointed Lecturer scheme being put into operation because both J. A. Hobson (who had arranged Cronwright-Schreiner's lecture tour) and J. M. Robertson were involved in South African affairs, both paying visits to the country. Furthermore, Herbert Burrows was ill, so the triumvirate could not really set to work until 1903. Their tenure was permanently and formally established in the spring of 1907, when Joseph McCabe was appointed to join them.[15]

At the turn of the century the identity of South Place was defined by its choice of permanent lecturers – and by the lecturers' agreement to serve, which said something in public about the society.

The most senior in the group was Herbert Burrows (1845–1923) who proved to be the best 'society man', regularly attending meetings, while the others only turned up for their own lectures. As a civil servant, an official in the Inland Revenue Department, he was closest in profession to the members. Burrows was born in a Suffolk village in the hungry 1840s. He educated himself with Cassell's shilling handbooks, becoming a pupil teacher at the age of thirteen. At eighteen he moved to a school in Redhill, soon leaving for a post as an excise officer, which took him all over the country. He became a non-collegiate student in Cambridge, did not take a degree, and became interested in spiritualism. In 1877 he went to London, where he joined radical clubs and fell under the spell of Mazzini. He helped found the Metropolitan Radical Federation, and Bradlaugh in his opposition to the blasphemy laws. Through this connection he met Annie Besant, with whom he collaborated in the incident of the Bryant and May match-girl strike. Under her influence he turned to Theosophy. Burrows was a founding member of the Social Democratic Federation, 'a committed Socialist', according to his fellow-lecturer, J. A. Hobson.

Burrows was probably the only Theosophist at South Place – which is not to say that the members were only either rationalists or theists: one leading member, Wallis Mansford, brother of the architect of Conway Hall, experienced visitations from the other world. But Theosophy was not out of tune with the ambience of South Place or its 'object'. Quite apart from its cosmogony, Theosophy had three drives: to seek the brotherhood of man, to study comparative religion, and to maintain a tolerant investigative attitude to nature. All three were compatible with 'rational religious sentiment', with what was known at South Place as the 'new tolerance'. In the late 1880s an ambitious series of lectures was given in its Institute on religion (naturally the one on Theosophy was delivered by Annie Besant), published as *Religious Systems of the World: A Contribution to the Study of Comparative Religion* (1890). The book has this epigraph:

The old intolerance has disappeared, and the old indifference which succeeded it has well-nigh disappeared also. The new tolerance of faith recognises as Divine all the creeds which have enabled men to overcome their bestial appetites with visions of things spiritual and eternal.

Burrows's phrase for this tolerance was 'constructive rationalism', which is prepared to see physical reality as an unfinished book: 'We find that almost every day we are approaching the borders of a realm of thought, reason and experiment in which the subtler unseen forces of physical nature are more and more coming into play.' The society wanted to have one of its lecturers sensitive to 'subtler unseen forces'; so much the better that Burrows was a radical as well.

In the summer of 1907 Burrows retired from the Inland Revenue, giving over all his time to his voluntary activities, to the Women's Trade Union League, the Women's Industrial Council, the S.D.F., the International Peace and Arbitration Committee, and to the three east London schools of which he was a manager. He went on lecturing until halted by illness in 1917.[16]

Burrows, the sweet-natured socialist, occupied one end of the panel of lecturers. At the other extreme was John MacKinnon Robertson (1856–1933), militant secularist and Liberal. (J. A. Hobson considered himself to be the fulcrum.) With the appointment of J. M. Robertson the society finally turned its back on Stanton Coit. When in office Coit made overtures to the secularists, though he castigated their (to him) obsession with the blasphemy laws. They retorted that he, too, would be obsessed if South Place, like the National Secular Society, was prevented from receiving endowments as a result of these laws. In their view Coit fudged the issue of neo-Malthusianism, which for secularists was *the* issue that underlay all others. J. M. Robertson worked on Bradlaugh's 'radical advocate and free-thought journal', *The National Reformer*, which regarded Coit derisively: 'A simple desire to do good will not suffice to constitute an "Ethical Movement" in the narrowest sense of that elastic phrase; and secularists want logic, and historical and mental and social science, as well as ethical aspiration.' This is what Robertson was hired to supply.

The society characteristically ignored public opinion. Robertson was a hot potato, described by Hobson as Bradlaugh's 'chief intellectual lieutenant', and associated in the public mind with atheism, republicanism and birth control. On the platform he had considerable charm in his man-of-letters brown velvet jacket, with an attractive Scottish lilt in his spoken delivery. He edited *The National Reformer* from March 1891, starting *The Free Review* when it folded. He wrote for *The Morning Leader*, under the pseudonym of 'Scrutator', which sent him to South Africa in 1900 to report on the operation of martial law. His dispatches were published as *Wrecking the Empire* (1901). By that year Robertson was in his forties and author of nearly thirty books, including two massive surveys, *A Short History of Freethought: Ancient and Modern* (1899) and *An Introduction to English Politics* (1900). He had just embarked on his career as a Shakespearean commentator with *Montaigne and Shakespeare* (1897): one of his first publications, *The Religion of Shakespeare* (1887), had originally been lectures delivered at South Place. His very first book, published when he was still a journalist on the Edinburgh *Evening News*, in a team of Bradlavian atheists, was on *Walt Whitman, Poet and Democrat* (1884).

Robertson was an ideal Liberal for South Place. When Bradlaugh died his supporters wanted Robertson as a replacement candidate for his parliamentary seat in Northampton. Though selected for the general election of 1892 he withdrew, offering himself, but unsuccessfully, as a Liberal-Radical in 1894. But in the Liberal landslide of 1906 he was returned as M.P. for Tyneside, which seat he held until 1918. Asquith appointed him parliamentary secretary to the Board of Trade in 1911, which, until 1915, made his appearances at South Place less frequent. Robertson was an abrasive Cobdenite who took every opportunity of reminding his own party, as well as the Opposition, of the highest Liberal authorities. His political philosophy was shown vividly in the foreign policy debate in July 1909 on the forthcoming visit to Britain of the Tsar of Russia, which was opposed by Keir Hardie as a protest against the savagery of Russian domestic policy. Robertson countered Hardie with the view that it was unwise even to debate the issue, because democratic and anti-democratic interventionism could provoke international hostility. He thought it irrelevant to speak of the wickedness of the Russian authorities: 'It is no business of ours whether there is a case or not. The whole question is . . . what the Russian people think of the matter.' Backs should be turned on the old habits of putting the wrongs of others right, especially when there were some foreign affairs which certainly *were* the business of Britain – like Egypt, on which Robertson spoke frequently, to the displeasure of the leaders of his own party.

South Place had acquired a combative rationalist, but also someone who spoke for the old Liberalism, the old standards of moral nobility and earnestness, to use the terms employed by Robertson himself to demonstrate what was currently lacking in public life, a deficiency which he was to bring to the door eventually of the detested Lloyd George. South Place also acquired a polymath. Robertson published continuously on politics, philosophy, history, economics and literature. Even his smaller projects, like his edition of Shaftesbury's *Characteristics* or his encouragement of Trechmann's translation of Montaigne, would have graced an orthodox academic career. When Harold Laski summed up the career of Robertson for the *Dictionary of National Biography* he singled out for comment the work on H. T. Buckle, on the evolution of states, on German racial theories, on free trade and on 'thrift', in the last instance with reference to the pre-Keynesian under-consumptionist theories which Robertson shared with Hobson. There was another thread in his career which was important for South Place and which later assessment may find to be central in his work.

When South Place decided to appoint a panel of lecturers instead of a quasi-ministerial leader it made a move for pluralism and against in-dividualism. Robertson was in a definite sense an anti-individualist, though perhaps only in one sense, because it was difficult for a Liberal admirer of Bradlaugh to be thoroughly anti-individualist. But a distrust of the conception of individual genius was an important strain in Robert-son's thinking. On that concept in its connection with literature he believed that literary capacity came from 'the totality of intellectual and economic conditions'. Some of his very early work, only published at the turn of the century in *Christianity and Mythology*, was on the mythical element in Christianity, going beyond Renan in its conviction that the Christ-figure was a focus for collective ideas. Robertson used Frazer, but diverged from his conclusion that great religious movements could spring only 'from the conscious and deliberate efforts of extraordinary minds'. Robertson believed that the totality of conditions counted for more than the extraordinary mind, and for this emphasis he was valued by one later South Place lecturer, the Marxist Archibald Robertson. The doubts of the first Robertson about 'extraordinary' minds were germane to his work on Shakespeare which belongs to the main stream of his thought and was not merely the pastime of an incorrigible investigator. Robertson believed as little in Shakespeare's solo responsibility for his creations as he did in the individual genius of Christ. He was a 'disintegrator', employing the methods of the Positivist scholar, F. G. Fleay, who died in 1909. So he was concerned with Shakespeare's in-debtedness to others and in hypotheses of collaboration. In this field the issue should not be clouded by argument about the plausibility of Robert-son's particular authorial attributions. His theory of authorship does not have to be damaged by his unconvincingness in this or that respect. In an age more committed to the concept of genius than our own his boisterous expression of his theory caused some bristling. Here is one of his more provoking accounts of Shakespeare.

What emerges for us thus far is the conception of a very plastic intelligence, a good deal led and swayed by immediate circumstances, but at bottom very sanely related to life, and so possessing a latent faculty for controlling its destinies; not much cultured, not profound, not deeply passionate; not particularly reflective though copious in utterance; a personality which of itself, if under no pressure of pecuniary need, would not be likely to give the world any sign of mental capacity whatever.

This piece of bardolator-baiting exaggerates Shakespeare's mental condi-tion before his discovery, through Florio, of Montaigne by 1603, in order to heighten the main point that Robertson wishes to make, that ac-complishment, or genius, is dependent on circumstances: 'all mastery roots in lower precedent . . . every masterpiece implicates in itself the past attainment of a thousand other men'. Robertson's case is that the momentous event in the maturing of Shakespeare was his reading of Montaigne, the first great modern thinker and the one from whom Robertson draws the idea which he applies to Shakespeare, that of the collaborativeness of creation. This idea would have appealed at South Place, whose members felt dependent on each other for their education, and which, of course, just before appointing Robertson had committed itself to the authority of 'evolving knowledge'.[17]

Changing the chapel, 1912–1930

South Place set its house ideologically in order with its new system of Appointed Lecturers, and by its articulation of an 'object'. The same brooms swept round *Hymns and Anthems*, the collection by Fox and Eliza Flower, which was replaced in 1900 by *Hymns of Modern Thought*. Some of the old favourites were brought up to date, in spite of criticism: one of the most telling points made was that the old hymns encapsulated the society's history, representing 'landmarks of emotion', so they should be left intact to maintain 'bonds of association' between members. One verse by Fox was significantly altered in the 1900 revision:

> 'Make us a god', said man:
> Then Religion followed Art,
> And answered, Look within:
> God is in thine own own heart.
> Within that temple is the holiest shrine:
> Silent revere, and be thyself divine.

'Religion' in this stanza was changed to 'Reason'.

But in spite of all the changes, members and visitors still attended a chapel at South Place, even though the red mahogany platform, with 'To Thine Own Self Be True' inscribed on its back wall, faced seats, not pews. In one respect the Sunday services were somewhat more like those of a chapel than in the time of Fox over fifty years before. The reading was shorter, 'about five minutes' requested the service sheet, which also reminded the lecturer to maintain the right tone by waiting for silence before allowing the service to proceed. The chapel was also somewhat dingy, even though it was cheered by electrification in 1904. In the early Edwardian years several of the old guard passed away, including W. J. Reynolds, William Sheowring and Clarence Seyler. Membership was fairly low: between 1901 and 1911 it hovered between 270 and 280 with occasional booms, but never went above 300. Takings from seat rents dropped, as the cheaper seats were preferred for purchase. That the society needed restoration was grasped most fully by Frank Overy, a young recruit from the South London Ethical Society, who set about reviving a plan which had been first mooted in 1901 to rebuild the chapel.[18]

In 1913 the problem of sale and move was debated, but the outbreak of war prevented progress. In 1919 the society returned to the issue, but nervously withdrew from it, even rejecting the old plan of 1901, because numbers had dropped steeply and only just got back to about 250. However, Frank Overy as secretary persisted, persuading members to consider establishing a link with the Rationalist Press Association to plan joint premises. The society agreed, turned about face, and considered sale and establishment nearer central London. Once its mind was made up the R.P.A. link was forgotten. Overy himself searched for a site in Bloomsbury, which with the growth of London University was in process of becoming an academic centre. He found one in Red Lion Square, just east of Southampton Row. Overy's enthusiasm was infectious and a grandiose scheme for a new free-thought centre evolved, including a thousand-seater hall with organ, cinematographic facilities and a flat roof for recreation. A hall rather than a chapel was planned. It was to be the second and major tribute to the memory of Moncure Conway, to be named after him. (In 1907 a guest lectureship had been endowed under his name, the appointment being decided by a committee dedicated for the purpose, not by the general committee – a characteristic example of the society's cellular structure.)[19]

While Conway Hall was planned there were new lecturers to hear. Two were appointed during the war.

On the eve of the 1914 disaster there was an abundance of subject-matter on both social and international ethics. The Liberal era was ending in varied rebellions; Apart from the suffragettes, Syndicalism was active in the trade unions, and the Guild Socialists were a troubling element. The Kaiser's war stimulated interest in German theories of the State and the biological necessity of war. South Place speakers were better qualified than almost any group in London to discuss such things.

Thus wrote one of the new lecturers, Samuel Kerkham Ratcliffe (1868–1958). He first lectured in the chapel in November 1912 on Rudolph Eucken, who was enjoying 'a reputation among religious liberals'. J. M. Robertson disapproved 'always against trading with the enemy'. S. K. Ratcliffe was appointed as a member of the panel in 1915: in the course of forty years he became one of the most reliable speakers, and author of an excellent brief chronicle, *The Story of South Place* (1955).

S. K. Ratcliffe knew the chapel in the 1890s. His father had a flour mill in King's Lynn, but moved to Manchester to work as a railway clerk when the business collapsed. Ratcliffe was boarded and schooled in London with an aunt. He picked up journalistic work, mainly on the evening *Echo* (owned by the Spencerian Liberal, J. Passmore Edwards), eventually becoming a leader-writer on it. He then was successively assistant editor and editor of the Calcutta *Statesman*, returning to London to work on the *Daily News*.

The second war-time appointment, in 1918, was of Cecil Delisle Burns (1879–1942) who was a great inspiration on the chapel platform in the 1920s, invited to give as many as twenty lectures a year. Delisle Burns was a former Catholic, trained by Benedictines. He was brought up in the West Indies, from which he was sent to the ancient Catholic school in Hertfordshire, St. Edmund's College. He read for the Classical Tripos at Cambridge, graduating in 1900. He then studied mediaeval philosophy, and virtually professed it in the delivery of Latin theses and disputations, at a Benedictine seminary in Rome. He was fascinated by the material relics of the Roman Empire and early Christianity. He returned to teach at St. Edmund's, but his superiors deemed that his interests had become heretical: he was dismissed and excommunicated. Delisle Burns proceeded into extension teaching in London, and took a London doctorate. He became associated with Patrick Geddes. During the war he took a post in the Ministry of Reconstruction, and after it in the intelligence division of the Ministry of Labour, moving to a similar post in the research department shared by the Trades Union Congress and the Labour Party.

Delisle Burns wrote copiously. His most popular book was *Political Ideals: Their Nature and Development* (1915). After the war he regularised his teaching with posts at Birkbeck College (on which he published a history in 1924) and the London School of Economics and Political Science. In 1927 he took the Stephenson chair of citizenship at Glasgow University. In the 1930s tuberculosis claimed him; he suffered considerably before his death in 1945. Nonetheless from 1935 he worked on a subject in which his interest had been aroused in Rome, the decline of the Roman Empire after the barbarian invasions, and the growth of mediaeval Europe. *The First Europe: A Study of the Establishment of Mediaeval Christendom, A.D. 400–800* (1947) appeared posthumously, partly through the agency of R. H. Tawney and the Hammonds. Delisle Burns identified with his period, depicting the irresponsibility of the wealthy and the deterioration of their security as having more than a touch of Edwardian plutocracy. As an administrator himself, the author 'learnt to appreciate such difficulties as a Roman official in the sixth century had to face'. Essentially *The First Europe* is about moral authority:

All men have certain tendencies or impulses which are stimulated when they become aware of something beautiful, something good in human conduct and character or something true in statements or judgments. Certain men and women, either as individuals or as agents of social institutions, have the ability to excite in others these tendencies or impulses so that their influence is accepted – all the more readily if they have neither wealth nor power of their own. Against such men and women the holders of wealth and power contend in vain. These men and women have moral authority.

This could have been a flattering conception at South Place, where members could see a Europe resembling the first Europe, which had been characterised by what Delisle Burns termed 'nomadism', seeing, too, the acquisition of power by modern barbarians, the agents of capitalism and the post-1870 'mass'. He found in modern Europe

the same 'failure of nerve' among the civilised when they see that the traditional system has not abolished poverty or war; and the same simple belief among the 'have nots' – the barbarians – that can appropriate the results of civilisation or the applications of science without adopting the process which has made them possible. This is a fundamental problem in the history of civilised life. Those who do not play a part in the establishment and maintenance of a particular type of civilisation – who therefore look at it from the outside – see only its final results and cannot understand the nature of the methods by which alone those results have been attained.

South Placers liked to hear that they needed education and why. They were moved and disturbed by Delisle Burns's more abrasive denunciations – for example, by his address of October 1924, inaugurating a South Place branch of the League of Nations Union, in which he graphically explained the research into poison gas that was undertaken in the United States.[20]

During the 1920s preparations were made for the society's new home, Conway Hall. It was designed by Frederick Herbert Mansford (1871–1946), a member of a South Place dynasty. His brother Wallis was the mediumistic author of *Bridging Two Worlds* and founder of the Stationers Association. His sister Amy married E. J. Harrington whose sister in turn married F. G. Gould, an editor of the society's journal. Harrington and Gould had senior positions in the Post Office; the latter was an expert on fungi and president of the British Mycological Society. F. H. Mansford was one of the first to suggest a new building for the society when he was a youth at the turn of the century. He became an architect and architectural historian of repute, with a special interest in restoration. He put many hours into work for the Architectural Graphic Records Committee of the Royal Institute of British Architects: he was its secretary from 1931 until it became the National Buildings Record in 1940. Apart from his practice and scholarly interests Mansford shared with his friend Paul Waterhouse a concern for town planning, serving on the R.I.B.A. Western Exits of London committee.

Conway Hall was Mansford's largest project, demonstrating his ingenuity and knowledge of modern materials. The society had acquired a wide strip of land running from the north corner of Red Lion Square along an alley (Lamb's Conduit Passage) to the nearest thoroughfare to the east, Red Lion Street, and also a narrower strip, at right angles to the main one, running across the block to the nearest thoroughfare to the north (Theobald's Road). Mansford planned a main entrance on the angle of this L-shaped site, with a narrow arch rising to the top of the upper floor. This arch is flanked by two columns in silver-grey brick, the colour of the building as a whole, varied with red brick detailing. The two columns do not look heavy because there is so much glass in the façade – wide windows on the upper level (of the library) as well as in and above the entrance doors. The glazing bars are in tidy criss-cross patterns. The entrance lobby has doors to the auditorium (the main hall) and curving stairs up to the library. Straight ahead is the corridor of the narrow arm, off which is a smaller hall and offices. The general feel is that of the Royal Shakespeare Theatre at Stratford-on-Avon, the old Shakespeare Memorial Theatre.

If in the late twentieth century Conway Hall looks drab it should be remembered that in 1930 it was freshly modern with excellent lighting. The auditorium has a glazed ceiling, accommodating 300 at ground level and 180 in a gallery. Mansford had light panelling nailed directly to the brickwork and used acoustic plaster, which contributed to the creation of the best hall in London for chamber music. Because of the nature of the site, with only the entrance visible from Red Lion Square, Mansford was aware that his design could appear incoherent: he tried, not quite successfully, to make the elevation hang together by disposing six handsome stone urns, bought from a City bank, along roof level, two of them on top of the entrance columns.[21]

In September 1929 Conway Hall was ready. The society was delighted, and in debt to Frank Overy for the conception and planning of the new home. He was appointed manager of the hall. Tragically he was to kill himself in 1932, so he never saw what the society made of itself, at last out of chapel.

Conway Hall in Holborn, 1930–1980

Though chapel no more, in 1935 twenty members signed a document stating that Conway Hall was their regular place of worship. It was therefore certificated for marriages by the Registrar-General. South

Place hymns continued to be sung in the clean, light hall, though the organ was not brought to it. In the mid-1930s membership increased to over 400; in the 1920s it had never reached 300. There was plenty for young people to do, especially popular being the Conway Discussion Circle, which had well-known speakers and arranged two full-scale debates a season. Young members campaigned for divorce law reform, world government and progressive education. They got together in a Federation of Progressive Societies and Individuals in 1931, the basis of the still-existing Progressive League. Its mentor was the 'it depends-what-you-mean' philosopher, C. E. M. Joad.

The old guard liked listening better than campaigning. Ratcliffe was the most regular lecturer of the 1930s. The Edwardian group of Appointed Lecturers survived but were aged. J. M. Robertson died in 1933 and Hobson in 1940, but he never lectured after 1934. After 1934 McCabe was occasionally to be heard. Delisle Burns stopped about the same time, kept away by his post in Glasgow, and by illness.

After the outbreak of war one of Ratcliffe's friends became a popular Appointed Lecturer. Archibald Robertson (1886–1961) had joined the Communist Party in 1937, having published as 'Robert Arch' for some years, first to escape the attention of his father (Bishop of Exeter, died in 1930), and then that of the Admiralty in which he was a civil servant. Robertson never joined the society – Appointed Lecturers did not have to; and they could not hold office – as he did not share its sympathy for, if not betrothal to, Christian civilisation, which was alien to his scientific humanism. But members liked him. His radicalism had three sources: Shelley (especially *Queen Mab*, 'with its devastating notes'), J. W. Draper, the important physicist and chemist, also author of *A History of the Conflict between Science and Religion* (1874), but above all Ernest Belfort Bax, the S.D.F. barrister and collaborator with William Morris in *On Socialism, its Growth and Outcome* (1894). Robertson read Bax's *The Ethics of Socialism* (1889) in his last year at Winchester. In his Tory Anglican boyhood it was bad enough to be a Liberal, but Robertson went to Labour after the Liberal landslide of 1906:

> It seemed silly, if you were a Socialist, not to be in the Labour Party. If organised labour could not be led in the direction of socialism, how much less could the unorganised mass outside? In reasoning thus I was nearer Marxism than I knew. Long before my time Engels had censured the S.D.F. on exactly that ground.

Robertson's materialism may have made an impact on members that can be judged by their answers to a questionnaire distributed at the time of his death in 1961. Of the 114 members who replied only 28 called themselves ethicists, but there were 72 humanists. Agnostics and atheists came about level, with 42 against 38. As for retaining hymns, 26 were in favour and 46 against.

Two of Robertson's successors, leading speakers of the 1960s, deserve note. John Lewis (1878–1976) was also a communist. He had been a Presbyterian and Unitarian minister, then a Marxist and national organiser for the Left Book Club, from which he especially promoted the work of Christopher Caudwell. After the war he lectured on philosophy at Morley College, and for the Workers' Educational Association, publishing prolifically. Lewis had been close to the roots of the British ethical movement, having known well Coit's experiments at the Ethical Church, at which he took an occasional service. As late as 1974 he stood up for Coit, rebutting the charge that he reduced religion to mere ethics. On the contrary, he lifted ethics to the level of religion,

but without the least suggestion of theology or metaphysics. You don't reduce religion to ethics, *you locate it there*. The ultimate demand of our loyalty and devotion is in the ethical demand, not in general, not in theory, but in actual fact, in the specific occasions on which we are confronted with our responsibility for and to actual people in their sacredness as persons. A demand not to be argued about as an ethical theory, not just to be only *formally* recognised, but *felt* in the way religious people feel the command of God's will: 'Here stand I, I can no other.'

This shows very well the position of the post-war South Place ethicist, and is comparable to that of a figure to be shortly encountered, Albert Lovecy, arguably the society's philosopher of the 1970s (though he was not an Appointed Lecturer).[22]

The second important post-war lecturer was Harold J. Blackham (born 1903), appointed in 1965. He joined the Ethical Church soon after Conway Hall was opened, but had contact with all spheres of the ethical, and humanist, movement. After the war it was Blackham's distinction to have interested Julian Huxley in the Ethical Union, persuading Huxley to open the International Ethical and Humanist Union in Amsterdam in 1952: Coit had always wanted Huxley to participate but never succeeded in enlisting him. From Huxley came one of the strongest ideas of religion possessed at South Place. It was probably his connection with Blackham that persuaded the society to join the Ethical Union in 1951, having long disdained the body that originated in Coit's early ambitions for ethicism, even though the quarrel with Coit was over: he had delivered the Conway Memorial Lecture in 1937. Huxley's religious sense was provisionally expressed in *Science and Religion* (1923), and definitively in *Religion without Revelation* (1927), revised with the help of Blackham for 1947. Huxley considered his 'evolutionary humanism' could be a 'developed religion' if it satisfied the following requirements:

It will not merely be confined to man's more or less immediate reaction to the mysterious or sacred; it will not be content with a system (often incomplete or self-contradictory) of mythology or of primitive rationalisation as to its theology; nor only with traditional ritual or formalism as to its code of action. *On the contrary, it will always extend its conception of what is sacred and a proper object of religious feeling to include man's destiny and his relation with the rest of the world;* it will apply the pure force of intellect to its ideas, and shall attempt a theology [*sic*] or intellectual basis which shall be both logical and comprehensive, accurate and coherent.

Blackham thought that Huxley, more than anyone, handled 'the essential task of Humanism' to create a secular faith.[23]

Besides Lewis and Blackham, two other chapel leftists, somewhat in the mould of Harry Snell (like him raised to the peerage), were appointed as lecturers in the 1960s. Reginald Sorensen (1891–1971) went to the House of Lords and Fenner Brockway (born 1888), veteran Labour Party anti-imperialist, was created a Life Peer in the same year. Both concentrated on issues of Commonwealth, like Snell. Brockway said with authority that 'Reg did more for Indian independence than any man appointed to [the] parliamentary commission.' Both had originally been under the spell of R. J. Campbell's 'new theology' at the City Temple. Both were Labour M.P.s for constituencies in the same east London borough. Sorensen was a Unitarian who called himself an agnostic. His view of worship was invoked in 1980 when South Place presented itself as a religious organisation in the Chancery Division of the High Court.[24]

This last-mentioned incident was a very important one in the history of the society. From the mid-1960s it was seldom able to forget that a costly legal hearing was ahead. The society was set on the path to it by an event, not of its own making, in 1967; its conduct upon this path was partly determined by a decision it took in 1966. The event was the revocation of the society's charitable status; the decision was to create a new post, that of General Secretary.

The post of General Secretary was created, partly, because it was felt that the world outside should be able to identify a managing administrator. A group of Trustees is responsible legally for Conway Hall; administration and policy are determined by a general committee which delegates to autonomous sub-committees. On significant issues the Trustees and the general committee have to be instructed by a general meeting of members. Up to the move to Conway Hall much organisation had been done by one lady, Caroline Fletcher-Smith, for fifty years. After 1933 several other secretaries were appointed, and after the war there were two of opposing persuasion in Hector Hawton of the Rationalist Press Association, and J. Hutton Hynd, a protégé of Coit who returned to London in his fifties after many years with the St. Louis (Missouri)

Ethical Culture Society. After his retirement in 1953 there were two interim incumbents and then the first General Secretary, who was meant to be a mediator with the public and within a society then riven with personality conflicts (exacerbated by conflict between the humanists and the old ethicists). The first General Secretary was Harry Knight who resigned in 1969. He was succeeded in 1970 by a recent member who had got to know Conway Hall from attending anti-nuclear war meetings, Peter Cadogan. It eventually fell to him to pilot the society into court.

Peter Cadogan (born 1921) converted from Anglicanism during wartime R.A.F. service. He joined the Communist Party in 1946, and, having opposed the Soviet invasion of Hungary, was expelled ten years later, at which he joined the Labour Party, from whose branch in Cambridge (where he was a schoolteacher) he was also expelled. He was founder-member of the Socialist Labour League which he left for the liberalism of the anti-nuclear movement, 'though I am not and was not a pacifist'. After the 1959 protest march to Aldermaston, Cadogan organised many demonstrations in East Anglia, becoming full-time secretary of the Committee of 100. In Conway Hall the portrait of Paine and the bust of Holyoake disposed him to join. Cadogan was a vigorous radical, of somewhat naval manner, 'forward-looking for some years', remarked a long-standing member, but as General Secretary 'unfortunately began to develop ideas that he *was* the Society, so had to go'. Perhaps: certainly the part he played in the charity legal case caused his downfall; but there was another issue which made him unpopular as well.[25]

As General Secretary one of Cadogan's responsibilities was to administer the renting out of rooms in Conway Hall, which provided a crucial source of income. A series of incidents created a bitter debate within the society on its lettings policy.

In the autumn of 1973 a fascist organisation, the National Front, held a meeting in the main hall. The building was protected by a police cordon which was attacked by demonstrators mainly from the International Marxist Group. In June 1974 a group called Liberation previously known as the Movement for Colonial Freedom, representing a fairly wide spectrum of opinion to the left of the Labour Party (including the I.M.G. and the Communist Party), booked a smaller room for 15 June. The National Front was booked into the main hall for the same night. Cadogan anticipated a clash between the groups, arranging with the police that they were to be directed into the building by different routes. On the day the N.F. marched to its meeting without incident, but a demonstration by Liberation sympathisers in Red Lion Square developed into a violent scuffle in which a young man, Kevin Gately, was killed. The N.F. was widely held responsible for his death and South

Place (effectively Cadogan, its spokesman) censured. A public enquiry under Lord Scarman was initiated.

Cadogan issued a statement defending the society's open lettings policy, arguing liberally that vicious renters put themselves self-evidently in the wrong. He moderated his defence when reminded by the Appointed Lecturer John Lewis that indirect sponsorship of the National Front contravened the Potsdam Agreements which forbade advocacy of national socialism. In April 1975 the National Front returned, this time to disrupt a televised meeting of the Common Market Safeguards Committee. Racist stickers were plastered about the lobby of Conway Hall. Cadogan banned the N.F. for six months. The general committee favoured a total ban, but a limited motion was passed at the A.G.M. in May, allowing rental to anyone so long as 'the terms of our contracts and the law of the land' were not contravened. This, however, did not satisfy a large and thoughtful minority which believed that it was not enough for an avowedly *ethical* society to invoke in general terms 'the law of the land'. Should not higher standards apply within Conway Hall than in Red Lion Square? This view had been adumbrated earlier in 1975 by Albert and Ray Lovecy in 'An Ethical Memorandum' in the society's monthly journal *The Ethical Record*. They pointed out that freedom of discourse was not freedom 'to proclaim the unthinkable', 'a system for which no ethical case can be made'. The Lovecys reminded members that there was precedent for excluding offensive hirers: in 1893 anarchists were banned after a meeting at which 'murder and outrage' were advocated as a means of political activity.

In the coming years the issue arose again in a form which posed a moral and material threat to the society. In September 1977 an obscure organisation known as Paedophile Information Exchange, meant to improve contacts between adults wanting children as sexual partners, was allowed to hold a meeting. There was some local outrage and Lovecy called a meeting to put pressure on the society either to enforce its 'law of the land' motion (which had arguably been broken) or get members to 'cease to "simply *defend* the XYZ's right to meet" and turn their minds to our proper concern, i.e. "simply to *think about* the XYZ's right go meet *here*" '. Then, in 1979, the National Front was allowed to rent space for an agents' meeting. Late in the year the mind of the society was drastically concentrated when, under financial pressure from the impending Chancery case, it applied to its local authority, Camden Borough Council, for relief from rates (that is, local taxes). The appeal was refused. South Place offered a reasonable case: many of its members came from the borough, and Conway Hall was a public asset. However, in November 1976 the borough had agreed that organisations which incited racial hatred should not be allowed to use council facilities: grant-aided bodies were urged to apply the same policy. South Place stood to lose £4,350. At the A.G.M. of 1980 it was voted (30 to 27) that the N.F. should henceforth be excluded.

Neither Cadogan nor Lovecy was satisfied, the one impatient with the mundane materialism of the motion and the other also believing that the occasion called for something better than an invocation of 'rational commercial practice'. But the society did put its appeal again to Camden Borough Council and in return was allowed the equivalent to a grant in the form of rate relief in 1981.

During the free speech debates of the 1970s Cadogan possibly did not begin to 'develop ideas that he *was* the Society' – and his ideas did not command its assent. However, he was certainly identified with the society in the public mind. In 1980 the right-wing Shavian columnist of *The Times*, Bernard Levin, seized on the society's dispute with the left-wing borough council, identifying a posture of intransigent tolerance with General Secretary Cadogan, whom he called 'probably mad . . . but if so there are an awful lot of people I wish he would bite'. The society was undoubtedly tolerant, but it had not consciously exercised the policy of toleration which Cadogan defended. He began to look suspiciously like a leader.

Throughout the arguments on free speech Cadogan was also under attack for the way he handled the society's problems when it lost its charitable status – and for his understanding of the society when he (legitimately) spoke as its representative in court. Until 1960 South Place was, in the eyes of the law, a chapel, and so a registered charity enjoying tax exemptions. But in that year a new Charities Act became law requiring all such bodies to register again. South Place applied early in 1967: because of the scale of the operation the Charity Commissioners had not asked its potential clients to hurry. The Commissioners replied, swiftly, that the society could no longer be regarded as charitable. On appeal, through the Attorney-General, who is ultimately responsible for charities in Britain, the situation became more difficult. The society may have hoped that while it was distant from the group of protestant dissenters, worshipping One God the Father, as stated in the Deed of 1824, at least it acted in tune with its deeds as amended in 1907 and, to mark the move to Conway Hall, 1930. The 1907 amendment was a general statement, referring for elucidation of the society's beliefs to its Rules, which contained the reference to cultivation of a 'rational religious sentiment' discussed above. However, the Attorney-General was advised that the twentieth-century amendments were actually invalid. It appeared that the society had to stand by its original Deed. A further appeal was made to the Commissioners on this basis, and it was rejected. South Place had no option but to seek a judgment of its case in the High Court of Chancery, a costly matter, compounded by cessation of tax relief and rising local taxes.[26]

From 1967 to the summer of 1980 the problem of going to Chancery nagged into the crannies of the society in a manner reminiscent of *Bleak House*. Inevitably the new General Secretary, Peter Cadogan, played a leading part, at first eagerly (at dealing with a genuinely historical issue), later with exasperation. The Trustees, on whom it fell legally to make the appeal, agreed before Cadogan's appointment to submit that the society had in fact not deviated from its original religious remit, doing so largely on the advice of one Appointed Lecturer, Peter Cronin, and the society's Queen's Counsel, Owen Swingland. They decided to stake the case on the original Trust Deed, rather than argue the validity of the then-questionable later deeds. At a members' meeting on 16 April 1975 the general committee was authorised to go to the High Court on these terms. Affidavits were prepared, by Peter Cadogan, H. J. Blackham, and by the Professor of Religious Studies at the new University of Lancaster, Ninian Smart.

A related legal problem affected the conduct of the society. In the winter of 1975 a local London newspaper reported on a marriage that had been solemnised at Conway Hall, long registered as the 'place of worship' of 20 members. South Place had an established tradition of performing services, for funerals, memorials, and for the 'naming' of children, in which great interest had been aroused by an 'open access' B.B.C. television programme about the society in January 1975. In 1977 the Deputy Registrar-General ruled that Conway Hall could not be used for weddings under the terms of the Places of Worship Registration Act (1885). He was probably influenced by the 1970 ruling of Lord Denning that marriages could only be solemnised in places whose principal use is for 'the worship of God or [to do] reverence to a deity'.[27]

By 1978 the Chancery hearing was on a nearer horizon. Cadogan confidently declared that 'we are manifestly the same Society that engrossed the Title Deed in 1825'. In the same year two new lecturers were appointed. Both were secular (or, as they will be called later, 'simple') humanists. Harry Stopes-Roe was chairman of the British Humanist Association and Nicholas Walter, grandson of S. K. Ratcliffe, was managing editor of the Rationalist Press Association, editor of *New Humanist*, and enjoyed affectionate notoriety as the anti-theological scourge of British newspaper correspondence columns.

Members may have been perturbed to read on one page of their *Ethical Record* that two militant secularists had been appointed, while on another

Cadogan stated that the society 'retained an essentially religious identity'. The history of South Place, in which 'religion' was defined very broadly indeed, may have consoled them. But it was becoming uncomfortably clear that rather specific meanings were to be given to 'religion' in the claims that would be made about the society in Chancery, by those chosen to be its expositors. Agitation surfaced in July 1979, when a special meeting was called, very late in the society's normal calendar, to consider a paper by Albert Lovecy and vote on the motion 'that the Society has no theistic creed and does not practise worship'. Cadogan eventually managed to have this amended to 'does not practise worship of a deity'. In this form the motion was passed. Within days Nicholas Walter resigned as Appointed Lecturer, later remarking that 'many people . . . have joined the society as part of their rejection of religion'.[28]

Less than a year later in June 1980 in the High Court, Chancery Division, Mr. Justice Dillon heard the claims of the society to be religious. A good proportion of the members who listened from the public benches were not at all sure it was religious, at least not religious in the sense propounded by Peter Cadogan, the only expert witness called to give verbal testimony for South Place. He argued that it believed in 'religious humanism'. Outside the court room his view was contested by claims for two other forms of humanism, which could be called simple humanism and ethical humanism. We shall briefly consider these three humanisms.

Cadogan's case was that South Place remained in the tradition of protestant dissent, convinced like the old Puritans of the sovereignty of individual conscience. (His own passion for the individual was related to a plan for political regeneration outlined in a booklet called *Direct Democracy: An Appeal to the Professional Classes, to the Politically Disenchanted and to the Deprived*, published in 1974, revised a year later.) Out of respect for the individual grew the society's 'humanism'; awe at the depth of individual experience made the humanism 'religious'. South Place held these depths as sacred as the God of Christian modernists (like Don Cupitt in the tradition of Paul Tillich). From reverence Cadogan moved to the sacred and to 'sacralities' – reverence for the beautiful, the true and the good, for belonging to other persons and to groups. He thought that there was emerging 'a new liberal religion that is still seeking definition', glanced at in such labels as 'modernism', 'ethicism' and 'Christian humanism'. He claimed that at South Place reverence issued in a kind of worship, but not a kind recognised by English law, at any rate in 1980. He enlisted support from the findings of a commission on religious education in schools of 1967 which said that 'an act of worship has in practice many facets and evokes various levels of response'. (It concluded, however, that 'it can only be worship if it is indeed the appropriate response of creature to creator', which is not what Cadogan meant.) Cadogan was aware that his 'small "h" humanism' did not recommend itself to rationalists or secularists, but thought it in sympathy with the ecologists, the environmentalists, the decentralists, the networkers, and the women's movement. He hoped that free-thinkers, rationalists and secularists would come round. These were the people who professed the second of the three South Place humanisms, that is, simple humanism.

This humanism was not simple in any derogatory sense. It was straightforward, belonging to the old tradition of secularism. If in the late twentieth century it looks archaic it should be stressed emphatically that there were crucial issues which the free-thinkers made their own, such as voluntary euthanasia. Simple humanism appreciated whatever there was to be heard at Conway Hall, but it was not committed to its subtle (or nebulous) communal position: it could see no reason why the society should have a philosophy different from that of the Rationalist Press Association. One simple humanist was a prominent member of South Place. Barbara Smoker was brought up a Catholic, like Hector Hawton whose writing inspired her after she left the faith in 1949. She joined South Place in 1950, became a member of the general committee but worked as vigorously for the National Secular Society. A militant humanist, she espoused secular education, reform of the blasphemy laws, and campaigned courageously for the Voluntary Euthanasia Society. She was in demand to give addresses at secular funeral services. A buoyant figure, she claimed to have financed the manufacture of the first 'Make Love Not War' badges that were popular in Britain in the 1960s. At South Place she was from the beginning of the charity issue critical of seeking redress on religious grounds. Her humanism was simple only in the sense that it was clear cut. It needed less explication than the third humanism which attempted to be specific to South Place.[29]

The third humanism, ethical humanism, was espoused by Albert Lovecy, and explained in a paper of January 1975 called 'A Plea for Constructive Thinking on Charity Law'. Instead of taking the charity issue as one which descended arbitrarily upon the society he saw in the nature of the concept of charity a clue to its meaning. Lovecy argued that to be on the receiving end of state benefit, as opposed to charitable benefit, may feel like 'taking charity', but in fact the two types of benefit are different. State benefit is political, offered after ratification by decisions about how known resources should be allocated. Charity responded to the call for what should be done, 'granted our will and our aspirations for the future', and was concerned with relief as opposed to redress. It could *pioneer* benefit in advance of the social services. In its identification with aspiration Lovecy found in charity an element which could be called religious: in the debates that led to Chancery he took the view that the society may be religious because it was charitable, not religious because it worshipped. In his paper he recognised that 'encouraging attitudes of mind' was not held to be charitable in law, but he believed this was due for revision and that moral suasion should be admitted to have the kind of worth, relating to 'our wills and aspirations for the future', normally defined as charitable. He knew that moral suasion varies:

The real task is to distinguish between attitudes of mind that are worthy of encouragement and those that are not. Here we must apply our highest standards, 'above the law' [that is, *pioneering* benefit] and thus in the province of religion. Religion which had no effect on the 'attitude of mind' would be unworthy of the name. However, it is no longer honest to pretend that the immense wealth of objective knowledge won by mankind must *ever* play second fiddle to the intuitive 'soothsayings' from bygone days (with or without recent exegesis) as the bedrock of conscientious judgments. (My italics.)

Respect for 'objective knowledge' distinguished Lovecy's ethical humanism from Cadogan's religious humanism. Some of Cadogan's thought about the 'sacralities' was echoed in Julian Huxley, who was respected by almost all parties at South Place. But Cadogan neglected an element in Huxley which was prominent in Lovecy, the scientism. Lovecy was progressive and scientific, in conflict therefore with the Arnoldian, 'cultural', religious humanism of Cadogan.[30]

This religious humanism was brought to the Chancery Division of the High Court on 3 June 1980, '*In re* South Place Ethical Society: Barralet and others *v.* Attorney-General and others', before Mr. Justice Dillon. In a seven-day hearing the judge ruled that the objects of the society were *not* for the advancement of religion, though it could be deemed charitable 'as for the advancement of education'. He concluded that the aim, stated in the Rules, to disseminate ethical principles, was clearly educational, but he was dubious as to whether the same could be said of 'the cultivation of a rational religous sentiment'. He concluded eventually that this was educational, because the society did it not only for its own benefit; but he had difficulty with the use of 'religious', which 'while giving the flavour of what is in mind, is not in my view used in its correct sense'.

The society was relieved to find itself again a charity – and not a religious one: for some it had been embarrassing to hear in court of their coffee-drinking being described virtually as sacramental. The society's simple humanists were not fully satisfied with Mr. Justice Dillon's view that the members 'are not atheists: the existence of God is neither affirmed nor denied'. But at least the decision opened the way for the British

Humanist Association, which had also suffered under the Act of 1960, to receive recognition as a charity.[31]

There were still plenty of problems within the society: a fear that the Inland Revenue would appeal against the judgment (dispelled in March 1981), the need to re-state the society's beliefs, and personal friction, especially with Cadogan, who continued to speak for his religious humanism (which was clearly not *excluded* by the court's judgment). The simple humanists opposed him, including Barbara Smoker who had kept up a campaign against his (and some of the Trustees') supposed religiosity since 1969, and Harold Blackham, the elder statesman of humanism who contributed a note to the *Ethical Record* rejecting outright the contemporary relevance of the old formula, 'rational religious sentiment'. Cadogan's position became precarious and in the summer of 1981 he resigned. Another voice was also lost to the society: Albert Lovecy died in February 1981. His widow, Ray, continued to work for the society, becoming its next spokesperson, the 'Honorary Representative', a new post designed to eliminate the past ills of General Secretaryship.[32]

The most articulate personalities of the society in the 1970s were Cadogan, Smoker and Lovecy. Each represented one element in a history that stretched back before their times. Cadogan's position illustrated the problematical rôle of a leader in the society, who had no right to lead; and his ideas of religious humanism illustrated the conceptual juggling act that had often been performed by the society's intellectuals. Barbara Smoker represented its strain which was naked of any reassuring superstructure (like Marxism) or prestigious social base (for instance, in the communications industry). For Lovecy, retirement from his post in a government research institute supplied him with time to think: especially he pondered the nature of charity, the concept of which was thrust upon the society. He wanted South Place to become more of an *ethical* society than it had been, that is, one which considered and acted upon the words, ideas and experiences which taper from the religious to the secular. For Lovecy the problems of South Place lay germinating within the very word 'charity'. Because of this he, if anyone, was perhaps truest to the total history of the society. It was founded in the late eighteenth century out of a new conception of God's charity and discovered new energies (by means of the catalytic Stanton Coit) in the epoch of semi-secular charity (or philanthropy) at the end of the nineteenth century.

Chapter 3

Bloomsbury and the Strand:
the London Ethical Society

By faith, not by sight

In Chapter 1 we noted that T. H. Green preached in the lecture room on the front quadrangle of Balliol, on the text, in the heading above, from 2 Corinthians (5:7). J. H. Muirhead heard him and counted this sermon, along with the 'Concluding Remarks' of F. H. Bradley's *Ethical Studies*, as a key document in the Idealist rejection of agnosticism. Muirhead was the founder of the London Ethical Society, actually the original British ethical society; South Place preceded it, but did, after all, adapt itself to ethicism. The L.E.S. was first an Idealist society, but not merely sectional because it had a general ambition to improve the current state of philosophy teaching at large. To this ambition we shall turn in the second half of this chapter; at present we are concerned with the Idealist 'faith' that makes 'sight' meaningful.

Idealism was dealt a blow by G. E. Moore's 'Refutation' of 1903. Just how it prospered in the 1890s, and how it was understood, is well illustrated by an interview which F. J. Gould conducted with J. H. Muirhead. Gould was not an Idealist, but politely conceded the rule of Hegel. He went on to ask whether Hegel was, however, only popular in the universities, and, if so, whether the universities actually represented the best in British thought. Question and answer ran as follows, cast into dramatic form with stage-directions deriving from Gould's prose.

Muirhead: At one period of this century the great thinkers stood outside the Universities – such as Grote, Mill, Spencer. That is not the case in the present day, though there are, of course, some distinguished men of letters who, though themselves University men, are not identified with University teaching. I might quote Mr. Leslie Stephen and Mr. Frederic Harrison.
Gould: And has this triumphant Hegelianism left any mark on the Church?
Muirhead: It has had one very remarkable effect and that is the complete disappearance of the Broad Church . . . [Gould looks astonished] . . . in *this* way: the new movement has taken hold of the people who have refused to go into the Church. They find it too radical to permit them to enter the Church's orders. It

absorbs the elements which otherwise would have contributed to the maintenance of the Broad Church party.

Gould: Perhaps you will also claim that Idealism has impressed itself on our literature?

Muirhead: (Imperturbably.) Yes, it has done so since the days of Coleridge and Wordsworth on to the time of Matthew Arnold. Carlyle acknowledged its power. Browning is its great popular exponent. It has left traces on Tennyson – *e.g.*, in the 'Higher Pantheism'.

The Idealists of the L.E.S. group saw themselves in the romantic line. T. H. Green in 1868 identified three aspects of romanticism which he believed should be understood by philosophers if they were to cope with the spiritual 'unsettlement' of the age. There were the 'deeper views of life which the contemplative poets originated' (notably Wordsworth). There was the conception of freedom and right popularised by Rousseau, which 'even in his hands had a constructive as well as anarchical import'. And, finally, there was the revival of evangelical religion. Philosophers had to assimilate these ideas and experiences if they were to be released from 'the prone and poring gaze of a false philosophy' – that of Hume, who consigned humanity to 'the dark chamber of a passive sense'. Hume showed men to be *of* nature, not ones who participated *in* nature. According to Green the 'natural man' of Hume could never actually have become a Hume himself. 'If he were merely the passive receptacle of natural impressions and not at the same time constructive and free, he could not enquire what nature was to him and he to nature.' Green believed that those who had learned the lessons of romanticism, and so were able to take philosophy further than Hume's *Treatise*, constituted 'a second Oxford movement'.

Gould turned from poetry to ask whether Muirhead valued Huxley.

Muirhead: Huxley never showed much interest in what is properly called philosophy, except in his *Hume*, and he nowhere touches deeply on its problems.

Gould: Idealists do not appreciate the Unknowable of Mr. Herbert Spencer?

Muirhead: (Decisively.) They are its most relentless critics! To assert that it is unknowable is to assert a knowledge of it. Idealism affirms that there can be no object that is not relative to a subject. An Absolute object or Unknowable object is a contradiction in terms.

Gould: Then do you go as far as to say –

Muirhead: Idealists do not say they know the Absolute. But we say that all knowledge is a progress *towards* a knowledge of the Absolute, while, to Spencer, knowledge is permanently shut up in the field of the relative.

Gould: But is not all knowledge relative?

Muirhead: Undoubtedly.

Gould: And you say we never can, as a matter of fact, do more than travel *towards* a knowledge of the Absolute?

The reference to the Unknowable leads to the idea of religion possessed by the L.E.S. group. They did not believe in the autonomy of ethics, but that 'religion was a fundamental element in human life in the sense of a faith in the reality beyond the sight of things that makes life worth living'. The L.E.S. aimed to *justify* the religious life (so it said in its first manifesto), and to re-interpret existing creeds. In January of 1893 its lecture-card stated in bold type that 'sympathizers with the Ethical Society are especially informed that membership in [it] does not imply severance with any religious organisation'. More than any other, this society was interested in concepts such as 'atonement' and 'justification by faith'. In saying to rationalist Gould that 'all knowledge is a progress *towards* the Absolute' Muirhead is describing faith, or expressing in his own terms the thought of F. H. Bradley in the last chapter of *Ethical Studies*, which Muirhead considered to be 'scriptural': 'It is by faith in our reconcilement with the invisible one reality that we are justified.'[1]

For the L.E.S. Bradley was the first sage of faith, T. H. Green the second, especially in the lay-sermon on 'For we walk by faith, not by sight'. There Green dealt with 'religious consciousness'. He compares the consciousness *that* God exists with an artist's consciousness *that* there is a beauty remote but in view (of a kind) while a work is in the course of creation. Green avoids what God is for the sake *that* He is. People may be as unclear about what He is, as an artist may be unclear about what beauty is in view: the artist travels towards the unknown as does the person in possession of religious consciousness. Gould asked Muirhead whether or not what is travelled towards by the religious Idealist is, at any rate, as remote as Spencer's Unknowable. The reply was straight out of Green:

Muirhead: Put in that way, it does seem a riddle. We know It and we know It not? But is it not the same with art and morality? An artist tries to express Beauty in a picture, but the Beauty he dreamed of has escaped him, or he has only expressed a part of it. So with morality: we fail in living up to our ideal, yet we do not say that it is an unrealizable ideal, any more than that beauty is inexpressible. The picture and the action bear witness to the reality of Beauty and Goodness, though they fail to express the whole. It is the same with knowledge. All knowledge is knowledge of the Real. In knowing anything we know the Absolute. Yet it remains true that we only know in part. In recognizing it as a part we show that in some sense we know the whole.

In saying that 'all knowledge is knowledge of the Real' Muirhead is giving in his own words the Hegelian doctrine which Edward Caird had communicated in his Glasgow classes. The doctrine supplied the analytic reassessment of Kant which is to be found in his *Critical Account*, published in 1877, the year after Henry Jones was 'born again' in the Glasgow moral philosophy class-room, and found also in the long essay on 'Metaphysic' which Caird contributed to the Ninth Edition (1883) of the *Encyclopaedia Britannica*.[2]

By the time Muirhead reached epistemology the attention of Gould began to fray. Changing tack, 'half dubiously, I questioned as to whether Idealism in any way linked itself with politics'.

Muirhead: I look to Idealism as providing a basis for the newer Liberalism.
Gould: What is this basis?
Muirhead: The idea of freedom as consisting not merely in the liberty of every man to do as he likes, but in the power of each man to do something that is worth doing. Hence the function of the Liberal politician is to develop capacity in the citizen. Spencer sets up the State *versus* Man; Idealism, on the other hand, affirms that, with Aristotle, 'the State is prior to the Individual', and that 'man is a political animal'. It is the citizen within man that we are called upon to develop. Government does not simply exist in order to secure liberty and the spread of contentment. Government should develop a spiritual *dis*content, and then satisfy the created want as far as is reasonable.
Gould: And do you put aside the old democratic ideal of self-government?
Muirhead: That is an element in the freedom, but it does not constitute the freedom.
Gould: Then it is only a means to an end?
Muirhead: I don't exactly say that. The self-government is a means in so far as it tends to the betterment of material surroundings and the spread of capacity. But the power to take part in the civic activity is not only a means; it is in itself a part of the Good Life. I hope to see this idea more and more take hold of our younger politicians. The man by whom it is, perhaps, most consciously grasped is Mr. Haldane [then, of course, over forty]. He is one of our few philosophic politicians. He is a Hegelian.

In the 1890s young thinkers had to manoeuvre past the bulk of Herbert Spencer. The Idealist had to ensure that his Absolute was not confused with Spencer's Unknowable. In social theory it was Spencer's attack on Liberalism, and his concept of organism, that had to be contested by those that respected him but wished for subtler definitions of freedom. In 1860 Spencer had published 'Parliamentary Reform: the Dangers and the Safeguards' in *The Westminster Review*; he returned to the theme in four essays for *The Contemporary Review* in 1884 which were published as *The Man versus the State* in the same year. Spencer enlisted his theory of social organism against a Liberalism which had transformed itself, in his view, into a system of coercion by the state. He satirically listed a multitude of pieces of legislation which encroached on individual freedom. Muirhead considered this theory in *The Elements of Ethics* (1892), based on a course for the London Ethical Society, valuing it for its critique of outmoded utilitarianism: it did recognise the evolutionary nature of society and saw that neither society nor pleasure were atomistic. Muirhead also gave qualified approval to the theory of organism of Leslie Stephen, expressed in *The Science of Ethics* (1882). But, while he found organism an indispensable conception, Muirhead believed that it was unusable while it remained tied to a hedonistic ethics. Spencer and Stephen were, he thought, flawed because neither advanced beyond the pleasure principle of utilitarianism. Or rather, Stephen only advanced involuntarily beyond this principle, for Muirhead did discover an unexpected concession in the *Science of Ethics* which he remarked in an appendix to his chapter on 'Evolutionary Hedonism' in his *Elements*. While considering self-sacrifice Stephen dealt with the case of the un-mitigatedly bad man who cannot be tempted to a good act by the promise of a benefit which would bounce back from his charity. Stephen realises that this bait to a good action may be irrelevant: whether it causes him pain or pleasure, the good action may be equally uninteresting to the scoundrel. The only thing he may have in common with good people is a lack of interest in getting personal benefit, because good people certainly do things which cause them pain. 'There is scarcely any man, I believe, at all capable of sympathy or reason who would not, in many cases unhesitatingly, sacrifice his own happiness for a sufficient advantage to others.' Muirhead was surprised to find Stephen mention 'reason' in this context. 'Sympathy', of course, was expected because this is a kind of pleasure and belongs in the utilitarian calculus. Muirhead thought that in this context the introduction of 'sympathy' failed to assist Stephen's case because the capacity of people to experience sympathy is not a reliable basis for developing altruistic action: it is a matter of feeling and 'you cannot tell a man that he *ought* to have a feeling'. You might make more headway with the scoundrel by simply ordering him to do the good thing, or appealing to his 'reason', the term which appears to slip, by acci-dent, from Stephen. Once out it admits the non-utilitarian view that the end of life is not happiness but good, and that the route to good is not through feelings (like 'sympathy'), but from 'reason'. In making this ad-mission Stephen allows the reader to appeal to the rational self, 'which can be shown to be essentially social, and therefore only capable of find-ing satisfaction in a *common good* [apart from which] there can be no categorical imperative and no morality'.

This discovery of a non-utilitarian element in Stephen helps to il-lustrate what Muirhead meant by telling Gould that civic activity 'is itself part of the Good Life', but the place of the discovery in the *Elements of Ethics* is also worthy of notice because it contains a reference to a thinker who was much appreciated in the world of the ethical societies (not only that of the Idealist L.E.S.). W. K. Clifford, the mathematician who died at the age of thirty-four in 1879, was an ethical evolutionist, ad-vancing beyond Spencer and Stephen by seeing that right is founded upon a contrast between a true or extended self, and a false or constrained self. Instead of appealing to reason (as Stephen should not have done, according to Muirhead – though he was grateful for it), Clifford used a conception of the 'tribal self'. Muirhead quoted the following passage with approval:

'If you want to live together in this complicated way' – called society [says Clifford] – 'your ways must be straight and not crooked; you must seek the truth, and love no lie'. Suppose we answer [Clifford continues], 'I don't want to live together with other men in this complicated way; and so I shall not do as you tell me', – that is not the end of the matter, as it might be with other scientific precepts. For obvious reasons, it is *right* in this case to reply, 'Then, in the name of my people, I do not like you', and to express this dislike by appropriate methods. *And the offender*, being descended from a social race, *is unable to escape his conscience, the voice of his tribal self*, which says, 'In the name of the tribe, I hate myself for this treason which I have done.'

Here, thought Muirhead, 'we have got beyond the pleasure theory; we have further exchanged the empirical for the teleological point of view, in so far as the "self" is made the centre of interest. All that is wanted is to ask what is implied in the idea of such a self.' Muirhead sought and found the answer to this in F. H. Bradley's *Ethical Studies* and especially in its chapter on 'My Station and Its Duties'. For the voice of conscience to speak as Clifford intimated, the person whose conscience it is must know that he is 'descended from a social race'. As a pupil of Green, Muirhead knew that 'our ultimate standard of worth is the ideal of personal worth. All other values are relative to the values for, of, or in a person.' The tribe must be taught to realise its worth. This was to be a basic task of the London Ethical Society, one of its functions as an organ of the 'educative state'.[3]

The L.E.S. group examined their station, their duties and the tribe. They were aware of the dangers of undue reverence for station and duties (Bradley himself had shown them), but the risks were worth it when this conception of ethics was compared to the atomist pleasure-principle of utilitarianism. The Idealists rejected 'parcels' of pleasure, contemplating in and beyond themselves the reason revealed in communal (tribal) life. Bernard Bosanquet mused many years after the L.E.S. on this, having particularly in mind the contribution made by Bradley:

It appears to me absolutely plain that by developing the conception of 'law universal' into that of a concrete system, embodied in the actual whole of existing institutions, and yet furnishing through its particulars a content in which the universal end lives and grows within the individual will, a meaning is given to the Kantian ethical idea which Kant very likely would have disowned, but which really satisfies the theoretical demand which his system recognised and failed to meet.

Even in the extracts above from Gould's interview with Muirhead a certain irritation is evident in Gould's questioning. There were several reasons for this. Gould was self-educated; Muirhead had an elaborate education in three institutions in Glasgow, Oxford and London. Gould taught in one tough school and was sent to teach in a tougher one because the London School Board disapproved of beliefs for which he had to fight, while Muirhead could speak with some complacency in his belief that the Hegelian revolution was complete. Personally, he was not so very secure: he was never to find a post in Oxford, or (the next best thing for a philosopher) in Scotland; but Gould may be excused for thinking he was stand-offish. However, what created the most friction among leading London ethicists was the fact that Muirhead's Idealism was essentially conservative, respectful of (Bosanquet's phrase) 'existing institutions', not through mere deference, but for the philosophical reasons sketched in this section. Muirhead thought it was 'reality beyond the sight of things' which made life worth living, that this reality could be detected in existing institutions. Gould, on the other hand, apart from being sympathetic to the more rebellious convictions of Stanton Coit, was moving towards Positivism, of which he became an orthodox exponent. Years after the demise of the L.E.S. Muirhead mused on his early ethicism. On Christmas Eve of 1922 he wrote to Bosanquet, wondering what it was that had attracted them to ethicism: 'I suppose it was the Kantian element rather than the Comtean element in it. These elements are struggling with each other still and are likely to break it up.' They began to break up the movement even at the turn of the century because the L.E.S. could not work with the other ethical societies. There were other reasons for its decline, as we shall see in the next section, as we examine the achievements and ambitions of the Idealists' ethical society.[4]

Philosophy in London

In Chapter 1 we observed several arrivals in London, including that of Muirhead. He came from Glasgow University where he was employed as a junior assistant under his former professor of Latin, having completed his term as a Snell exhibitioner at Balliol. The force of Idealism had come through to him from Edward Caird. In Glasgow he felt he had found neither the right career nor a vocation, so he took the drastic step of applying for admission to the Unitarian institute in London, Manchester New College.

Muirhead was admitted in the autumn of 1885, when he was thirty. On the graduate list for 1888 he is entered as a Unitarian minister for Ealing but he gave up ministerial activity almost immediately. He primarily wanted to be a teacher of philosophy, then as much as in Glasgow. Though small, Manchester New College, in Gordon Square, Bloomsbury, provided unique opportunities for getting new qualifications in philosophy.

Today the building to which Muirhead went in Bloomsbury is called Dr. Williams's Library which points to the history of this Unitarian stronghold in London. In 1699 a Dr. Daniel Williams purchased books from a clergyman who left the Church for non-subscription at the Great Ejection of 1662. Dr. Williams was one of the many dissenters put outside the pale – Quakers, Seekers, Antinomians, Congregationalists, Independents and Presbyterians, the last eventually becoming known as Unitarians. The Unitarians' denial of the divinity of Christ was illegal until 1813; they were not fully rescued from heresy, in the legal sense, until the Dissenters' Chapels Act (1844). To commemorate this Act the Unitarians built University Hall in Bloomsbury to provide a home and some tuition for young dissenters who were studying for London University degrees. Its wardens included Arthur Hugh Clough (who detested the place and was signally unsuccessful in recruiting students), R. H. Hutton, Henry Morley and E. S. Beesly who, as we saw in Chapter 1, was there in the time of J. R. Seeley. Because the Hall proved less popular than its founders hoped, many of its rooms were taken over by Manchester New College, which moved in from the north in 1853, somewhat confusingly retaining its former name. This college-within-a-hall took about a dozen students a year, some of them Hungarian, as befitted the Transylvanian origin of the anti-Trinitarian heresy. The college curriculum was devised by J. J. Tayler and James Martineau, the former envisaging a 'School of Theology and Religious Philosophy' which would benefit from the proximity of University College, a few steps away from the back yards of the Hall. Martineau came permanently from Liverpool to teach in 1857. His emotional or 'gothic' Christianity, as it was sometimes called, did not appeal to the rationalist Unitarian seniors, schooled in the traditions of Belsham and Priestley. In 1889 Manchester New College moved to Oxford. Some rooms were let off to the Mary Ward (later Passmore Edwards) settlement, which was meant to translate into actuality the 'New Brotherhood' which excited so many readers of *Robert Elsmere*. In 1890 Dr. Williams's collection of books, then much augmented, was moved in from nearby Grafton Street. Thirty-five years later space was made, as we shall see, for a newly founded British Institute of Philosophical Studies.[5]

James Martineau became Principal of Manchester New College in 1869, so it was essentially to his institute that Muirhead came. Its nature affected his decision to form an ethical society when he graduated. The college provided unique opportunities for study. The Christian theism of Martineau had much to say to young people who were religious but convinced by the case against miracles or (as Muirhead put it) were prepared to believe *with* Christ rather than *in* him. Muirhead moved beyond this theism which was still metaphysically committed to a personal deity and ethically to a concept of conscience created by this deity. For Muirhead individual conscience was too limited an expression of the religious sense. He did believe in an incarnation but one widely manifested in nature and in the evolution of history. This he called 'the larger outlook that was then opening out as to the foundations of the religious consciousness, as this had found expression in the great religions alike of East and West'. He found 'the larger outlook' in Martineau's subordinates, especially Charles Barnes Upton and J. Estlin Carpenter. Upton assisted Martineau in philosophy and was working on Rudolf Hermann Lotze; Carpenter took Hebrew and Old Testament studies, but he also worked on eastern religion, notably the editing of Buddhist texts. The younger men were relatively unworried about relating their thought to Unitarianism. In them Muirhead saw possibilities for a new institute, 'a centre of enlightenment on the meaning and place of religion in human life and a meeting-place of the best religious teaching at once of the Eastern and Western worlds, of the Catholic and Protestant churches and of Church and Dissent within the latter'. But Manchester New College itself was still Unitarian, committed to a personal deity – and politically it was reactionary, ironically considering its earlier battles for freedom of thought. It was an oasis in a philosophical desert, nonetheless, making Muirhead realise how much his subject was neglected in the metropolis.[6]

It was also neglected by London University, as was recognised in 1876 by George Croom Robertson, Professor of Mental Philosophy and Logic at University College, who wrote in the first issue of *Mind* that while there was no university which in principle made 'so systematic a stand for the cause of Philosophy in Education', the neglect in practice of the subject was deplorable, the ideals having been compromised by the necessity of setting examinations for a host of often ill-qualified non-resident students. In 1857 the examinations were opened to all comers, with the result that they became merely a test of what 'a fair proportion of candidates for the time being are found able to pass'. Matters did not much improve in a decade. The London professors, and aspirants like Muirhead, yearned for a proper teaching university, with examined students in direct contact with teachers who exercised sensitive control over examinations. A solution did not come until after the report of the Haldane Commission in 1913 and the University of London Act. The London Ethical Society grew out of a desire to campaign for tuition in philosophy in London.[7]

89

In the spring and summer of 1886 Muirhead worked on a manifesto promising to organise 'systematic Ethical Instruction', using 'every endeavour to arouse the community at large to the importance of testing every Social, Political, and Educational question by moral and religious principles'. On the third Saturday in November a meeting was held in Manchester New College, at which Muirhead gave a paper on 'The Ethical Point of View', and a three-man committee was appointed. On the Sunday evening the first of a series of lectures was given at Toynbee Hall on 'Morality and Modern Life', sponsored by a new 'Ethical Society'. It was at Toynbee Hall (natural resort for a lonely Balliol man in London) that Muirhead had heard that there were such things as ethical societies in the United States, first from Stanton Coit, and then from an American visitor to whom Muirhead warmed, John Graham Brooks, who seemed to epitomise the spirit of Concord and Emerson (without the crankiness), and handed round some leaflets about the Chicago Society for Ethical Culture. Muirhead was secretary of the new society, remaining so until he could take up a chair of philosophy in Birmingham in 1896. From 1890 it was called the London Ethical Society, and in 1897 it metamorphosed into the London School of Ethics and Social Philosophy.[8]

Muirhead had two particular friends to help him start the society. James Bonar was of the 'class of Caird' at Glasgow. In 1881 he began a career in in the Civil Service Commission, later distinguishing himself as a writer on economics. In 1885 he started a co-operative for bookbinders in Bloomsbury. Percival Chubb, a frustrated pen-pusher in the Post Office, came to London from Newcastle-upon-Tyne; he was largely self-educated through university extension classes. He was taken up by Thomas Davidson, the charismatic Scots philosopher and traveller. Early in 1884 a group of Davidson's disciples decided to extend their belief in self-development to social reform and founded the Fabian Society, from which there was a break-away group, of those keener on 'being something' than 'doing something' called the Fellowship of the New Life. Chubb was a founding New Lifer, Fabian and ethicist. He was to follow Davidson to America where he taught at the ethical culture school in New York; in 1911 he became leader of the St. Louis, Missouri, Society for Ethical Culture. Chubb and Bonar were not systematic Idealists, and neither stayed long with what was in the end essentially Muirhead's ethical society.[9]

Muirhead's mainstay, the figure for which the L.E.S. was virtually invented, was Bernard Bosanquet (1848–1923). Seven years Muirhead's senior, Bosanquet belonged to the academic generation of F. H. Bradley. He had known Green, and R. F. Nettleship, at first hand. He lectured in classics and philosophy at University College, Oxford, from 1870. It was Bradley's *Ethical Studies* which brought him to London by invalidating his own plans for a book on ethics. He wished, also, to have direct contact with practical, personal social reform: he joined the Charity Organisation Society, serving on the Shoreditch District and General Administrative Committees, alongside Helen Dendy whom he married in 1895.

Bosanquet was valued by the L.E.S. not least for his critique of socialism. In a lecture to the Fabian Society in February 1890 he confronted the doers of something with their philosophical confusion. He thought the Fabians were caught in a conceptual trap. They rejected economic individualism, from which it appeared that they would also reject moral individualism as materialist and Epicurean, preferring moral socialism, for which society is 'the moral essence of the individual'. But, he argued, morality depends on the individual mind being moved by a social purpose, moved on its *own* will. Economic socialism makes this will redundant because it is 'an arrangement for getting the social purpose carried out by the force of those compulsory motives or sanctions which are at the command of the public power . . . If you want to treat your social units as bricks in a wall or wheels in a machine, you cannot also and at the same time treat them as elements in an organism.' The Idealists were dyed deep in the idea of organism. In the late 1880s, according to Muirhead, the concept of society as organism was nothing new, in its best-known form being merely 'watered down to a vague physiological metaphor by Herbert Spencer, or identified by others who ought to have known better (Bryce and Dicey among them) with views casually picked up from the newspapers or from particular social groups, and dignified by the name of "public opinion" '. Bosanquet gave a Hegelian charge to the term, retrieving it from the socialists. He reminded the Fabians, in his paper of 1890, that Hegel would give them no support for their view of private property.

Bosanquet's conservatism epitomised the attitudes that marked off the L.E.S. from the majority view of the Fabian Society, as was noted by G. B. Shaw in July 1895 when he wrote to Sidney Webb about the embryo London School of Economics. Webb had disingenuously remarked that academic research was ideologically neutral. Shaw maintained that this was an illusion: was there any research so abstract that 'Bosanquet and Miss Dendy would arrive at exactly the same conclusions and produce the same information as Wallas and Miss Stacy?' The pairs of names represent the L.E.S. (with the Charity Organisation Society) and the Fabian Society, in whose executive Graham Wallas and Enid Stacy were active, as polar opposites. (Muirhead had diggings next door to Wallas, whose sister he married.) It would, however, be wrong to conclude that the L.E.S. was a Charity Organisation Society think-tank or that it was isolated in Idealist doctrine. It was committed foremost to education (how else could Idealism be understood?) and to spreading all types of philosophical study. And if it was anti-socialist it was fully aware that Liberalism needed new vitality.[10]

Apart from Bosanquet three others dominated the society. Mary Sophia Gilliland Husband came from County Derry and married a civil servant, T. F. Husband. She was the main L.E.S. organiser and a frequent contributor to the review pages of *The International Journal of Ethics*. Sophia Bryant was the daughter of a Dublin clergyman. She was married for only one year, her husband dying when she was twenty. She won a scholarship to Bedford College where she specialised in mathematics, which drew the attention of the formidable Miss F. M. Buss of North London Collegiate School for Girls, where she became a teacher in 1875. She was the first female holder of a doctorate from London University, studying part-time while still a teacher, for the B.Sc. and for the D.Sc. which she took in 1884. In the 1890s she taught the Bloomsbury and north-west London liberals what to think, 'in a costume of green cashmere with pale blue piping to define the outlines, broad-brimmed hat of the Kate Greenaway sort, adorned with a green ostrich feather'. This was typical costume for female Bloomsbury intellectuals: the Liberty dresses of Stopford Brooke's daughters adorned the congregation in the Bedford Street chapel. In 1895 Dr. Bryant served on the Bryce Commission on Secondary Education, the first to appoint a female commissioner. Both Bryant and Husband worked at the construction of a non-utilitarian theory of education. Both were devotees of Bosanquet. Finally, Muirhead relied on a Bloomsbury figure who deserves a chapter of his own, Philip Henry Wicksteed (1844–1927). Wicksteed came from an old Unitarian family, educated in the 1860s at University College and Manchester New College. From 1874 to 1897 he was minister at the Unitarian chapel in Little Portland Street.

The L.E.S. was, then, based on the work of two men and two women: Muirhead and Bosanquet, Husband and Bryant. Its practical remit was to provide ethical instruction 'in connexion with such educational agencies as the Society for the Extension of University Teaching, Working Men's Colleges, Clubs, Co-operative Societies and [those concerned with] the education of the young'. The speakers in the first series of a dozen lectures at Toynbee Hall represented charity, Unitarianism and Idealism. For charity these was the Reverend Barnett himself and C. S. Loch of the Charity Organisation Society; for Unitarianism there was J. Estlin Carpenter and the eminent worker for women's education, Anna

Swanwick. But it was the Idealists who held the stage from the first in a society which was to be a cradle for academic philosophers. Of the first twelve lecturers, Muirhead took a chair in Birmingham (1896), J. S. Mackenzie one at Cardiff (1895), and Bosanquet at St. Andrews (1903). Henry Jones had been professor at Bangor at the University College of North Wales (1884); he was later appointed at St. Andrews (1891) and Glasgow (1894) where he succeeded Caird on his departure to become Master of Balliol. Of the non-Idealists there was Samuel Alexander who became professor at Manchester in 1893. J. Estlin Carpenter was successively Vice-Principal and Principal at Manchester New College and Wilde Lecturer in Comparative Religion at Oxford (1914–24). So the first ethical lecturers were to radiate outwards in a ring of philosophy schools about Britain.

The L.E.S. soon moved from Toynbee Hall to the Strand. In 1886 the Unitarians opened a new building, Essex Hall, just off the south side of the Strand. It had 'well-lighted offices' and 'excellent accommodation for Public Meetings'. There the L.E.S. established its programme, soon running to thirty lectures a year. It also engaged in practical social work by opening a group of 'guilds' (youth clubs), supervised by Mrs. Husband about a mile to the north in White Hart Street, Drury Lane. This was a notorious Irish slum (which partly explains Mrs. Husband's commitment), little changed since William Hogarth depicted the area in *Gin Lane*.[11]

It was, however, neither in lectures nor in youth clubs that the essential work of the society was done, but in organising classes for the study of philosophy. These were initiated in collaboration with the London Society for the Extension of University Teaching (founded in 1876) which first offered classes in five centres, which number of centres and classes quadrupled by the late 1880s. The L.E.S. was indeed part of a large pattern of expansion in this field. The university extension authorities supervised academic standards, acting as a parent body which set up partnerships between itself and on-the-spot committees which were responsible for paying class teachers for whom fees were raised from attenders. The L.E.S. used this system. With the help of a small financial guarantee from J. Estlin Carpenter, Muirhead set up adult education classes at Essex Hall from 1888 to 1891. From then on, the society, having proved itself, ran courses without the supervision of the L.S.E.U.T. until 1897. The subject matter of the courses was divided between economics and social history (including socialism), and philosophy. In the first category the prominent course directors were Philip H. Wicksteed (three courses between 1888 and 1897), F. W. Flux and Graham Wallas (two courses each). One course each was given by

W. M. Childs, Helen Dendy, J. A. Hobson, John Rae and G. Armitage
Smith. On the philosophy side some teaching was done by Dr. Bryant
and J. S. Mackenzie (two and one courses respectively), but the lion's
share was taken by Muirhead and Bosanquet. Muirhead took philosophy
for three years. Bosanquet gave his first class in 1891 and continued to
take at least one course a year until 1897; in four of these years Muirhead
took classes as well.

The L.E.S. courses, which consisted of ten meetings, were arranged to
combine three activities. First, a lecture was given, to be followed by a
class in which the lecture material was explained and discussed, and in
which written work was set. Regular attenders who attained a satisfactory standard in the written work were allowed to take an examination
from which could be earned a certificate of pass or pass with distinction.
The lecturer produced a printed syllabus, sometimes virtually con-
stituting a small textbook. Some published works derived from the lectures, like Muirhead's *Elements of Ethics* (1892) and Bosanquet's *Companion to Plato's 'Republic'*. Sometimes the L.E.S. courses evolved from the
students' interests. Having experimented in 1889–90 with the first purely philosophical extension course in London (on 'Elements of Ethics'),
Muirhead mounted a course on Aristotle's *Ethics* and Green's *Prolegomena* because of enthusiasm expressed by the students. This course
was equally successful, so the group sought to make Essex Hall a centre
for what it called (in the report of the class secretary, always appointed
from among the students) 'consecutive work' in 'Social Subjects,
Economics and Philosophy'. When Bosanquet came to give his first
course, on 'The Nature of Knowledge', he was astonished to find that the
largest room in Essex Hall had to be used. 'I shall soon scatter them', he
murmured. But he did not. The allure of his teaching is shown in Mrs.
M. S. G. Husband's remark that his course on Plato (1892–3) had 'a
loveliness of spirit . . . a kind of blend of Plato and Jesus Christ'. A similar
testimony came from Mrs. Marian De Glehn, the extremely sophisticated sister of F. H. Bradley who wrote to Bosanquet in 1895.

Your lectures have given me a new possession, and are [*sic*] not merely an im-
petus at the time. I know my Plato has lived at my elbow, and joined the medley
inside me ever since . . . It is such a mercy that he shows some slight touches of
human frailty here and there – just enough to make one feel one dare consort with
him – instead of that awful feeling of constraint which I imagine is the proper
holy feeling a disciple should have and which always makes me want to go and roll
in the gutter at off-times . . . well some big men put me straight into prison by trying to force one *out* of oneself, and it is so splendid the way Plato seems to help one
live one's *own* life well, and be one's own best self. He has helped me to be more
reconciled to Nettleship's death than anything else could have and see it not
simply as a horrible purposeless waste.

Mrs. De Glehn is referring to the death of R. L. Nettleship in the Alps, at the age (like Green) of forty-six. He was a Platonist, inspired by Benjamin Jowett who played a key part in the transmission of Hegelian Idealism to Oxford. Platonism and an enthusiasm for adult education could go hand in hand in this milieu, as shown in Jowett's section on 'The Education of Later Life' in the introduction to his translation of *The Republic*. (Idealism and adult education were also scorned by more downright characters. In 1899 an Oxford undergraduate, Henry Balfour Gardiner, later a composer of the Roger Quilter school, studied Green's *Prolegomena*; against the famous passage in which the Greek idea of self-fulfilment is unfavourably compared to the Christian he scribbled in his text the words 'One would think that this was written by a flatulent product of the University Extension system'.)

The philosophy of the L.E.S. was Idealism, and that imbued with Platonism. Muirhead shows with nostalgia in his late book *The Platonic Tradition in Anglo-Saxon Philosophy: Studies in the History of Idealism in England and America* (1931), the excitement of a philosophical adventure. He believed that Idealism could restore civilisation to the nineteenth century. His optimism supplied him with pioneering similes to describe the growth of the movement: J. H. Stirling, the first British interpreter of Hegel, has his work compared to 'the forts and shacks built by the early settlers in California to secure the rivers and mines they had won by their enterprise. The country itself had still to be won for civilisation.' It was in a similar spirit that Henry Jones once compared Green and Caird to Arthurian knights, the first a sturdy Sir Bors and the second the more tranquil Sir Galahad.[12]

After Muirhead left Manchester New College in 1888, 'for the next six or seven years I became a kind of bagman in philosophy'. Through Jowett's influence he acquired some classics teaching at Royal Holloway College in Egham, Surrey, and some at Bedford College for Women, then in Baker Street. More philosophy teaching came his way after the revision of the London University B.A. syllabus by which logic was offered as an alternative to mathematics in the second (intermediate) examination. Muirhead was able to fight alongside Samuel Alexander in committee to help philosophy become 'a more important subject than it had even been before in the university colleges', whose students took the London examinations, and which 'by this time existed in all the more important provincial towns of England'. In the 1890s he wished that the Essex Hall classes of the L.E.S. could become something less occasional. In 1896 he was appointed to his first permanent post, a chair in one of the provincial towns, Birmingham. He still hoped that the L.E.S. could become a school of philosophy and he had an eye to a place for this school in the newly organised London University that was under discussion.

The Selborne Commission (1889) proposed a new scheme for London University which was taken up by the Gresham Commission (1895) and after much parliamentary travail incorporated into the University of London Commission Act (1898). The plans were urged on by R. B. Haldane who envisaged an ideal university in which there was the kind of close contact between teacher and taught he had experienced with R. H. Lotze at Göttingen. He worked for and with Sidney Webb, and the putative London School of Economics and Political Science. Muirhead and Bosanquet at the same time were thinking of making their L.E.S. into a School of Ethics and Social Philosophy. They tried out their scheme on Sidgwick in Cambridge and Caird in Oxford, both of whom were dubious about a school for students who lacked the Classics. The ethicists pointed to the advantageous maturity of the Essex Hall students, highly motivated 'teachers and educationalists . . . lecturers and journalists'. William Wallace supported them strongly, believing that such students could work from translations. In March 1897 a meeting was held at the house of W. S. Sonnenschein to launch an appeal for funds. Just about enough was raised, so the L.E.S. was dissolved and a London School of Ethics and Social Philosophy opened in the autumn.

For three seasons to spring 1900 the L.S.E.S.P. ran courses on the same pattern as those of the former ethical society. The most popular course (sixty students to the class) was given in 1899–1900 by G. F. Stout on 'Fundamentals of Psychology'. The presence of this course, and its popularity, showed a change in intellectual priorities which had occurred since the beginnings of the ethical society. Psychology had become a central subject, having grown in status since James Ward's article on the subject in the Ninth Edition of the *Encyclopaedia Britannica* (1883). The change was, according to Richard Wollheim, part of 'a general European movement of thought which aimed at rescuing psychology from its "sensationalist" bias to refurbish it as a study of mental activity. "Act", "attention", "activity", "will" – these were the basic and irreducible concepts of the new science.' However, psychology at the L.S.E.S.P. caused problems which may have helped to scupper the school. James Sully, Croom Robertson's successor at University College, resented the course given by Stout in the late afternoons in the non-academic precincts of the Royal Palace Hotel, Kensington. Bosanquet had to prepare a memorandum disclaiming competition. The appearance of the new subject did not improve the reputation of the new school.

In May 1899 the L.S.E.S.P. applied to the University of London Commissioners for recognition as a constituent school of the university.

Bosanquet believed that 'any decent school which can support itself' would be accepted. 'So if one can't find one's millionaire – a beastly business, too – one simply drops through.' The L.S.E.S.P. could not find its millionaire and drop through it did. For the London School of Economics and Political Science a sum of £1,000 for a library was donated by Charlotte Payne Townshend (later Mrs. George Bernard Shaw), who also paid for the school's first rooms. The L.S.E.S.P. had for its library only £18 3s 11d. At a general meeting in spring 1900 the school was dissolved.[13]

The school and the L.E.S. which produced it had two memorials. There was the 'Library of Philosophy', published initially from 1886–7 by W. S. Sonnenschein, under Muirhead's editorship. It continued to produce important texts until his death in 1940. The first volume of the library was significantly J. E. Erdmann's *History of Philosophy*: it was Erdmann on whom Jowett called in 1844 for advice about 'the best manner of approaching' the study of Hegel. Jowett's efforts at comprehension inspired the Oxford Idealists, from whom the L.E.S. stemmed. Muirhead was sympathetic to Erdmann as an Idealist, but also as an evolutionist intellectual historian. 'Ideas', Muirhead remarked in *Elements of Ethics*, 'have a history in time like all other forms of conscious life.' The purpose of the library was to do justice to a neglected aspect of evolution.

The second memorial is the Royal (originally British) Institute of Philosophical Studies, founded in 1925 with an office in University Hall where the first ethical society meeting was held. The Institute aimed to do for philosophy what the L.S.E. did for economics, exactly the aim of Muirhead's society and school. To it Bosanquet bequeathed a carefully chosen collection of his books, annotated with his commentaries. To Muirhead the foundation of the Institute appeared 'to tell me my own dream'.

When the Institute opened Muirhead was on a post-retirement lecturing visit at the University of Southern California. In the United States he was awed by the scale of campus business and technical schools, expecting that philosophy would be neglected. He was delighted to find this was not so, and even embarrassed: he brought with him a lecture entitled 'What is philosophy anyway?', which he had to set aside as elementary and patronising, when he discovered a prosperous discipline. Philosophy, he began to think, was only a Cinderella in England, where 'the new universities grew for the most part out of colleges scientific and technical or commercial, [while] in America they were continuous with the older university system where they were both held in honour'. When he returned to England he may have speculated. Supposing Manchester

New College, an eminently 'decent school', had not departed the very building which housed the Institute in 1899? Supposing the L.E.S. or L.S.E.S.P. had been able to establish a treaty with the Unitarians in it? In that case *it* could have become a school of philosophy in the new university. If this had happened there would have been another L.S.E. in London.[14]

Chapter 4

Bayswater: Stanton Coit's Ethical Church

Wholesome objectivity

On the night of 14 April 1865 the end of the Civil War was celebrated in the streets of Columbus, Ohio. Jefferson Davis, president of the confederate states, was burned in effigy and the eight-year-old George Stanton Coit flung a hot stone at it. His hand was still smarting the next day when he was told that Lincoln had been assassinated. A fortnight later he saw the President lying in state under the dome of the Capitol.

Vehement action was characteristic of Stanton Coit (1857–1944). Moncure Conway was to warn South Place chapel that he was 'a mildly inflexible man'. Coit was never a pacifist, remarking that 'periods of peace, organised on a principle of cut-throat competition [are] meaner and baser than periods of war'. Remembering the hot stone Coit reflected that 'in a childish way I hated slavery even more than the horrors of the War which ended it'. So did his parents. They were abolitionists, assisting in the administration of an escape route from Kentucky to Canada. Mrs. Coit was a campaigner for the political education of women and the president of the first suffrage society in Colombus. She was also a Spiritualist, and from this Coit had to work himself free. Mrs. Coit was a convert, not long before his birth, to a faith which was in the 1850s extremely popular in the mid-Western states. A Catholic congress in 1854 estimated that eleven million out of twenty-five million Americans were Spiritualists. The Spiritualists themselves claimed less influence, but there was still a substantial membership figure of between one and two million. There was a strong connection between progressive political and progressive religious positions. Many Spiritualist leaders were Unitarian ministers, and a coalition of Spiritualism, abolitionism and female suffragism was not unusual. At first Coit accepted his mother's faith, though it was not forced upon him; he appeared to possess some power as a medium, which he claimed to retain into later life, though he never used it. It was not until he was at college that he rejected 'spiritism' (the name of the time) at the age of nineteen. He had before this been distressed at séances, on one occasion repelled by the evident materialisation of his sister; but his disillusion with Spiritualism sprang not so much from a suspicion of quackery or rationalist distrust of the supernatural, but from ethical grounds. He rejected a theology which interpreted life as under the control of disembodied phenonema, a control which delegated human responsibility to non-human agency. Coit found the system morally humiliating. He could not accept that good and bad deeds 'shall ever be traced to any other moral agencies than those actually inhabiting living human beings and recognised by other human beings as fit subjects of human rights and privileges'. This is how he explained his position in *National Idealism and a State Church* (1907) in which a critique of what an average Anglican would understand by supernaturalism is given extra bite by Coit's early knowledge of the delegation of moral autonomy that his mother's 'spiritism' required. The rejection of this faith was precipitated, at Amherst College in 1877, by an illness. Coit had been reading *Alice's Adventures in Wonderland* (1865) whose fantasy fed physical fever with a delirium that posed a sickening question.

How did I know that I was really I and not a thought in someone else's mind? . . . I felt my body swelling up until it filled the room, and went up the open fireplace into the chimney. Naturally, I have ever since loathed and hated Alice, her wonderland and the author of this clever portrayal of a mind disintegrating into the chaos of lunacy . . . Is not the explanation not only of its popularity, but of its having been written by a gifted Oxford don, that already the nineteenth century was beginning to be permeated with, and relaxed in fibre by, the subjectivism, and individualism, and even the solipsism which began to infect the philosophers of the West either with the scepticism of David Hume or with the teaching of Emmanuel Kant that time, space, the laws of cause and effect and all the orderliness of the natural universe were but emanations from our rational consciousness itself?

Even so, Emmanuel Kant possessed prophetic standing for Coit, because he recognised 'the absolute worth of the good will, of the dignity of the moral law; of the imperative nature of the inner commandments; of the self-law, when presented to the mind, to constrain the will to obedience through holy awe and reverence'. But Coit rejected the epistemology, and refused to regard this moral law as that of God.[1]

At Amherst Coit recovered from his mother's Spiritualism, thirsting for what he called 'wholesome objectivity'. He was starry-eyed for Emerson whom he had discovered at the age of fifteen: his enthusiasm was so well-known that he was the only student chosen to address the elderly Transcendentalist when he visited the college. Emerson's effect on young Americans resembled the influence of T. H. Green some years later in England. The American equivalent of Green's lay sermon on faith was Emerson's address at Harvard in July 1838, a more public event which shook New England orthodoxy. Emerson told the Senior Class at Divinity College that the life of Christ had become 'uncharmed' to the degree that worshippers could no longer feel themselves entering into a relationship with a divine 'person'. Churchgoers neither understood nor spread the word of the moral genius of Christianity. 'Where now sounds the persuasion, that by its very melody imparadises my heart, and so affirms to origins in heaven?' Not in modern church or chapel, nor even among those who tried 'to establish a Cultus with new rites and forms . . . Rather let the breath of new life be breathed by you through the forms already existing.' Amherst in the 1870s was as orthodox as Harvard in the 1830s: the students were awed by the free-thinking Coit who 'fairly reeked' of Emerson, though was still 'the most spiritual man in his class'. He was respected by the professoriate, so much so that after graduation he was the first non-communicant to be invited to teach for the college. Although in late life Coit devised many 'new rites and forms' for a church of his own invention, he tried to follow the spirit of Emerson's advice to breathe life into 'the forms already existing'. He insisted that the ceremonial in the Ethical Church was not meant to be a substitute for Christian rite, but an experimental alternative from which the Anglican Church could learn. He was certainly consistent with the Emerson who wrote ten years after his Harvard address that there should be

a new church founded on moral science: at first cold and naked, a babe in the manger again, the algebra and mathematics of ethical law, the church of men to come, without shawms, or psaltery, or sackbut; but it will have heaven and earth for its beams and rafters; science for symbol and illustration; it will fast enough gather beauty, music, picture, poetry.

This was the template for Coit's Ethical Church in Bayswater.

We see in the young Coit 'wholesome objectivity' and Emersonian idealism. What linked them was 'feeling', in which there was special significance brought home to Coit at college by means of a lecture on modern physics from Professor Elihu Root. His account of a mechanistic, nightmare-inducing universe dismayed the Amherst undergraduates, but he restored their morale by reading from lyric cxxiv from Tennyson's *In Memoriam* (1850):

> I found Him not in world or sun,
>   Or eagle's wing, or insect's eye;
>   Nor thro' the questions men may try,
> The petty cobwebs we have spun:

> If e'er when faith had fall'n asleep
> I heard a voice 'believe no more'
> And heard an ever-breaking shore
> That tumbled in the Godless deep;
>
> A warmth within the breast would melt
> The freezing reason's colder part,
> And like a man in wrath the heart
> Stood up and answer'd, 'I have felt.'

The heart did not reveal to Coit a loving personal God; perhaps it did not to Tennyson. He found in 'warmth within the breast' a power 'which pours down supernal [*sic*] beauty and meaning upon and into the godless deep of mechanics and psychology'. This 'meaning' consisted of three related layers or worlds – the ordinary material world, the world of 'finite minds co-operating in collective unity' (as in Professor Root's rapt student audience), and the world of essences 'impinging creatively' on the first two worlds, and understood through feeling. The schema is clearly Platonic.[2]

Coit graduated from Amherst in 1879 and was soon after given a post at Amherst High School. In this transitional period he had ample time to contemplate what he did *not* believe – the 'argument from design'. His first employment after graduation was to coach up an Amherst youth in Paley's *Natural Theology* (1802), in which, according to its sub-title, 'the existence and attributes of the deity are deduced from the appearances of nature'. Coit's deity was, on the contrary, 'a warmth within the breast', as was known well to a friend who remarked to him in 1881 that he should meet a man named Felix Adler, 'who is doing the very thing you are dreaming'. Coit promptly entrained for New York City to hear Adler deliver a Sunday address for the Society for Ethical Culture. He was delighted and first thing on Monday knocked on Adler's door to tell him that he was ideally qualified to become forthwith an ethical lecturer himself. Adler agreed. He offered Coit some lecturing from the platform of the Society of which he was the leader; there were also plenty of ethical lessons to be given to the children of its members, so Coit was able to leave Amherst High to set up in the abrasive city. Adler, however, was not quite ready for him: he wanted lecturers of the Society for Ethical Culture to have high academic credentials. So that Coit could acquire them and be exposed to European philosophy, he ordered and helped him to travel. Coit, in 1883 aged twenty-five, followed a path to enrol at the University of Berlin which had earlier been taken by Adler himself.

Like Adler, Coit was exposed to socialist thinkers in Berlin, but unlike Adler he became a socialist. His conversion was caused largely by reaction to the teachings of non-socialists like Adolf Wagner and especially

Heinrich Von Treitschke who in lecture hall and as a member of the Reichstag declaimed an aggressive nationalism. He declared that the state was power and that war was politics. He was contemptuously anti-democratic and anti-British.

Just before Christmas 1885 Coit submitted a doctoral dissertation on 'Die innere Sanktion als der Endzweck des moralischen Handelns' ('The inner sanction as final purpose for moral action'). He then embarked for London, to stay at Toynbee Hall, which had been recommended him by a friend. Here he was able to give out news of ethical culture in New York, which stimulated J. H. Muirhead and others to start the London Ethical Society. If London lacked ethical culture, New York lacked settlements such as Toynbee Hall. Coit's stay in the East End convinced him that he should graft the idea of communitarian dwelling on to Adler's Society, which he attempted in the summer of 1886 having returned to New York to teach in Adler's Working Men's School. Coit mustered clients by calling door-to-door at houses between Houston and Grand Streets, asking boys and girls if they would like to go to a party on Staten Island. When the cold weather came he rented three rooms for them in the Tenth Ward, the Jewish quarter near Hester Street. The district was bad, but there were more lethal slums, with a higher death-rate, in black areas. The unique quality of 'Jewtown' was its combination of a young population and abnormally high crowding: between 1880 and 1890 the number of souls to an acre rose from 432 to 522. Coit found a suitable house for a settlement, on a more modest scale than the custom-built Toynbee, at 146 Forsyth Street where he was warmly received by the locals as a rich boy gone to the bad. By November a brass plate proclaimed the house to be 'The Neighbourhood Guild', accommodating 'A Young Men's Club', 'A Young Ladies' Club', 'A Boys' and Girls' Club' and 'A Free Kindergarten'. From the club-meetings there emerged various semi-political campaigns, as Coit tried to make his young people aware of the political jobbery which affected their environment and opportunities for employment. His efforts anticipated later settlement work, notably that of Jane Addams of Hull House.

In 1887 Coit visited London again. South Place chapel still had no minister, and Moncure Conway invited Coit to deliver four Sunday lectures. We saw in Chapter 2 how Conway sponsored Coit's application to become his successor, how Coit demanded that the chapel be called an ethical society and buffeted his way through South Place from which he departed late in 1891. It is now time to consider this episode from Coit's point of view rather than that of the largely bewildered South Place.

Coit's basic ambition was to work as a social missionary and religious educator on both sides of the Atlantic. He left New York for London probably because his relationship with Adler began to chafe. The dictum 'Deed not Creed' did not mean for Adler what it meant to Coit – which was work with and among the poor. Adler was anti-socialist, and, despite his reverent attitude to women, anti-suffrage. He differed from Coit in another respect. In the Standard Hall address of 1876, the growth point of ethical culture, Adler promised to exclude from ethical culture meetings 'prayer and every form of ritual'. But Coit was much interested in the Emersonian theory that new life could be breathed into 'forms already existing', and he was not averse to making treaty with the practices of Christian churches, which was in itself at odds with the Jewish origins of ethical culture and in any case contrary to Adler's careful non-denominationalism. Coit must have been intrigued by the prospect of fashionable South Place – from New York he may not have been able to distinguish between what he heard of visitors to the chapel and its membership – in the care of a celebrated American, and apparently in a transitional phase. He knew of its Unitarian origins – had not Emerson been Unitarian? Charles B. Stover could cope with the neighbourhood guild, so Coit left buoyantly for London. No one would have guessed from his first stinging lectures on *Robert Elsmere* that he was unnerved by the complicated social assumptions of the metropolis.

Coit lectured energetically and started clubs among the society membership, but this did not exhaust his desire to live among working-people, to restore their self-respect by various means. He could not reproduce a Forsyth Street guild in respectable Finsbury so Coit sought a working-class location and a sponsor for a neighbourhood guild. He began by renting a school-room in Kentish Town. In the autumn of 1889 he found permanent premises in the same area, two adjacent semi-detached houses in Leighton Crescent, which he persuaded a lawyer to purchase from whom he could rent it at £100 a year. Coit moved in with a friend from New York, Samuel F. Fechheimer (later Fletcher), and three young South Placers. They occupied some of the twelve rooms in each house. The houses had been purchased partly because they had a hall at the back, formerly used by the Sacred Song Association. Coit called the residence Leighton Hall.

From the upper windows of Leighton Hall he could see the depredations of the new railway, amid a wilderness of brick box houses, hazed by smoke. The Hall was not a tenement: the gardens in Leighton Crescent were quite large and the general area precariously respectable. The guild within the Hall was attended by plumbers, coal-shovellers and workers from the nearby organ and piano factories. Dressmakers came, of frail constitution, prone to faint at evening functions. They were not, noted Coit, coarse of feature like factory-girls: he thought that they were innocent enemies of the self-supporting woman because they worked at home for minimal wages. Coit deliberately selected this locality and clientele because he believed he should begin with 'the best people', those whose lives were 'hard and barren', but who could just keep their heads above water. He explained his theory in a short book on *Neighbourhood Guilds: An Instrument of Social Reform* (1891), in which he claimed that if he started at a lower social stratum he might alienate the moderately capable people who could be organised into an autonomous self-help and communication system, intended to be on the lines of Mrs. Octavia Hill's rent-collectors, or the Salvation Army, both of whom were admired by ethicists for their means if not their ends. Coit wanted the neighbourhood to help itself, for example, by organising an urban bush-telegraph for the exchange of information about job opportunities, a method which had kept the Forsyth Street guilders in work. The younger members were taught their rights: they investigated the law pertaining to public wash-houses with a view to supplementing the meagre local facility which philanthropy had bestowed. Coit wanted the latest inventions installed in the Hall, like the economical 'Atkinson' stove, and he acquired heat-retentive trays so that meals could be cooked centrally and taken up the street. In the Hall there were classes and plenty of social events, at which the local intelligentsia assisted. Felix Moscheles, painter, pacifist and Esperantist, donated a piano and gave his name to the Guild magazine. Henry Holiday, painter and well-known enameller who had been converted to socialism by Edward Bellamy's recent *Looking Backward* (1887), decorated the walls of the meeting-hall with murals illustrating a transition from the Reign of Mammon to the Reign of Humanity. Self-government was attempted by means of a series of democratic clubs on the Forsyth Street pattern. By 1891 the guild had 230 members, representing one hundred families, which reached the limit Coit set himself, because he sought not size but proliferation, or, in his term, 'radiation'. He planned a second branch in a slum, Litcham Street, deliberately moving one social stratum lower for his next enterprise. It was not successful, though a small social club was started in Allcroft Road. Work there, and at Leighton Hall, went on until the turn of the century, some of it later continuing at the St. Pancras Ethical Society (later North London Ethical Society) which dissolved in 1911. Coit himself resided at the Hall until his marriage, hoping that it would become a fraternal dwelling place for newly graduated university men; he appears to have had few contacts with women at this stage of his career. In 1892 the residents included St. John E. C. Hankin, theatre critic of *The Saturday Review*, and Findlay Muirhead, publisher of the Blue Guides for tourists. A later resident was a respected member of the

Finsbury society, Alfred J. Clements, who initiated the series of chamber concerts which still bear his name at South Place Ethical Society.[3]

We saw earlier that many members of South Place distrusted Coit's evidently socialistic activities in Kentish Town. Perhaps his desire for a graduate community irritated those who had to acquire an equivalent to university education at the chapel meetings. We saw that the hostility of the self-educating party at Finsbury eventually forced Coit's resignation. Early in 1892 he retreated to Leighton Hall to lick his wounds. He still had supporters. Besides Clements, there was also from South Place W. C. Coupland, whom Conway had nursed away from Unitarianism and who was at work on a commission from the society of a book of pieces for meditation, *Thoughts and Aspirations of the Ages: Selections in Prose and Verse from the Religious Writings of the World* (1895). Coit also knew Muirhead from his earlier residency at Toynbee Hall. He decided to set up his own ethical society, the West London Ethical Society, and appealed to Muirhead that it run in conjunction with the London Ethical Society. In July 1892 the two societies declared a union; but by May 1893 it was clear that Coit had made another false start. The L.E.S. found it could give neither financial nor intellectual backing to Coit's ambitions. The philosophers were irritated by his methods. Most of Coit's work for the joint societies consisted of Sunday lecturing at Prince's Hall, Piccadilly, in a distinctly liturgical atmosphere with a string quartet in attendance. The shy Bosanquet thought that Coit blurred a necessary distinction between teaching and preaching. And on the other side. Coit's hostility to Hegel could not have helped, about whom he expressed this unequivocal opinion in 1898, a few years after his break with the L.E.S.:

I went to Germany and soon accepted as true Schopenhauer's judgment of Hegel as the arch word-charlatan and sophist of the century. I think he was a great genius; but with an insolent contempt for the common mind and common speech, he perverted the legitimate meaning of terms. He does not lack insight. Yet it seems to me that what scientific minds express honestly Hegel presents in brilliant and startling paradox. Hegelianism stripped of Hegel is good common sense.

'Wholesome objectivity' again, whose manner of expression could be brusque; an alliance with the London Ethical Society was doomed if Coit spoke with a fraction of this bluntness in 1892. The equation of 'legitimate meaning of terms' with 'common sense' was precisely what the philosophers' ethical society tried to combat. The ill-fated union of London and West London Ethical Societies proved to Muirhead, on the L.E.S. side, that there was a gulf between the 'more or less congregational organisation', sometimes with roots in the American ethical culture movement, and the type of society he preferred, which had no idea of forming a 'church', yet was felt to be religious, though not because ' "morality" was everything'.

In June 1893 the bond between the two ethical societies was dissolved. In July the West London Ethical Society – destined to become the Ethical Church – was reconstituted and Coit offered a permanent appointment as leader at a salary of £400. (Though there was a committee, it is only fair to add that the Society *was* Coit; but it took nerve to remind the fiery democrat of this fact.) Coit spent most of the winter in America, returning to his post in the spring of 1894.

Having established his West London Ethical Society, Coit concentrated on the process of 'radiation', to create societies in the new mould (unlike South Place and the L.E.S.) in new ethical parishes. He had a hand in forming an East London Ethical Society 1889, coaxed a South London Ethical Society from 1892 and a St. Pancras Ethical Society from 1895, with a catchment area between Euston Road and Archway Tavern. In 1896 the four new societies federated into a Union of Ethical Societies, which invited representatives from similar societies to join them. This was to become the official body of British ethicism, out of which was eventually formed the British Humanist Association. With his society, other 'young churches' he could epistolise and even a Union, Coit had plenty to occupy him in London.[4]

Some great and unique service?

A momentous event occurred for Coit in 1898. On 21 December he married Fanny Adela Wetzlar (1863–1932), the daughter of a Frankfurt industrialist. After the civil ceremony Frederic Harrison conducted a service for the couple. In his address Victorian and Positivist merged. The Coits were doomfully advised of the abhorrence of divorce and that the modern passion for equality should be resisted, for the dignity of marriage was impaired when wife usurped the function of husband: the wife's mission was to make the home and be its 'Moral Providence'. Evidently Coit was not embarrassed by these injunctions because he allowed the form of service to be published. Adela Coit worked for the International Suffrage Alliance and founded a London Emerson Club. She bore three daughters, Adela, Gwendolen and Virginia. Virginia collaborated with her father in his old age on the translation of a huge treatise on ethics by the German phenomenologist, Nicolai Von Hartmann, which we will consider at the end of this chapter. With his marriage Coit became a wealthy man: he and Adela made large donations to the ethical movement. Henceforth, as a man of position, Coit moved in to an address in Hyde Park Gate.[5]

Soon after its formation the Union of Ethical Societies thought it should have a journal, edited by Coit, to be called *The Ethical World*. Coit did not want to be responsible for a merely diocesan paper, so he astutely formed an independent company which regretfully informed the Union that its adoption would be inadvisable 'for the present'. He was right to go for independence: before long the Union was to dislike being even indirectly associated with the *Ethical World* whose wings would have been clipped if the Union had owned it. Coit edited this Saturday weekly of sixteen pages for three years, with considerable flair: it was an excellent ethical society – in print. (As we shall see, its name was changed several times: to avoid confusion it is always called the *Ethical World* hereafter.) From 1 January 1898 the *Ethical World* kept up a high standard of commentary on home and foreign affairs. It was rather weak on ethics, except on the political implications of ethics, because in this field the contributors were understandably liable to be diverted into sometimes tedious disquisition on the ideological demarcation lines between ethical societies, a characteristic of the movement at large. Coit himself may have undervalued his work for the *Ethical World*, committed as he was to personal moral leadership in the public domain; but in its years under his care it yielded over 2,500 pages of often penetrating comment, notably on imperialism, on education and on the woman question. Coit managed to capture the service of some brilliant writers at growth-points in their careers, first among whom was J. A. Hobson who was able to continue in its pages the work he had begun in the short-lived *Progressive Review* (1896–8). He was a prolific contributor, composing many of the anonymous current affairs notes. He was co-editor from April 1899 to February 1900, though for five of these months he was in South Africa, reporting for the *Manchester Guardian*.

Thus Coit had his ethical society, a Union, a journal. He also wanted a team of missionaries, so in April 1898 he marshalled a group which he called the Society of Ethical Propagandists. He envisaged ethical propagandising as a career 'for young men, who for conscience sake, cannot take holy orders, but who still desire to become teachers of social righteousness'. Initially a dozen Propagandists were paid an emolument; later four others were added to the list. The plan faltered because all of them eventually had to pursue real careers. Some were associates from Leighton Hall, like Fechheimer, who had followed Coit's path, having been taught by Adler in New York, taking a doctorate at the University of Jena in 1897. He became a lecturer in education in Cambridge. The Norwegian Christian Collin also resided at Leighton Hall. He was responsible for some of the few contributions to the *Ethical World* about literature, as well as contributing an interesting organicist piece to the essays published for 'the Society of Ethical Propagandists', *Ethical Democracy* (1900). He argued that Darwin's 'great creating Nature' delegated its powers to human beings, which in their turn developed 'supplementary' or 'unattached organs' by means of which still greater power was acquired. However, the human race relied too much for its own good on these excrescences, because it was inherently feeble and unable to cope with the wealth of information delivered back to it from the unattached organs. Collin claimed that human beings need art to re-learn their own natures. Within literary works energy is stored, with 'coal-like, or diamond-like, compression', and this energy can be tapped by means of correct ways of reading, in an anti-eclectic fashion,

to incorporate at least a few of the greatest works of creative genius. There is, perhaps no greater obstacle to the artistic education of mankind, than the modern habit of making our brain a kind of inn or hotel where the visions of artists arrive and depart in ceaseless succession.

Collin did not stay long with the London ethicists, returning to Oslo to become a professor of English literature. A fellow Propagandist and former warden of Leighton Hall was F. B. Kirkman, the most uncompromisingly secularist of the team. He quarrelled with Coit's concessions to theological terminology, insisting that 'God' *never* meant 'the moral ideal'.

Dr. Coit does not seem to understand. I would almost venture to say that the words 'God' and 'prayer' stink in our nostrils, if this expression, by its intensity and unpleasantness, will help him to realise that his attitude in this matter and that of many of his sincere admirers, among whom I am proud to count myself, are irreconcilable.

But this was not said until the winter of 1904. Kirkman contributed several pieces to the *Ethical World* on education, but the main educationalists among the Propagandists were F. J. Gould who ran a series of model lessons in moral instruction until he left for the Leicester Secular Society in 1899, and his successor, Hugh H. Quilter, an Oxford graduate and Sunday school teacher for the St. Pancras Ethical Society. From April 1899 Quilter contributed sample lessons to the paper, more evolutionist in approach than Gould's, and especially observant of human body language: 'Our gestures or "bearing" in conversation are a most important part of our whole behaviour.' He published a beautifully illustrated evolutionist school book on natural history (with moral implications) called *Onward and Upward: A Book for Boys and Girls* (1902). Quilter later became a Board of Education school inspector.

Another group among the Ethical Propagandists was that of journalist–activists, who lived by writing and lecturing and worked for political pressure groups and sometimes in municipal government. In this category there was G. H. Perris, son of a Unitarian minister in Liverpool, who followed his brother (editor of *The Daily Mail*) into journalism, first as editor of *The Hull Express* in 1889, and later as editor of *The Speaker*. He edited the pacifist paper *Concord*, was later foreign editor of *Tribune* and *The Daily Chronicle*, and became war correspondent for the latter from 1914. He became a leading internationalist and anti-imperialist. Perris was a close friend of J. A. Hobson, for a time a Propagandist, whom we have seen to be involved with the L.E.S., who later settled into a long relationship with South Place, but in between he worked with Coit, lectured at Leighton Hall, and worked with *The Ethical World*. Another journalist was the aggressive rationalist Joseph McCabe. He came from less fortunate circumstances than Perris or Hobson. The son of a Macclesfield draper, he attended Catholic elementary school and was selected for training in Manchester by the Franciscans. He became a lecturer in philosophy and ecclesiastical history at Forest Gate seminary. In 1895 he was appointed rector to a new college in Buckinghamshire, but he decided to abandon the church and monastic life, and was helped through to a life in lecturing, and indefatigable authorship, by Coit. One of his greatest successes was a translation of *Die Welträtsel* (1899) by the materialist–evolutionist sage of Jena, Ernst Haeckel. It became a best seller in English under the title of *The Riddle of the Universe* (1899). Like Hobson, McCabe eventually made a base for himself at South Place.

There were three other Propagandists who suffered more hardship than McCabe in their early lives – Ramsay MacDonald, Harry Snell and William S. Sanders. The early lives of Snell and MacDonald were noted in Chapter 1. By the time Coit assembled his team these three were of an age (between twenty-seven and thirty-three), having achieved a relative degree of stability. Snell had a post as secretary to the director of the new London School of Economics and Political Science; he became one of the lecturers funded by the Hutchinson Trust, the travelling for which brought him near to physical collapse, out of which he was helped (with a foreign vacation) by Coit. MacDonald married Margaret Gladstone in 1896, whose wealth enabled him to write, organise and travel. W. S. Sanders held a similar post to that of Snell. He started life with minimally greater advantages than Snell, leaving school at eleven rather than eight years old for agricultural work. He became a clerk in London. Both he and Snell were active in London municipal politics until the 1920s, when they entered parliament, Snell as M.P. for East Woolwich (in 1922) and Sanders for North Battersea (in 1929).

Besides Coit himself, there were four other Propagandists: R. W. D. Nankivell, E. Stewart Walde, Maurice Adams and F. W. Foerster. The first two were inactive. Adams was a senior progressive, a founder of the Fellowship of the New Life, at the time of the Propagandists in charge of the Croydon Ethical and Religious Fellowship. Foerster was marginal: at the Union congress in 1896 he enthused, but dragged his feet over the tasks assigned of him to arranging a second congress and establishing an ethical society in Zurich; he was to get a name for being soft on Catholics. All the Propagandists were male – though by virtue of sheer activity Zona Vallance (1860–1904) deserved membership. She was probably not included because the formation of the group followed hard upon that of the Moral Instruction League of which she was secretary, a more onerous post anyway than that of Ethical Propagandist. Zona Vallance, the daughter of an East End doctor, came from the East London Ethical Society and was the movement's leading spokesperson on issues concerning women. Her early death was a major loss.[6]

Thanks to the activities of Coit it was possible to think of an 'ethical movement'. But then in his forties Coit felt a failure. In December 1899 he wrote to Ramsay MacDonald:

Is there no possibility that the I.L.P. [Independent Labour Party] would change its name to 'The Democratic Party' and introduce some new ethical elements into its principles and programmes? . . . I pray, night and day, that somehow something to the good of the matter may happen through us Ethical Propagandists. But the Lord enshrouds my soul in darkness and fear. In one question I ask myself, how can I be of real service to the Labour Movement? I have an overwhelming but vague sense that it is . . . for me to render some great and unique service, and this is like a madness, as I do not see how and as nobody respects the things I have been preaching and teaching all these years, what ought I to do?

Emotionally Coit had to be *in* a movement – the world of 'finite minds co-operating in collective unity': it was not easy for an unorthodox American preacher to find a place in British labour politics. But the structure of the labour movement was becoming more complex, and Coit was right to appeal to MacDonald because the I.L.P. was gaining authority. The most important of the trade unions, the Amalgamated Society of Engineers, had an I.L.P. member as secretary in George A. Barnes. There was action to come of which Coit wanted a part: a great conference of labour organisations was scheduled for the end of February 1900. Coit announced in January in the *Ethical World* that the paper was henceforth to be committed to socialism, whose 'cloven hoof' had hitherto only 'peeped out' beneath the cloak of ethics. This could be one of his first steps towards rendering 'some great and unique service'. The paper was to be committed to 'make Society, in the church, in the school, in the playground, in the factory, in the legislative halls, a spiritual organism'. It backed the socialism of the Webbs' *Industrial Democracy* (1898), of *The Clarion*, of *The Labour Leader*, and the moderate Marxism of Eduard Bernstein. In February 1900 a front page article in the *Ethical World* by George A. Barnes called for 'a separate and distinct organisation' to enter parliament to force back the 'plutocrats who man both political parties'. Such an organisation should not, he wrote, draw its members only from the working class, so as to prevent labour's energy being wasted on 'sectional questions', 'such as have weakened and discredited trades unionism. The many disputes regarding demarcation of work will occur to the mind of the reader.' The way was becoming clearer for the participation of people of Coit's type.

When the conference came it did indeed reject the view that only working men were eligible to be labour parliamentary candidates. As Mac-Donald put it in the *Ethical World* in March, the conference repudiated the idea of the labour movement as a class movement, wishing it to become and be known as 'a party of opinion'. This redefinition made possible the major achievement of the conference, its creation of the Labour Representation Committee. A decision favouring middle-class representatives opened a door for Coit. He was still not sure which way to jump. In April 1900 he wrote again to MacDonald, hesitant of joining the I.L.P. because of its conflict with the Social Democratic Federation. Did not this conflict prove he was right, that there should be *another* political party, a 'Democratic Party into which men like [J. A.] Hobson could throw themselves?'. The idea of a new party simmered in an April essay in the *Ethical World* by H. W. Massingham, a disillusioned Liberal who had recently resigned as editor of the *Daily Chronicle*. He attacked the moral bankruptcy of the government and the impotence of the Opposition front bench. Coit rallied to Massingham in an editorial note in June, arguing that as an election could not be expected for at least seven months, until March 1901, there was time to prepare for a great democratic convention. Subsequent numbers contained much approving comment on this idea, though the more militant socialists were dubious. Parliament is not everything, said J. F. Green; S. G. Hobson was sceptical of loquacious 'New Liberals' trailing their coats with news of the supposed death of Liberalism. However, speculation was halted. Plans for a convention of democrats were thwarted by the 'khaki dementia' which brought a dissolution earlier than anyone had anticipated. The General Election was to be in October. Coit took off for America, to promote a similar scheme for a national labour party with local paid staff which would take 'a strong stand against trusts, and [would] have neither political nor religious affiliation as which interfere with their work'. There was even talk of his standing for election as mayor of New York.

Coit returned to busy himself with a campaign for a Democratic Party in the *Ethical World*. From the beginning of January 1901 it was re-named *Democracy: In Religion, Education, Art, Industry and Politics – An Organ of Ethical Progress*. In the following months the campaign received strong support from the collectivist William S. Sanders, who was in the process of writing *The Reorganisation of the People* (1902). But divisions were showing through the ethicist ranks. On 19 October 1901 Coit had to announce that there was to be another change of title for the paper, from *Democracy* to *Ethics*, with the sub-title, 'An Organ of the Ethical Movement'. He gave into this after pressure from some shareholders, who thought the title inflammatory. This brush with the shareholders in-duced in Coit a 'cynicism and contempt towards his fellow men', not to-wards the 'ignorant and illiterate masses', but for the 'small enlightened public' which found *Democracy*, as a title, too red-blooded. It had to be, expostulated Coit: 'socialism' was tame and fashionable ('We are all socialists now . . .') and anyway the word socialism

had no association or contact whatever with the history of the masses in their struggle towards liberty and light . . . Not so with the passion-torn, mud bespat-tered divine word 'Democracy', which suggests all that has been great in France and ancient Greece, America and Republicanism, and which is alive with pas-sion, electric with the joy of liberty, and quick with creative energy.

By comparison 'ethics' was too clean, neutral – and meaningless to the populace. In February Coit resigned from the editorial chair of the newly named journal, no longer able to tolerate the non-socialists (or non-democrats) of the ethical movement, though he continued to write plenty of its material. He announced that he wanted more time to write, as he was planning a book on 'Ethics for Teachers' and an expanded version of his *Neighbourhood Guilds*. In fact, as we shall see in the next section, Coit became involved in two ambitious treatises of a different kind.

Coit's resignation coincided with a charge in the *Daily News* that the Union of Ethical Societies was a 'socialistic organisation'. The *Ethical World* hotly denied it on 22 February and the following week on 1 March a 'personal word' from Coit was published, entitled 'Socialism and the Ethical Movement'. 'I probably out-socialist every other socialist in England', he claimed. *He* was no mere 'nationaliser of land and capital': *he* would carry the principles of social democracy into the church, de-mand state organisation of entertainment, recreation and art, 'all this besides the necessity of the collectivistic ownership of the general sources of material wealth'. The Union of Ethical Societies was not socialist because, democrat that he was, he abhorred the very idea of forcing ethical societies to his socialist opinions. So, most of the ethicists were non-socialist, with his theoretical blessing. Although between 1900 and 1903 the annual congresses of the Union were chaired by collectivists (MacDonald and Sanders) the council was nervous of avowing socialist aims. In 1899 there had been a move, albeit defeated, to impede the admission to the Union of the Battersea Ethical Society by enquiring whether it was affiliated to any political body, which it certainly was, nearly all the members being supporters of John Burns and the Battersea Labour League. After the *Daily News* accusation, the council of the Union moved that a letter should be sent out once and for all repudiating the charge of socialism. Coit pursued a series of bids in the *Ethical World* to win over groups outside the ethical societies with which politically concerned ethicism had natural affinities, like the Labour Churches and secularists. He was beginning to think in terms not so much of a Democratic Party as a 'Democratic Church' for the masses, to serve them as the established church served the ruling class, supplying – his emphasis – 'a *background* for measures, institutions, and customs as well as establish and preserve *the whole nation, without class distinction, in its moral, intellectual, and economic unity*'.[7]

Coit's 'personal word' of 1 March 1902 was naive and impetuous; naive because by 'outsocialisting' everyone else he effectively depoliticised himself, and impetuous because he gestured at projects on which he had never really worked (like the nationalisation of entertainment), or ones which he had hardly mentioned in the context of actual British conditions. (Though there had been thought on some of these issues in the *Ethical World*, for instance, on the press, that 'hypnotic apparatus', as G. H. Perris called it in a piece applauding John Morley's idea of 'newspaper classes' showing 'how to discriminate the essential from the sensational'.) Coit's offer to carry the 'passion-torn' word to the administration of religious bodies must have seemed a red-herring even to sympathetic socialist readers. But Coit was becoming increasingly interested in such ideas. He had always claimed that there should be ethical missionaries leading a Coleridgean clerisy. If ethicists formed a kind of clergy, was not an ethical society a kind of church? On 16 March 1901 he contributed an article called 'Shall it be an Ethical Church?', answering with a resounding affirmative. In 1902 he began to move away from stimulating and logical analogy (like that between clergy and 'clerisy') towards the more risky realm of factual proposition. He began to believe that the ethical movement could not only be engrafted on to the Labour Churches (themselves analogical organisations), but even have an attachment to the established Church. On 6 June 1903 Coit confessed that he found himself for the first time in his life 'in the midst of a meeting, chiefly of clergymen, sympathetically agreeing with everything said, and occasionally crying out with the others, "Hear, hear!" '. He was referring to the annual meeting of the Churchmen's Union. An old flame had been fanned. Years before he fell out with Adler over his own readiness to make treaty with the Christian churches; the parting from his mentor came after he expressed a wish to relate a Boston ethical society (of which he had been offered leadership) to a Christian church. But then the desire was only a tendency, an interest among stronger ambitions. In June 1903 he joined the Churchmen's Union, in order to promote 'the ethical democratisation of religion in England'. Ironically, within a few weeks an opportunity arose which promised to gratify his ambition for political authority, to perform 'some great and unique service' in public life. On 26 August he was adopted as a parliamentary candidate for Wakefield in Yorkshire, with strong union support. In September he signed the I.L.P. constitution. In the same year he received naturalisation as a British subject.[8]

The Wakefield constituency had been fought in 1902 by Philip Snowden, after its Liberal member had gone to the House of Lords. Snowden was defeated, after which a local Labour Representation Committee was formed which adopted Coit who then visited the town regularly. At national level the Labour Representation Committee had recently gained authority when the House of Lords ruled in favour of the Taff Vale Railway Company. Coit worked hard in Wakefield. In the spring of 1905 he purchased a newspaper, *The Wakefield Echo and West Yorkshire News and General Advertiser*. It was a cheap Friday paper, younger than its two rivals, the *Wakefield Express*, progressive and Liberal, founded in 1853 and the solid *Herald* which for a century had spoken for church and state. Coit brought out the first issue of his *Echo* on 5 May 1905, having installed Linotype machinery. This caused four redundancies, but he unionised the works and it was accepted for the Typographical Society's 'fair' list. He had recently appointed George O'Dell (1874–1957) as personal assistant and made him editor of the *Echo*. O'Dell was to become a well-known ethicist. He was educated at a polytechnic school in London, and, besides working for Coit, earned his living from journalism and as what he called a 'character counsellor'. In 1913 he joined Adler in New York, acting as leader of several ethical culture groups, helping to found the journal of the American Ethical Union, *The Standard*. He eventually became a Unitarian minister and retired to England in 1947.

Coit had several lines of action in Wakefield. He organised a labour movement, running the first May Day rally the town had seen, and arranging for a deputation of the unemployed to demonstrate at the council offices against the Unemployed Workmen Act of 1905. He campaigned for better housing, publicising the town slums which had long been condemned to little effect by the Sanitary Aid Society, and he mounted a 'Kitchen Gardens For All' movement, urging the council to act on his discovery that a disused sewage farm could be made into allotments. (He remembered seeing in his student days 'the whole of Berlin surrounded by allotments'.) When officials claimed that working people were not interested in kitchen gardens, Coit used one of his favourite retorts: the numbed foot does not feel where the shoe pinches. Adela Coit also got to know the constituency, and promised to help finance a local 'social science centre'.

The General Election was called abruptly for the beginning of January 1906, allowing only a brief campaign. Coit was called a political adventurer, 'unblushingly advocating the extravagances of socialism'. The *Echo* explained that he was not a doctrinaire socialist, but committed to 'an advanced labour policy'. Adversaries made play with his nationality and his academic title – there were rumblings about imaginary American 'degree factories'. The candidate responded with a haughty reference to his Berlin credentials and to his naturalisation in 1903. Many years later, O'Dell remembered that Coit's naturalisation document was sent down to Wakefield only within hours of the poll: undeniably he was something of an adventurer. His electoral platform proposed nationalisation of (notably) railways, canals, mines, gas, electricity, water supplies, and tramways; the introduction of old-age pensions, protection of trade union funds, revision of the Unemployed Workmen and Education Acts, the establishment of community control of the liquor traffic, Home Rule, and the abolition of Chinese slavery in the Transvaal. There were certain personal preoccupations in his election address: 'Home Rule All Round', meaning devolution from Westminster, and the creation of municipal workshops for public facility improvement schemes ('the State as a model employer'). He did not hide his ethicism and his eloquence was unashamedly in the strain of Matthew Arnold: few, if any, parliamentary candidates before or since have declared in the market-place that, 'I believe there is a power not myself, which makes for righteousness, and I believe that that power is what is defined as God in the Old Testament. That power is my God.' That power did not protect him from a plague of fly-posting, denouncing him as an atheist. Coit successfully sought an injunction in court against the libel.

Nor did this power carry him to Westminster. He performed respectably at the polls, but came second to the Conservative candidate, who was returned with a slender margin of 217. Unfortunately for Coit the anti-Conservative vote which could have helped him was split by the late appearance in August 1905 of a Liberal with a similar platform; he polled many fewer votes than Coit.[9]

Coit went back down to London with at least the satisfaction (he said) of seeing one enemy of the working class defeated. It was not the end of his campaigning. In 1907 he was considered for the East Birmingham seat, but the local I.L.P. representative decided that although he was 'a good man', he would not suit because of his 'peculiar religious views' in a constituency where the voters 'are very anti-agnostic'. In the same year he allegedly helped Mrs. Emmeline Pankhurst set up an office in London, in which William S. Sanders's wife, Beatrice, worked as an accountant. But he was to dissociate himself from violent suffragette activity. Ramsay MacDonald continued to support his labour candidacy, and approved him for a second attempt in Wakefield. He campaigned for the General Election in 1910: 'The great question you are to decide is whether the *Peers* or the *People* rule this country.' On this occasion there was no Liberal candidate, but again he was narrowly defeated. This was the end of Coit's parliamentary ambition. He was soon, in any case, to become alienated from his old socialist associates when, never a pacifist, he refused to oppose the war. During his involvement with Wakefield he was immersed in the question of transforming his West London Ethical Society into an ethical church. It is likely that one reason for contesting Wakefield was that he knew that if successful he could take his ideas about Prayer Book reform into the House of Commons, up to the legislature. After his second defeat, the West London Ethical Society and religion had his total attention.[10]

Shall it be an Ethical Church?

'There's a red-headed chap in a church in Queen's Road who spews God out of his mouth – you ought to go and hear him.' A young man on active service during World War I received this message. He duly told his brother and in the early 1920s both visited the church and were invited to tea by Coit. The brother, Alex F. Dawn, became his secretary. Everyone who knew Coit says that he was difficult: according to Dawn he was 'highly strung', phenomenally quick to grasp a point, but on occasion 'very light-hearted and amusing'. He also noted one important feature of Coit's self-image:

Dr. Coit was not strictly a humanist. He disliked the name and was indignant that Gustav Spiller . . . referred to the humanist movement. Coit was a Platonist in the sense that he believed that the ideal of Truth, etc., had an independent existence. In fact he was annoyed with me for holding the view that they were abstractions.

We shall see how Coit's Platonism was related to his Ethical Church, and return to his rejection of pragmatic humanism mentioned at the beginning of this chapter.

'Shall it be an Ethical Church?' asked Coit in 1901. He argued that the Sunday meeting occupied the same place in an ethicist's life as did Sunday service in that of a Christian churchgoer. So wouldn't the societies attract new members, converts to ethicism or even emancipated Jews, if they frankly offered themselves as churches? Undoubtedly the argument was fallacious. Felix Adler, in New York, made the Ethical Culture society successful by carefully keeping it free of church-like associations. The Jewish community knew that supporting his society did not imply a conflict with the synagogue, and, of course, continued to respect Adler's distinguished Jewish lineage. As for attracting doubting Christians, Bernard Bosanquet could have told Coit that 'the general rule is that different forms of the same thing are hostile'. Nonetheless Coit's wish for a church was psychologically plausible in the context of his longing to perform 'some great and unique service' and his more significant desire, less dependent on a private psychological drive, to establish unity among the ever-shifting cohorts of socialism.[11]

We saw that after his resignation in 1901 as editor of the *Ethical World* Coit planned to use his time for writing. But his thought was flowing away from his intended project, on neighbourhood guilds, towards religious behaviour. As an ethicist naturally he turned to consider the Ten Commandments. He became fascinated by the Decalogue and set about devising a version of it that might satisfy ethicists at Sunday meeting. By this time a Moral Instruction League had been founded. F. J. Gould had produced copious practical teaching material, but there was a need for a general study of ethics – and in any case Gould had in Coit's eyes marginalised himself by converting to Positivism and what he wanted was to experiment with a scheme that would command the widest assent. As we shall see, 'normality' was his fixation. The idea of worship began to figure in his thought about ethical imperatives and the Decalogue. In 1904 he published in the *Ethical World* a 'modern naturalistic substitute' for the Decalogue, fully aware that he was inviting ridicule from 'the all-round radicals of the old-fashioned sort'. He adapted the commandments to the nationalism of the J. R. Seeley type:

The real organic unit of the religious life, of which any man is a member, is always the nation to which he belongs, *in so far as the nation stands for social and personal ideals and principles*. (Coit's italics.)

He had learned from Seeley about the combination of religion and statesmanship in the Old Testament and was enthralled to find a similar combination in the Prayer Book, or, more precisely, in the second Prayer

Book of Edward VI, *The Book of Common Prayer and the Administration of the Sacraments, and Other Rites and Ceremonies of the Church of England* (1552). This Prayer Book was for Coit a work of fundamentalist protestantism, an *ethical* document, which had a message both for his own movement and for the Church. It spoke for social democracy, in its requirement, for example, that communion wine be no longer withheld from lay persons, in the way it played down the supernatural – omitting exorcism for the baptism service, and in the burial service showing as much care for the souls of the living as for that of the deceased – and in the new prominence it gave to the Athanasian creed which it required to be said on thirteen days rather than on the six specified in the first (1549) Prayer Book. Most important of all the second Prayer Book placed the Decalogue, 'the most decidedly ethical document of the whole of the Old Testament', at the beginning of the form for Holy Communion. If the divines of the sixteenth century could effect such a revolution in attitude, was there not hope for the Church of the twentieth century, especially if its clergy took note of enlightened ethicists?[12]

We saw that Coit felt at ease at a meeting of the Churchmen's Union in 1903. In the winter of 1904 he proposed a five-point plan to the ethical movement: stay within 'the historical stream of religious consciousness', state clear principles, introduce ritual at meetings (for the sake of 'decency and order': earlier in the year Coit reproved ethicists for applauding), institute an ethical society to be called the Church of Social Democracy, and introduce the word *God* into ethical discourses. He knew what kind of ritual he wanted. It had been tried out on a hundred ethicists from twelve societies in July 1904 at a service which concluded the annual congress of the Union. The order was as follows.

Opening Words
Canticle: 'Woe unto him that buildeth his house by unrighteousness,
And his chambers by wrong.'
Declaration of Ethical Principles
Silence
Hymn
Discourse
Anthem
Announcements
Hymn and Collection
Closing Words

The pattern was that of the service already in use at the West London Ethical Society, but leaving out the parts in which the 'congregation' made choral responses, its 'Invitation to Fellowship' from the leader, and its organ voluntary; from 1911 Coit had a first-rate musician, in the person of Charles Kennedy Scott, to devote his gifts and time to the cause of ethical worship. To Coit the congregational answers or responses were essential. One of them was a non-supernatural (or 'naturalistic') Decalogue called 'Ten Words of the Moral Life', first used three times a year at the welcoming of new members and later (after 1912) monthly. Coit also devised a 'Universal Litany' for monthly use. From the records of the West London Ethical Society it is clear that Coit forced through the adoption of the responsive elements. Much later, in 1934, he was to say that he cared more for his creed than for the Ethical Church itself.

Thus Coit had in 1904 a programme for a church. In the summer, following his defeat in Wakefield, he gathered with the help of O'Dell a collection of materials for ethical services, eventually to be published in two sumptuous volumes, to celebrate the twenty-first anniversary of the West London Ethical Society, as *Social Worship: For Use in Families, Schools and Churches* (1913), edited by Coit, with music selections edited by Charles Kennedy Scott. At the same time he worked on two books to explain the rationale of ethical worship, *National Idealism and a State Church: A Constructive Essay in Religion* (1907) and *National Idealism and the Book of Common Prayer: An Essay in Re-interpretation and Revision* (1908). The first of these books was revised for American publication as *The Soul of America: A Constructive Essay in the Sociology of Religion* (1914), its title displaying that in the interim Coit discovered Emile Durkheim's *Les Formes élémentaires de la vie religieuse* (1912). But Durkheim did not make his full impact on Coit until after Swain's translation of 1915. To this experience we shall shortly return.[13]

Coit's concern for ritual was growing in momentum. He secured some support from the ethical societies. In 1902 the council of the Union agreed that its book of ethical songs should be retitled *Ethical Hymns*. But he did not get much further. It was not that ethicists objected to spells of meditative silence, or singing, or listening to readings. What they resisted was the alliance Coit offered with the Church, however much he insisted that it was the Church which should follow the ethicists, not the other way about, and that he was thoroughly re-interpreting and revising its forms. He believed that an ethical church could stimulate the Anglican modernists, but mostly ethicists were uninterested in obliging with lessons an institution they had rejected. They respected Coit, without whom there would have been no Union and probably no ethical societies; but no societies wanted to follow the example of the West London Ethical Society, and if individuals did, they simply joined it.

The chance to turn tendency into actuality came in 1909 when O'Dell noticed that the lease of a gothic United Methodist Church in Queen's

Road, Bayswater, was up for sale. At the time the West London Ethical Society was based in Kensington, holding its meetings in rented halls to the south of the borough, often in Kensington Town Hall, and running a settlement, with day-nursery in charge of Mrs. O'Dell, in Notting Hill to the north. It wanted a home of its own and struggled to raise funds for the chapel, which it finally accomplished with the help of Mrs. Coit who bought the lease for £1,000. The society considered calling it an 'Ethical Temple', but gave in to Coit's wish that it should be the Ethical Church. The building was so called, though the society did not formally change its name until 1914. But, because this chapel immediately became the scene of Coit's experiments, it is fair to say that 1909 is the founding year of the Ethical Church. It captured the interest of Londoners. In 1909 it had 470 subscribers, the highest in the history of the West London Ethical Society. And of course the number of visitors exceeded that of members.[14]

A visit to the Ethical Church

What did these visitors find at the Ethical Church? The atmosphere was accurately caught by one member who was a novelist. The following is an extract from *The Prophet's Wife* (1929) by R. O. Prowse.

Anne stood just inside one of the swing doors through which you passed from the vestibule to the hall, ready to hand a music book to every one who went in. She took the books as she wanted them from a pile that stood by her side on a chair against the wall. They were large thin volumes, well printed and well bound, that contained the words of the anthems and the music as well the words of the hymns and canticles of the service Hepworth [the 'minister'] had devised. It was early, and few of the rush-seated chairs were occupied. Well-warmed and well-lighted, with a little cheerful coming and going among the stewards (there was a second steward in the central aisle, and a third at the other door), and a faint murmur of talk from two or three persons in the vestibule, the hall had that air of confident anticipation to be found in a church in which a good congregation is expected. Indeed, the hall had so much the appearance of a church that 'church' seemed the appropriate word. The rows of rush-seated chairs, with a central aisle, the walls panelled to the sills of the windows, the pointed and raftered roof with the crossing beams from which hung blue and gold chandeliers, the pulpit placed against what might have been an eastern wall, and approached, on each side, by a finely curved flight of stairs, the beautifully worked curtain that covered the panelling on this furthest wall – the effect of all this was eminently reverent and devotional, and, if one's tastes were simple, was not without an element of beauty. Between the pulpit and the row of chairs was an open space, on one side of which an organ stood, while on the other, more oak benches on which the choir sat in two rows. Hepworth entered the hall by the curtained door near the pulpit, and mounted the curving stairs. He wore a black silk gown over a black cassock, and as he stood in the middle of the pulpit he made a dignified and impressive figure.

The service began with

an introit sung by the choir: after which Hepworth read, as 'Opening Words', a sentence or two from Emerson [*sic*]. The music of the service consisted of a canticle, two anthems and two hymns: poems of Shelley, Sir Henry Wooton, Edward Carpenter, Clough, Robert Bridges were set to the music of Palestrina, Bach, Richard Farrant, Rutland Boughton, Kennedy Scott. There were two lessons, chosen from Thomas à Kempis and the work of a contemporary author, and a pause for silent meditation or prayer. The Discourse was delivered before the singing of the last anthem and hymn. There was a collection after the Discourse, and the service closed with two or three 'Dismissory Sentences' from William Blake.

The picture is nearly correct, down to the 'large thin volumes', copies of the second volume of *Social Worship*, whose first, heavy, volume contained readings, and the curtain, acquired by Mrs. Coit from a church in Rome. However, the real Church was, by all accounts, slightly more ornate. On the 'eastern wall' above the pulpit and framed in the panelling, was set a large, wide painting by Walter Crane entitled 'The Torch Bearers', depicting seven naked figures running across the top of a globe, passing flaming torches from hand to hand. There was one woman in this relay, but seated to indicate the subjection of women without the suffrage. The male figures wore red caps to show they were freed men, except one just below the edge of the horizon with Coitian red hair. Above and below the painting was the legend, 'Still the race of hero spirits Pass the torch from hand to hand.' The globe was set in a blue firmament, a colour taken up in the carpet of the open space in front of the pulpit. The colour scheme of the Church was planned by Crane, who also designed the fussy stalks for the electric light standards on each side of the pulpit. The Church was loftier than that of *The Prophet's Wife*. It was semicircular, with two galleries curving round the central space, and for much of its history the choir sang not from one side but from the upper gallery, and so was invisible to most of the congregation. The Church was decorated with sculptures and reliefs. There was a Buddha and a Christ on fluted wooden plinths on each side of the pulpit. Above the pulpit there was on each side a Luca della Robbia relief, two from a set of four owned by the Church. A stand for a bust of Pallas Athene was built into the upper part of the frame of 'The Torch Bearers'. There were stained glass windows, showing Elizabeth Fry, Bernard Shaw and his Saint Joan. In the open space below the pulpit there was an ornate oak chair and lectern for a cantor. From 1923 a white marble column stood in front of them inscribed 'An Altar to the Ideal, the True, the Beautiful and the Good'.

In *The Prophet's Wife* the service is led by a figure somewhat less like

Coit than the appropriately named Dr. Quoin in another and earlier novel by Prowse, *James Hurd* (1913):

With a fair and well-trimmed beard and a complexion lightly and pleasantly tanned by the sun, Dr. Quoin looked a man of strong and reassuring personality. In a gathering [of 'provincial progressives'] so largely suggestive of protest and repudiation, of dislike, one imagined, of the hampering imposed by the smaller conventions, his well-dressed, well-groomed figure, with its comfortable conformity to the canon of taste, conveyed a very comfortable assurance of the normal. He had the look of fitness of a man who had lately come back from the sun, the look of substance of a man with whom you felt safe from anything fantastic or fanatical, anything unbalanced or sensational or perverse.

In Bayswater Coit himself stood before a less determinedly unconventional congregation. It was idiosyncratic, but mostly from the secure middle class, consisting of teachers, a bookbinder, professional men and women (including a woman doctor and woman estate agent, who ran a business in her husband's name), writers, artists, a celebrated theatre variety performer, to list those chosen as characteristic by Prowse in *The Prophet's Wife*. Bayswater and Kensington had wealthy households cheek by jowl with squalor. There were a few working-class members: it was possible for a colonel from the nearby Household Guards barracks to sit down at the American-style monthly church supper with a gas-fitter (who wore gloves to hide his chemical-stained fingers). There was something for these people to attend on Sunday mornings and evenings, and on Wednesdays and Fridays. In the period described in *James Hurd* (that is, around 1912) there were, over a period of three months, Sunday discourses on varied subjects. On Sunday mornings they dealt with different conceptions of God (including those of Bernard Shaw and the Christian socialist, W. H. Paul Campbell), on 'phases of the inner life', the irreligion of the future, the concept of civilisation as a sickness, on utopian communities, on Father Tyrell, on Norman Angell's *The Great Illusion*, and on 'the alchemy of thought'. There was a children's service, with a discourse on *Peter Pan*. On Sunday evenings there were lectures on 'personal responsibility', and a series on art, with lantern slides. On Wednesday evenings there were talks on politics, four on divorce law, two on current theatre productions (*The Winter's Tale* and *The Voysey Inheritance*). On Friday afternoons there were twelve lectures on the Psalms. The Sunday morning discourses were part of the full weekly service, at which, on the first Wednesday of each month, Coit's 'Universal Litany' was spoken. 'Ten Words of the Moral Life' was intoned once a month.

The minister in *James Hurd* possesses 'a very comfortable assurance of the normal', an accurate evocation of Coit's manner − but also indication of an attitude which he wanted to create in the proceedings of the Ethical Church. He wanted them to be reassuringly *normal*. In his choice of reading he

avoided, as untrue to common sense, both the platitudes that would please the undisciplined and incapable, and also the eccentricities which might delight the abnormal. Among the abnormal, as a sub-class, I would place those who count themselves, and who are accounted by their special admirers, the super-normal. Abnormality obtrudes itself today in many forms under this pretence, but in no realm of human interest more than in the domain of religion. We are flooded in our age with 'freak religions', as they have been denominated, which cultivate the occult, and, scorning the normal avenues of spiritual communication, strain at originating new senses.

The serene reference to 'normal avenues' evokes what Ivor Brown once called the Edwardian age of innocence: 'You ended or mended the House of Lords; you gave Ireland Home Rule and stood no nonsense from the bishops and the brewers; you extended the franchise to include even women; you developed education. The elector would see and follow what was good. How could he not?' Coit wanted normality to be within the very fibre of his Church's activities, and for this he had a full-scale conceptual justification. To this we shall come shortly, in the course of considering the theory of Coit's church.[15]

A Platonist's church

The ritual of the Ethical Church has inspired transports of superciliousness in its critics. A common complaint is that it was a naively nostalgic institution, the creation of those who were unable to resist an addiction to the ecclesiastical. This is not very plausible, partly because most people who attended the Ethical Church (and the ethical societies at large) knew what church was and did not like it. A more telling criticism is that of Susan Budd who finds Coit's rituals simply inauthentic. 'Ritual', she argues, 'can only express, reinforce and give numinous quality to that which exists already', that is, something already accomplished in such evidently spontaneous doings as those of the working-class secularists who 'rode out in in charabancs to picnic in the Pennines, carrying banners with pictures of Paine'. (The example shows how seductive the high-minded picturesque can be.) Budd rejects the ingeniously tuned rituals of the Ethical Church as inauthentic because they were *invented*. I suspect that this criticism is not far from the view of the churchgoer who believes his own rituals to be authentic because they formalise and enact something which once really happened, and finds

124

those of Coit factitious, self-referential, 'made up'. What is to be made of the charge of inauthenticity?

There must be agreement about at least one feature of the nature of ritual: it is not primarily a mode of expression (a means of getting *out* something already experienced); its real significance is in being a mode of action (a means of getting *to* a state which could not be secured by any other method). It is a form of ultimate action because participants in ritual are supposed to believe that it is only through performing the actions required of them can the power they seek be acquired; and ritual that has no connection with power is surely not ritual in any interesting sense. This view is taken by Emile Durkheim in a passage which is both important inherently and because it is one of which Coit took special note. He copiously annotated his copy of Swain's translation, *The Elementary Forms of the Religious Life*, during two readings he made in the summer of 1923. The passage in question occurs in Durkheim's 'Conclusion' in which he states, with almost Bradleyan force, that the first article in every creed is a belief in salvation by faith. Men seek strength through religion; men cannot be made stronger by mere ideas for 'an idea is in reality only a part of ourselves'. Since an idea is part of myself, it cannot confer upon me any power superior to what I already possess within my own nature. So the religious cult 'is not simply a system of signs by which faith is outwardly translated; it is a collection of the means by which this is created and recreated periodically. Whether it consists in material acts or mental operations, it is always this which is efficacious.' Durkheim goes on to state that members of a cult acquire strength through acts because it is from action that the content of their religion, their mythology, derives. Budd follows Durkheim in saying that ritual offers again something that once really happened. But this argument is not necessarily incompatible with Coit's ideas and practices at the Ethical Church, nor especially is Durkheim's major argument that religion derives from the system of actions *which is society*: 'It is action which dominates the religious life, because of the mere fact that it is society which is its source.' Society is the cause of 'religious sensations', sensations which are the matter of religion and which Durkheim says can be compared to sensory experience analysed by natural rather than social scientists:

We have shown what moral forces it develops and how it awakens this sentiment of refuge, of a shield and of a guardian support which attaches the believer to his cult. It is that which raises himself outside himself; it is even that which made him. For that which makes a man is the totality of the intellectual property which constitutes civilisation, and civilisation is the work of society. Thus is explained the preponderating role of the cult in all religions . . . And there is no cult without action.

Against this passage Coit scribbled: 'Work out this idea in the practice and teaching of the Ethical Church.' A little later he added, 'Preach the power of society, that worships the socialising spirit within it, *to redeem its members* [my italics]. Preach this in the Ethical Church. Embody this idea in our ritual!' 'This idea' refers to Durkheim's sentence, 'If religion has given birth to all that is essential in society, it is because the idea of society is the soul of religion.' To worship the socialising spirit within society is to be religious in Durkheim's sense; and it continues to be religious in his sense if Durkheim is to be believed that the freedom ethic of late nineteenth-century liberalism was also religious, though not because Coit subscribed to this ethic, but because his alternative to its individualism was at least *as* religious. However, the question remains of whether, despite Coit's impassioned wish, 'worship' of the socialising spirit did take place in the Ethical Church, and also the question of whether the Ethical Church identified this socialising spirit. Still another question can be asked of Coit's annotations to Durkheim, the answer to which shows, I think, an anomaly within the part of the Church ceremony which Coit cherished, its responsive part. In his marginalia Coit wrote that when a group worshipped the socialising spirit its members could be redeemed. The problem here is why the issue of *redemption* should arise. Was the congregation at the Ethical Church in a state of *sin*? For the concept of redemption is surely inseparable from that of sin. Let us consider how the problem of sin and redemption enters into Coit's ritual.

In *National Idealism and a State Church* Coit examines 'the most superb literary and liturgical composition of the Church – the Litany', and sketches a revised version of it, designed to accentuate 'the essence of its substance [which] is the love of social justice'. Here is the socialising spirit. This version was elaborated in a booklet, *Two Responsive Services* (1911), which also included the naturalistic Decalogue, forming a supplement to *Social Worship*. We saw that Coit was determined to make these liturgies figure prominently in the 'ethical year'. The 'Universal Litany' was, of course, based upon the Anglican Litany or General Supplication, which the Prayer Book requires to be sung or said after morning prayer on Sundays, Wednesdays and Fridays. This Litany is the central expression within Anglicanism of the state of sin. This is evinced by the responses in which the congregation makes supplication:

> . . . *O God the Father, of heaven:*
> *have mercy upon us miserable sinners.*
> . . . *O holy, blessed, and glorious Trinity,*
> *three Persons and one God:*
> *have mercy upon us miserable sinners.*

And after the introductory section:

> ... *Spare us, good Lord.*
> ... *Good Lord, deliver us.*
> ... *We beseech thee to hear us good Lord.*

The refrains confirm the statements of the minister, until the final, more rapidly intertwined dialogue addressed to God, and to Christ as the Lamb of God. The responses are those of unregenerate man. The purport of the Litany is not to seek help in face of the multiple temptations and afflictions of life (fornication, plague, sudden death, childbirth, captivity, widowhood), but to seek relief from a state of sin which renders these temptations and afflictions the *more* unbearable. When Coit revised the Litany he deleted, as might be expected, its 'magical' passage like

> By thine Agony and bloody Sweat; by thy Cross and Passion; by thy precious Death and Burial; by thy glorious Resurrection and Ascension; and by the coming of the Holy Ghost.

It would be easy enough to show that these passages were replaced with something comparatively lame; but this would not lead to a relevant charge because Coit was not seeking equivalents or substitutes. More to the point of criticism are Coit's changes in the responses. In his first proposed revision, in *National Idealism and the Book of Common Prayer* (1908), each plea or statement from the minister is followed by

> ... *We most earnestly desire.*

or

> ... *We long to be delivered.*

Later, in the 1911 version whose use became standard in the Ethical Church, he devised more varied responses, of which the following is a selection:

> ... *We ask for mercy from our fellow-men.*
> ... *We call upon all men to save us.*
> ... *Man by his foresight and mercy shall save us.*
> ... *Give us humility, peace and strength.*
> ... *By our faith in mankind we hope.*
> ... *Is the deep yearning of our hearts.*

Suppose the question be set on one side of whether or not the 'principle of social justice' is a viable substitute for 'God'; suppose the ministerial statements in this Litany be allowed without dispute; yet *still* the coherence, logic or even intelligibility of the responses are in doubt, because these responses cannot be related to the concept of redemption, because they express no sense of sin, or, in Bradley's words, no sense, fearful or whether, of being in a 'world alienated from God . . . the self . . . sunk in sin'. To have a Litany which resembles the Anglican General Supplication advertises that faith is a central necessity for the congregation which participates in it – 'faith', not belief, not hope, not desire. Coit's Litany cannot be said to express 'faith' in the religious sense (is there any other?) because 'sin', even in some paraphrased form, does not come within its frame of reference. His Litany gives hardly any scope for the expression of alienation. This is not to say that a secular equivalent for 'sin' could not be found – though perhaps it never has been; the point is rather that Coit, imbued ever with his wholly laudable 'wholesome objectivity' which was actually not vulnerable to satire, could not bring himself to think in this area.

Consideration of the Ethical Church inevitably comes down to the question asked of South Place Ethical Society in 1980 by Mr. Justice Dillon: religious or not religious? Coit's attitude to faith and sin must lead to the conclusion that it was not religious. T. S. Eliot once remarked that Tennyson's *In Memoriam* was religious not in the quality of its faith, but that of its doubt. 'Its faith is a poor thing, but its doubt is a very intense experience.' This epigram reversed shows why the Ethical Church was not religious: its doubt was such a poor thing that its 'faith' did not deserve the name, was not grasped at as a result of a consciousness of sin, doubt or alienation.[16]

It is not, however, enough to say that Coit 'could not bring himself to think' of sin. In fact, he set himself systematically against thinking of it, conceiving his church to be in explicit opposition to another agnostic thinker who made much of sin, doubt, and alienation. His books on national idealism were written to rebut the sense of nightmare (mentioned at the beginning of this chapter) of William James. James's *Varieties of Religious Experience: A Study in Human Nature* was published in 1902: Coit took issue with it because James was so much concerned with personal religion and in his view culpably set aside churches and their works as irrelevant. James's sense of religion was anti-Durkheim, and Coit disputed it before he knew Durkheim. For him religion had to be social, whereas for James it was individual; he was concerned, according to Coit, with religious 'geniuses', who attract disciples. For Coit, 'there was never a great religious innovator who was not nourished and fostered, as it were, in the very heart of an ecclesiastical organisation'. He meant it when he said he was a democrat: *National Idealism and a State Church* is a polemic against the individualism of James's preoccupation with the struggles of the isolated soul. Coit therefore passes by the moving chapters in *Varieties* on 'The Sick Soul' and 'The Divided Self'. 'A lamentable effect of Professor James's position is that, by commending spiritual isolation, it unwittingly panders to vanity, egotism and the fantastic vapourings of incipient insanity.'

Around 1904 the outlines sharpened on Coit's conception of an Ethical Church. He was probably pressed towards implementing his ideas by the progress that had been made in the establishment of James's Pragmatism in England. Influence, whether in the field of literature or philosophy, is often defined as a matter of imitation, the borrower liking what he has been 'influenced' by. Just as often the process is negatively reactive: the person influenced is set on a path of expression to differentiate his position from another which closely resembles it − and sometimes failing, if posterity only detects the similarity, and concludes the journey was made in tribute. In 1903 the Oxford philosopher and Pragmatist, F. C. S. Schiller, published *Humanism: Philosophical Essays*. 'We all', wrote F. H. Bradley in *Mind* in the following year, 'have been hearing the sound of the new gospel in philosophy.' The gospel of Pragmatism, or Humanism, was that 'man makes the truth, and the truth of any statement consists in its consequences. If a statement is useful, it is true and if it is not useful, it is not true. Truth is that which works and which helps us in the struggle for existence.' This is a summary by Gustav Spiller in an essay which gave a guarded welcome to Humanism. Bradley, of course, detested it and controversy flared through the pages of *Mind*, joined by Schiller and James himself. Spiller stated some doubts about Humanism which lead to those of Coit whose own optimistic gospel it seemed to resemble:

There appears to be an ambiguity in the reasoning of the Humanists the clearing up of which would probably lead to the settlement of the controversy. Speaking roughly, the Humanists are right when they contend that only that is true which is useful, which works well, and which fits into our way of absorbing experience; but they are wrong in concluding that, because they have selected the most convenient path along which to travel − have made that path if you please − they have, therefore, constructed it entirely out of materials supplied by their inner consciousness.

The last clause here indicates the problem over which Coit took issue in James's Pragmatism − and why he disliked being called a Humanist − for in it Spiller points to an individualistic element in Pragmatism. Spiller's first remarks in the passage above are not so far from Coit, who contended that the discipline of religious worship might as well be called true if it was efficacious. It could *work*, so following Seeley, the mentor quoted in Chapter 1, it mattered little if the worshipper believed in Hengist and Horsa. But Coit did not want to be associated with the individualist element in Pragmatism, or the Humanism which stemmed from it, so clarification of his ideas was urgently necessary. He needed to differentiate his position from that of 'the younger Oxford', as Schiller's Humanism is identified in Prowse's *James Hurd*. He had to explain that only social action, as in church, was fully 'useful' to the psyche. The necessity of a church seemed to him the more imperative as he observed the popularity, amongst the intelligentsia, of the individualistic solutions of James and Schiller.[17]

We have been considering how a church became a necessity for Coit and the way in which the Ethical Church was in some respects incoherent or contradictory in the rationale implied by its ritual practices. The rationale was most insecure in Coit's attempts to adapt features of the orthodox church. The enterprise is hard to justify from the grounds of Coit's convictions about church and state. On the other hand he was able to find much more sound justification for the Ethical Church from another source, from the work of the contemporary German phenomenologist, Nicolai Von Hartmann.

Hartmann's *Ethik* was published in 1926, and Coit did not read it until four years later. It had, therefore, no connection whatever with the Ethical Church in its evolutionary years. However, as Felix Adler was doing what Coit had been dreaming in 1881, so Hartmann explained to Coit what he had been striving for in his Church. He set about translating *Ethik* into English and when he advertised for a successor at the Church in 1932 he announced in the press that 'candidates should of course first be sure they are in active sympathy [with] the values and principles which have guided me in formulating [the] services . . . best set forth in Nicolai Hartmann's *Ethics*'. Hartmann's *Ethics*, in Coit's translation of 1932, completed the intellectual structure of the Ethical Church, rather than the altar placed before the pulpit in 1923. Coit thought that this enormous and now largely unread book 'told him his dream'. It shows why he – legitimately – thought of himself as a Platonist.

Coit first encountered Hartmann by means of an article by Sidney Hook in the *International Journal of Ethics* in January 1930. He was intrigued enough to write to Hartmann, then a professor in Cologne, asking him for permission to translate his book. Hartmann agreed, and so shortly did J. H. Muirhead to include an authorised translation in his 'Library of Philosophy'. *Ethics* was published with a preface by Coit dated October 1931. He must have worked fast, for *Ethik* is long (746 pages in German). Coit was then nearly seventy-five years old, but still master of his German, though he had some help from his daughter, Virginia. When the translation appeared expert reviewers made very few criticisms of Coit's rendering.

With the translation of Hartmann's *Ethics* Coit entered the debate on the source of moral obligation that had so much exercised Idealists, including those of the London Ethical Society from which he had parted so many years before. In the late 1920s Muirhead struggled towards a new philosophy of value in his *Platonic Tradition in Anglo-Saxon Philosophy* (1931). In his editorial note prefacing Coit's translation he pointed out the relation of this treatise to the problems which had been lived through by his generation of Idealists, the Kantian-ethicists. Kant had proposed that the 'ought' emanated from a transcendental or supranatural ego. The philosophers of Muirhead's circle adapted this concept, building into the ego a sense of human moral perfection, a perfect self which could be realised 'as the ultimate end of action and the standard of reference in moral judgment'. But, worryingly to the high-minded school of Green, this ideal of *self*-realisation came suspiciously close to plain egotism or hedonism, which diminished the authority of Kant's noble 'ought'. Subsequently a desire emerged to re-site the source of authority outside the individual, and his or her self-realising ego, in values which had autonomous existence. Muirhead found in this phase of Idealism a return to the Platonic view of the world as a repository of values, each with a claim to be its own 'ought', each related to an overall 'Good'. It was up to the trained philosopher to discern these relationships. It was with such a system of 'autonomous values' that Hartmann was concerned. *Ethics* is a passionate book, but also a very difficult one, calling for 'exceptional effort', as Muirhead warned in his prefatory note. Its appeal for Coit becomes clear if we briefly examine the essay by Sidney Hook which persuaded him to write to the author in Cologne as a kindred spirit.

Sidney Hook, it should be stressed, was not a convert to Hartmann. He wrote from a 'naturalist' position, believing human values to be relative to time and locality, as solutions to specific problems. For him ethics was 'the equilibriation of interests and adjustment to environment'. Hartmann, on the other hand, was a 'realist', believing in absolute, permanent values, which are *a priori* and even independent of human cognition, like mathematical formulae or natural phenomena (not saying, however, that these are equivalents). He knew that moral behaviour varied across centuries and continents, but he thought that human beings attempted to realise the same values in their behaviour. Hartmann argued that the degree of variation in what was considered moral behaviour was relatively slight when compared to the wide historical variations in non-ethical concepts (like the solar system, or the origins of human life). The early part of Hook's critical essay is devoted to discrediting Hartmann's realism from the naturalist angle. He concludes with an attack on the psychology of absolutism which seeks ethical certainty. According to Hook the absolute is sought because 'obligation, responsibility, and duty becomes too conditional'. If the naturalist claims that ethics is circumstantial and 'the goods of morality [are] developed in human activity', the absolutist may retort that human actors can, and indeed must, know what constitutes good and bad to start with. How could they be recognised without prior knowledge? The naturalist asks how the absolutist can prove that his goods and bads are in fact not disguised products of experience, 'unconscious hypostases or secret preferences or fantastic wishes'. Hartmann's answer was to call up intuition in the form of 'an obscure consciousness of value'. This 'valuational consciousness' is the subject of investigation in the first volume of *Ethics*, called 'The Structure of the Ethical Phenomenon (Phenomenology of Morals)'. Hook was sceptical about a 'primal, immediate capacity to appreciate the valuable' and of the intuition which supposedly discovers it. 'This retreat to Plato does not help matters much' – because Hartmann is dealing not with 'a clue to be investigated, but a revelation to be completed'. So intuition finds no route to certainty: how do we *know* that our values have autonomous or independent existence?

Coit was not at all dismayed by the fallacy which Hook detected. On the contrary, he found enfolded within it a rationale for his Ethical Church. Hartmann justified and even explained to him what he had been doing. Hartmann's concept of an intuition of value showed Coit the kind of insight that could be acquired in the Church. It also led into a justification for Coit's idea of 'redemption' which he so obstinately and paradoxically placed at the centre of his services. Redemption, as Coit understood it, was not from sin, but, after Hartmann, it could be redemption from ignorance, which he need not define as a kind of sin, but as an equivalent, not as simple ignorance or lack of enlightenment (as recognised by positivist or humanist, capitalised or not) but rooted in irreparable ignorance, the humanly inevitable ignorance of the inhabitants of Plato's cave. Values that exist autonomously, beyond the sway of individual human choice, which can only be grasped by 'valuational insight', are as far and near as grace is to fallen man. A kind of revelation is needed for them to be grasped. Earlier in this chapter we noted Coit's belief in a power 'which pours down supernal beauty and meaning upon the godless deep of mechanism and psychology', a meaning which includes comprehension of a 'world of essences'. These words were quoted from Coit's fragment of autobiography written after he had translated Hartmann. In them we see him reading back a Platonism into his youthful experiences at Amherst. But the experience outlined in the memoir is nonetheless consistent with Hartmann. There is no reason to believe that Coit was inventing, in his seventies, the key incident at college of Professor Elihu Root's declamation from *In Memoriam*:

A warmth within the breast would melt
The freezing reason's colder part,
And like a man in wrath the heart
Stood up and answer'd, 'I have felt.'

'Warmth within the heart' was actually a bedded part of Hartmann's 'valuational consciousness': he followed Pascal in believing that the heart has its reasons which the reason knows not of. Quoting his master, Max Scheler, Hartmann remarks that 'there is an inborn aprioristic *ordre de coeur* or *logique de coeur*, as Blaise Pascal happily expresses it'. From this Coit was given renewed confidence in the logic of his Church – and, as so frequently himself a 'man in wrath', he found an endorsement of his own tumultuous personality.

While Hook disputed Hartmann's sense of inborn or aprioristic logic, setting it aside as 'metaphysical fantasy', he still enthusiastically welcomed Hartmann's allegiance to 'an *ordre de coeur*'. He did not doubt that there was such a thing as 'valuational consciousness', and he was deeply impressed by Hartmann's compendious treatment of human values and his attempt to establish an order of priority among them, rivalled, he believed, only by Aristotle, whom Hartmann possibly exceeded in 'the most comprehensive treatise on ethics which has ever been published'. If the values themselves are not absolute essences, he thought that it was still legitimate to posit 'valuational consciousness' through which a scale of values is sought. Hook applauded Hartmann's analysis of the way in which values are, in consciousness, pitted against each other. Coit, too, found this analysis rich, and thought that Hartmann helped him to understand the play of values in life, just as they can be understood from works of art through the mediating power of the dramatic poet. Hartmann himself draws this analogy in an early passage in *Ethics* which must have impressed Coit:

When a poet moulds a human situation and sets it before our eyes, we easily see its constituent parts in their ethical fullness; we somehow suddenly feel their values throughout, although obscurely and with no consciousness of the complexity of their valuational structure. Thus we feel the great as great and the sublime as sublime. In actual life only one thing is different from what it is in dramatic art. *There is lacking the guiding hand of a master, who unobtrusively brings the significant into the foreground, so that it becomes evident to the eye of the common man.* But life throughout is a drama. And if we could only see plastically the situation in which we are placed, as the poet sees it, it would appear to us just as rich and filled with values as his creation. The proof of this is the fact that in looking back upon our past the highest points of value are for us those moments which hover before us in entire concreteness and fullness of detail – independently of whether at the time our sense of value realised the ethical content or not, yes, often in contrast to our former crude perception, and with perhaps a secret pain at the thought that it has for ever vanished, that it was ours and yet not ours. (My italics.)

Coit aspired to provide 'the guiding hand of a master' in his Ethical Church, the arena in which a master could be found.[18]

When Coit, in his seventies, translated Hartmann, it was time for the arena to be maintained by someone else. He advertised for a new leader, receiving many applications. Harold J. Blackham was appointed, becoming first joint-leader, with Harry Snell and Coit's daughter, Virginia. From 1933 he was 'minister', as the post from that year was designated. The Ethical Church was not prospering. It was in the early 1930s in competition with South Place which had its new Conway Hall. The liveliest members wanted discussion and information rather than worship, with which Blackham sympathised. Coit was no longer on the premises, but kept in constant contact with his minister by daily, sometimes furious, letters from his retirement dwelling, a bungalow on the cliffs at Birling Gap near Eastbourne in Sussex. In 1932 his wife died; Coit was hale still and continued to entertain in his retreat. One visitor reminded him of his work on the *Soul of America* and asked the Coleridgean nationalist what he thought of the soul of a Germany in which Hitler was rising to power. Coit replied that Hitler's racial nationalism was a 'state-egoism' in which the state is 'set up as an ultimate end and not . . . as an instrument of justice':

The greatest theologians, as well as the greatest social philosophers, have for ages recognised the state in its real social functioning as no more egoistic than a true church is. Church and state are twin creatures conceived of one spirit – the spirit of disinterested service. The ethics of the state cannot conflict with the spirituality of the church, unless the state itself perverts its own nature. This is what has taken place to an unprecedented degree in Germany within the last year [1932–3]. The state in its normal [*sic*] functioning is moral. There are two forms of perversion possible to it, however – the non-moral state which forgets justice as its aim and the immoral state, which, like a criminal lunatic, delights in cruelty and falsehood in defiance of the fundamental principles of Judaism and Christianity, and of the intellectual liberty which ancient Greece gave the world.

This could have been an Anglican Broad Churchman speaking – though one who had heard Treitschke in person and so was able to understand Hitler, and such fascist documents as Houston Chamberlain's *The Foundation of the Nineteenth Century* (1899, published in English in 1911). It was as a Broad Churchman that Blackham described Coit in the memoir of his patron. This memoir recalls the last years at Birling Gap. Coit outlived his elder daughter Adela, and his butler's wife, both of whom had looked after him. Finally he was nursed by his butler Lanchbery and by 1943 'there was no trace of the explosiveness of his temperament'. He spent hours looking out over the English Channel, perhaps imagining the clashes of nationalism in Europe at war. He died in the night of 15 February 1944.

The Ethical Church waned. In 1953 it was finally decided to dispose of the building and change the name of the institution back to West London Ethical Society. With the proceeds (£25,000) a tall terrace house was purchased, a stone's throw from Kensington High Street. The Society rented out space to the Ethical Union, which is why the successor to this body, the British Humanist Association, later had its headquarters in the house in Prince of Wales Terrace. Coit's will instructed the trustees of the Ethical Church that its success should be assessed when twenty years had elapsed. The time approached. In 1963 Coit's daughter Virginia proposed that the society's activities be drastically curtailed. In October 1965 it was finally dissolved.

In assessing the Ethical Church the scale of Coit's conception must not be forgotten. This is illustrated in an exchange between Coit and William Salter in 1903 in the *Ethical World*. Salter was surprised to read of a speech Coit had given to a Jewish group in New York, in which he criticised Felix Adler for maintaining his Society for Ethical Culture separate from the Jewish community. Surely, commented Salter, it made no sense to contest this: an ethical movement that remained within the Jewish community would have no room for Coits and Salters. Exactly, replied Coit: but Coits and Salters were expendable. Better to sacrifice the conviction of a sprinkling of ethicists or ethical culturalists for the sake of grafting a new movement on to 'the virile stock of the Jewish race'. 'Would it not have startled the smug theologians of orthodox Christianity out of their very boots to have seen spring, from the very bosom of that religion which gave birth to Christianity, a new religion, up-to-date, born at the end of the nineteenth century after Christ?' This reasoning led Coit to his treaty with British orthodoxy, but it was fatally misguided to think of enlisting the allegiance of 100,000 Anglicans as if they were 100,000 Jews. At the level of theory the idea was not outrageous, for at that level his views resembled those of a Broad Churchman or modernist (but those were still a minority of Anglicans); in practice, as minister of an eccentricity like an Ethical Church (inevitably it was so regarded), he was marginal. And most British ethicists did not regret the fact that Adler had made his society independent of Judaism, observing enviously the prosperity of the American movement. When Zona Vallance visited New York in 1902 she saw audiences of 1,500 for Sunday ethical lectures in Carnegie Music Hall. She found a refreshing 'absence of any plan or half-conscious wish to supplant or reform existing theological sects'. She wished that the British societies had abjured these ambitions. If only Coit's purposes had been allowed to grow independently – but with his principle as well as temperamental preference for the normal he had to attempt a treaty with the all-too-real Church.

Coit's purposes for his church were in many ways sensible. He believed sincerely that an Ethical Church could supply a form of psychotherapy. In 1912 he visited the Rockefeller Institute of Medical Research in New York, and asked himself why there should not be similar institutes of religious research for 'the moral cure of souls, of cities, of nations'. He argued that 'it is possible to know that the effect of a religious meeting has been morally curative as to know the effect of medical treatment has checked the disease and saved the patient'. He was not completely wrong. But his own congregation responded to more modest claims and the satisfactions it discovered can be found in a statement by Virginia Coit, a source which might be suspected of bias were it not so lacking in the grandeur of her father's proposals. The statement occurs in an account of the church, written in 1937, in which she tried to explain its purpose to those who could see little point in having quasi-Anglican services 'unless it be that a very brilliant speaker is to be heard'. She suggested that many people, including those who looked askance at the services, were 'often really in a very vague, confused state of mind', which was painfully exposed when they had (for example) 'the task of telling children what they think about ethical and religious beliefs'. The best purpose of the Ethical Church was

to help people clarify their convictions, to find firm points of departure from which they can order their thoughts, to help them find terms in which they can give simple expression, which even children can understand, to their own deepest experiences and convictions. It is not easy out of your own inner struggle and experience to formulate essential truths which can be conveyed to others, especially to children: and where your ideas are purely personal, just your own effort, contradicted to right and to left, they tend to seem too tentative to be handed on.

In its considerate way this passage isolates one of the major problems of secularisation. The person who is converted from religious belief does not give up a collection of concepts to be replaced by another set. He or she abandons genres of expression and methods of transmitting ideas. The convert to agnosticism finds him or herself with ideas whose only merit seems to be that they are true (or truer than the ones rejected), and it is not perverse, though it is paradoxical, to say that this may not be felt to suffice. Virginia Coit was not defining a quality to be found in the Ethical Church which contradicted or was irrespective of her father's ambitions for ritual: after all, those ambitions were to make value *explicit*. That he was so minded is shown in a passage in his introduction to the service book, *Social Worship*, in which he tells of having urged on 'a company of scholars' the necessity of preparing a modern equivalent to the Book of Deuteronomy which would set out, for all to see, 'the specific elaborations of social justice which are embodied in the living statutes of the land'. According to Coit one of the scholars interrupted to say that this might not be wise because 'the existing land laws of England were so unjust to the working classes, and the exclusion of women by law and custom from the great opportunities was inhuman and cruel, that it were better for the quiet, the safety and dignity of England that the prevailing ignorance should continue'. Never mind, said Coit: let the laws be stated, and, if they were unjust, an enlightened self-respect would 'the same day' set about their replacement with equitable decrees. In the services of the Ethical Church there was supposed to be summary, statement and illustration of the enactment of the spirit of the nation and its laws. It in no way invalidates the conception of 'enlightened self-respect' to say that it is not easily accessible. And in England, explicitness or the desire for it, was and is equally inaccessible. In his pursuit of the explicit Coit remained inevitably quixotic – or (and he knew it) irrevocably American.[19]

Chapter 5

The Ethical Movement

The other ethical societies

In the early 1890s several ethical societies were established, somewhat different from South Place, the L.E.S. or the Ethical Church. This period of growth is well described in an affectionate memoir of the first of them by F. J. Gould:

On a March evening, 1889, at the Unitarian schoolroom near Oxford Street, I heard Mr. Trevor (assistant to Philip Wicksteed, the Dante scholar) and afterwards founder of the Labour Churches, give a very useful account of the Moral Instruction (*La Morale Laïque*) in French Primary Schools, and I was deeply interested. Another member of the scanty audience was Dr. Stanton Coit . . . a fair-haired American from Ohio [who] preached an admirable Humanist gospel in happy alternation of smiles and hurricanes . . . A group of us met in Hackney (November, 1889) and planned an Ethical Society. The group included Gustav Spiller, an emancipated Jew from Buda-Pesth, much devoted to poetry and psychology, now [1923] a naturalized and excellent Englishman and attached to the Labour Office of the League of Nations at Geneva.

Next to Coit, Gustav Spiller (1864–1940) was the main maker of the ethical movement. He came to London in 1885, where he worked as a compositor. Inspired by Coit's South Place discourses in 1888–9 he set about starting a society in east London. Until 1901 he remained in the Bank of England printing works for six months each year, using the remainder for study. Coit then employed him as an ethical lecturer. In 1904 he became paid secretary of the International Union of Ethical Societies. Spiller's intellectual life's work was the devising of what he called an evolutionary psychology of human beings as 'specio-psychic', that is, developing by group assimilation of 'the substance of the expressed thoughts of their whole species', a view he opposed to the 'narrowly individualistic conception of human nature and reason, which traces the origin of the leading concepts to the superior minds of a few distinguished thinkers'. This reflected Coit's anti-individualism, and Spiller's own self-education, implied in the rather laborious titles of his main two, compendious, books, *A New System of Scientific Procedure: being an attempt to ascertain, develop and systematise the general methods employed in modern enquiries at their best* (1921) and *The Origin and Nature of Man: an enquiry into fundamentals reconciling man's proud achievements with man's humble descent* (1931). F. J. Gould continues to remember east London ethicism:

Early in 1890 we launched the East London Ethical Society at a dancing saloon by Mile End Road. Four years later (October, 1894) we – proud as Solomon at the erection of his Temple – inaugurated a corrugated iron hall in Libra Road, Old Ford, amid a hubbub of our East-end neighbours and the cheery yells of the boys. All – lectures, entertainments, Sunday-school for sixty children, boys' and girls' club – was done 'on a purely human basis'. I venture to affirm that, in a grey monotonous environment, we did, in a humble way, as penetrating and vital work as Toynbee Hall in Whitechapel. Today I feel a throb of gratitude to the pioneer spirits who came down into our wilderness and gave us of their store of philosophy, science, art, politics, and visions – Coit, Graham Wallas, Okey (basket-maker and Italian scholar), Bernard Bosanquet, Mrs. Gilliland Husband, Miss Foley (Mrs. Rhys Davids), J. F. Green, (now M.P. for West Leicester), J. Ramsay MacDonald, Halliday Sparling, and the devoted and enthusiastic Zona Vallance, daughter of a Stratford doctor. Socialists mingled with us cordially. Among them were Tom Mann, a staccato, emphatic orator, with pointed moustache and revolutionary menace; and George Lansbury, a man with a truly good heart, a half-cynical, half-pathetic pity for the unrighteous world, and more zeal than judgment – his editorship of the *Daily Herald* and his friendship with Lenin of Moscow being a perfectly natural evolution ... Tom Mann's four small daughters and four or five of Lansbury's children attended the Libra Road Sunday school of which, for some six years, I joyfully took charge.[1]

This East London Ethical Society was the first of the new ones, after the L.E.S. was founded and South Place changed its name. In 1897 it started a branch in Hackney which later became the Bow and Bromley society, and later still just the Hackney society. In 1892 Coit started his West London Ethical Society, which was (excluding South Place) always the largest of the societies, its rival being the South London society, which owed much of its appeal to the personality of the socialist secretary, Nellie Slous Freeman, a gentle school teacher from a free-thinking family. In the early years of the South London society mass meetings were held in Peckham Rye, with the headquarters at St. Mary le Strand House in the Old Kent Road. It survived until 1938, a small group called by other ethicists 'the highbrows of Peckham'. In 1895 Coit's friends at Leighton Hall formed the North London (later St. Pancras) society. A Battersea society started in 1897, influenced by John Burns. In that year societies opened outside London in Portsmouth, Bristol, Edinburgh, and Belfast.

The Belfast group was Coitian, and the Bristol society was started by a member of the London Ethical Society. The L.E.S. was the model of a Cambridge Ethical Society (1888). Its first meeting was to hear a paper by J. S. Mackenzie, from the 'class of Caird', who was still reading for the Moral Sciences Tripos at Trinity after a brilliant career at Glasgow and a fellowship at Edinburgh. His Edinburgh lectures were the basis of his *Introduction to Moral Philosophy* (1890), an Essex Hall textbook. He was a close friend of J. M. Ellis McTaggart ('at once atheist and a convinced believer in human immortality', according to C. D. Broad), who was co-opted on to the Cambridge Ethical Society organising committee which included the orientalist, Norman McClean, James Adam, editor of Plato, and S. M. Leathes (one of the triumvirate which planned and executed the Cambridge Modern History) and the mathematician and geophysicist, A. E. H. Love. All these men were in their twenties. From an older generation there was the psychologist and philosopher James Ward, who had graduated in 1874 as a mature student, having passed through a period of purgatory as minister in a Cambridge congregational chapel. There was also the vicar of Great St. Mary's, William Cunningham, who, besides lecturing for the Moral Sciences Tripos, was a pioneer in the promotion of the academic status of economic history, having published his *Growth of English History and Commerce* (1882). John Neville Keynes was on the committee. The Cambridge society's lectures and discussion groups survived until the spring of 1896.

Some of the other societies reacted against the influence of the founding fathers of ethicism, like the Hampstead Ethical Institute (1900), which disliked Coit's manner of claiming (it thought) 'a monopoly of morals'. It favoured the tradition of Spencer, Huxley and Mill, allying itself with the Streatham and Brixton society in 1901, rather than with the Coit groups of the four points of the metropolitan compass. Some provincial societies diverged from Coit for other reasons. The Merthyr Tydfil and Plumstead (1903 and 1904) societies moved from ethicism to labour politics. As might be expected several societies formed in process of non-conformity developing away from non-conformity, as had been experienced at South Place. The Rochester and Chatham (1898) society began as a debating club started by a Unitarian minister with the help of an agnostic town councillor and a Catholic priest. The Bradford (1898) society was an offshoot of the Reverend Robert Roberts's Independent congregation. In London, the Holloway (1905) society was started by a former Unitarian minister. The number of societies peaked at 42 in 1906 – enough for a 'movement'.

In November 1895 a meeting was held to federate the societies. The first congress of what was called the Union of Ethical Societies was held at Leighton Hall on 5 July 1896; in 1920 it changed its name to the Ethical Union. This, the official body of the British ethical movement, had limited authority because for most of its life the two largest societies, South Place and West London (Ethical Church), would not join. The movement developed on the continent after Felix Adler visited Germany, where a Berlin E.S. was formed, presided over by the rector of the university, Wilhelm Foerster. This society was led by a philosopher, Georg Von Gizýcki, a specialist in Shaftesbury's benevolence and whose book on ethics had been translated into English by Coit. The movement spread south and east from Berlin. In 1896 an International Ethical Union was founded. However, more important for the British movement was the foundation in December 1897 of the Moral Instruction League, largely run by ethicists, of which more will be heard in the third section of this chapter.

One society appears, from its name, to belong to the movement. In fact the Ethical Religion Society was a theist organisation on the fringe. One of its members, Ellis Thurtell, claimed that the other ethicists veered to Positivism: however strong was the moral sentiment enlisted on behalf of humanity, he argued, it should never exclude a religious sentiment awakened 'by that which is behind humanity'. What was supposedly behind humanity was a red rag to Coit who denounced this 'metaphysical addendum'. He replied to the theists as a pragmatist and as a scientific rationalist: 'Just as geology has been cleared of theistic implications so has ethics', and (the pragmatic line) 'ethics, science and religion are *public*: they hold good whatever metaphysical implications they contain'. The distinction between a God 'behind' ethicism (deplorable for Coit) and one 'implied' by it is a fine one. A puzzled ethicist complained that people who had rejected Christianity could not be expected to give up all supernaturalism at the first blast of an agnostic trumpet. Coit replied, in lordly fashion, that the distinction did demand some delicacy of intelligence. He may have made things worse for the convert by saying that a non-theist society was not necessarily an agnostic one.

Coit despised the Ethical Religion Society and its leader J. Washington Sullivan; and he had little time for the religiosities of what he considered to be kindred groups. He lectured frequently to Labour Churches, and got on well with them; but he was even to fire a volley across their bows when it came to his notice that some of these Churches had been apparently harassing members who believed in the ethical god of duty rather than in the 'fatherhood of God'. Coit smelled heresy-hunting in Labour Churchers who were too callow to accept 'with serenity the possibility that when dead we may be done with'. One member replied, saying that when dead we are certainly not 'done with like pigs'. No, said

Coit, not pigs, just done with like 'violets, or sunsets, or . . . melodies which only in dying become perfected'.

In the London Ethical Society it was, perhaps, the course of philosophy classes which mattered most. For many ethical societies it was the lecture or discourse which was at the centre of their existence. On a typical Sunday (20 March 1900) the following lectures were on offer in London. At the West London society an American academic, Earl Barnes, spoke on the American negro, at South London there was a morning discussion of Theosophy and an evening lecture on war by J. M. Robertson, who had in the morning played a home match at South Place on 'The Nineteenth Century: Modern Science – Its Moral and Philosophical Outcome'. The North and East London societies met only in the evening for talks on Pestalozzi, and on Bishop Colenso by Harry Snell who had spoken on the same subject in the morning at Hampstead Ethical Institute. Streatham and Brixton offered Sidney Lee on Shakespeare and patriotism. Washington Sullivan discoursed to his Ethical Religion Society on whether the Decalogue was the true foundation or morality.

The societies were a blessing for Londoners in search of Sunday stimulus. Ivor Brown, for example, was not enamoured of tramping streets called 'Belsize this or that' to sing rhymes of reason or chant the praise of progress, but still he appreciated meetings at which he could hear 'fairly uninhibited discussion at a time when inhibitions and taboos prevailed to an extent unbelievable today [1954]'. He particularly liked Harley Granville-Barker. He called Coit 'an expert on the dais', significant praise from a theatre critic in embryo.[2]

The committed ethicist, of course, found much more than intellectual entertainment. Harry Snell was such a one. In 1926 he described himself and his fellows as refugees from the crude terrors of orthodox religion, out of 'the shadow of a fearful faith: God was to be feared because he was a God of Vengeance; death was to be feared because of the pitiless reckoning-day beyond . . . The pioneers of a kindlier humanistic faith were assured by the orthodox that God would forgive men for the sins of the body, but not for sins of the mind.' Ethicists found what they called 'fellowship', of which the essence was the sharing of unspoken assumptions in tolerating what were hoped to be trivial differences. This toleration created some nebulousness in ethicist credos; when ethicists were forced to say what they really believed painful chasms could be opened, when the members discovered they had not realised how much they differed from each other. One way of maintaining fellowship was in ceremony, by singing and reading, often making use of Coit's anthology, *The Message of Man: A Book of Ethical Scriptures* (1895). It is facile to explain away these modest celebrations as nostalgia for Anglican or non-conformist services, disgust with which had created ethicists. Anglicanism could signify a young woman being told by her vicar that to tackle housework during parish visiting was unladylike, or non-conformity the spectacle of a Baptist minister tearing up and scattering across his congregation a letter of complaint about the strictness of his views on baptism. It was, in any case, a singing age. Socialists frequently closed meetings with a rendering of Edward Carpenter's 'England Arise!'. Ethicists enjoyed the lack of churchiness at their meetings, which often were refreshingly free of the 'church voice', the notorious, upper-class, ministerial drawl. Ethicist speakers did not *sound* like vicars, often having regional, or Scottish accents.

Because ethicist meetings were vaguely ceremonious comparison could be prompted with Positivist services. These were centred round an address, which, Frederic Harrison reminds us, was

in no sense intended to stand for the 'services' and 'worship' of the Churches. They serve but to give the more general ideas, and to keep the other work fast to its central aim. The business of a Church, as Comte thought, is to educate; to educate all round, in all useful things, in all spheres of human life: not merely to stimulate devotion (this most certainly), but furthermore to train the group and foster the sciences, to cultivate the arts, to regulate life: to consecrate, to teach and to humanise . . . So the bulk of the work of Newton Hall is done by systematic classes for the study of science – in geometry, astronomy, physics, chemistry, biology, and sociology.

The ethicists were further from 'services' than the Positivists (except in the Ethical Church). As for the educational element, there was certainly a drive for it in the societies: the ethicists wanted to learn, and to do well for their children in the doom-ridden world of church and chapel in which (said Harry Snell) the devil lurked in every place of youthful joy. Ethicists could take some symbolic satisfaction from appropriating and altering the garb of the priests in black gowns. But unlike Positivism, ethicism offered unsystematic teaching, and it was not markedly scientific. And there were two other differences: ethicists did not share, or were not aware of, the concept of the social function of the church (until Coit began to explore and exploit the idea after 1904); and the ethical societies were not millenarian.[3]

Though the societies depended on the bonds of fellowship, and were frequently inexplicit, ethicists still wanted to express corporate policies. For these it is necessary to go to the proceedings of their Union of Ethical Societies. It had a council which met regularly and it held annual congresses. Societies joined if they endorsed its objects. A fee was levied according to the numerical strength of a society. The Aims of the Union were formulated for the first congress in 1896, as follows:

1. By purely natural and human means to assist individual and social efforts after right living.

2. To free the current ideal of what is right from all that is merely traditional or self-contradictory, and thus to widen and perfect it.

3. To assist in constructing a theory or science of right, which starting with the reality and validity of moral distinctions shall explain their mental and social origin and connect them in a logical system of thought.

The Union intended to speak for as many societies as would join, sponsor classes for adults and children, and to publish. Its aims were elaborated over the decade that followed this manifesto, culminating in a more intricate statement in 1906, though with no gain in cogency. Notably additions were the requirement of an economic standard that would enable the moral development of citizens, and a rejection of supernaturalism emanating (as might be expected) from Coit. In 1904 he proposed an amendment to the statement on this subject which had been added to the Aims in 1901: he wanted the Union 'to affirm that moral principles and the love of righteousness are in their nature independent of the belief in life after death and in the existence of a creator or soul of the universe'. Interestingly, this amendment was rejected, but Coit's proposal did set in train a process of revision issuing in Aims for 1906, in which the article on supernaturalism was stated thus: 'The moral life involves neither the acceptance nor rejection of belief in any deity, personal or impersonal.' Representatives from sixteen societies agreed to the Aims in 1906, against the four of 1896.

The Union had views on social reform. In 1902 it deplored the 'reactionary and obscurantist' Education Act. In 1905 it called for municipalisation of hospitals, and for old-age pensions. In 1907 it counselled haste in legislating for the election of women to municipal councils. From 1907 the Union's grip on social affairs faltered. A social problems sub-committee was appointed which came up with a report containing some ideas which were eventually submitted to the congress of 1909. It stated that the moral life could not be realised when disorder and injustice were created by established customs and institutions. Six requests were made: (1) government guarantee of the physical necessities of life, which were to be 'scientifically determined'; (2) full education to the age of 16, in classes not exceeding twenty-five pupils; (3) universal suffrage; (4) a court of arbitration for international disputes, developed out of the Hague Conference; (5) the use of eugenics, both negatively (discouragement of marriage between those predisposed to disease, legally if necessary) and positively (young people were to be encouraged to marry those of 'high physical, intellectual and ethical standard'); (6) better social and medical treatment of women, especially mothers. This document made uneasy the delegates of the 1909 congress. They shelved it for discussion in 1910, when a motion that the report should receive the backing of the whole Union (rather than remain merely a sub-committee's set of suggestions) was lost. In the following years a number of resolutions were passed: a review of the blasphemy laws was welcomed (1914); sex instruction in the Board of Education Code was called for (1915); the Russian nation was congratulated for casting off the yoke of tyranny (1917); the government was censured for its 'appalling' mishandling of the Irish problem (1921); capital punishment was rejected (1923); the right of women to retain first citizenship after marriage to a foreign national was demanded (1924). But the repertoire of protest was a trickle compared to the 1909 rejected programme of reform. This was undoubtedly a reason for the decline in number of member societies. And, of course, the other reason was that the number of societies was dwindling.

The Great War was one reason for diminution of the movement. Fewer meeting places were available; young people were away from the cities, in which the mood was contrary to ethicism in places: the Hampstead Ethical Institute lost members because a distrust of aliens made people dubious of optimistic schemes of universal morality. The number of affiliated societies dropped to ten in 1917. After the war congress attendance was down to about fifty people, a third of the Edwardian number. Few societies federated: there was the hardy annual Forest group from Epping (with its 'verderers'), the Hampstead society, the London Women's Group and Nellie Freeman's South London society. The Ethical Church had withdrawn in 1916, and South Place was not to join until 1950. However, there was good fortune in 1927, a legacy from Horace Seal of £5,000 which swelled funds that before had never exceeded £400. The Union used about £300 to register as a limited company, so it prepared a new statement of its objects – which was notably less secular than the 'Aims' of 1896. In 1920 ethical 'faith' was specified for the first time, as was 'Religion of Human Fellowship'. The Object of 1927 confirmed this trend:

To promote by all lawful means the study of ethical principles; to advocate a religion of human fellowship and service, based upon the principle that the supreme aim of religion is the love of goodness, and that moral ideas and the moral life are independent of belief as to the ultimate nature of things and a life after death; and, by purely human and natural means, to help men to love, know and do right in all relations of life.

The religious orientation was maintained through the 1930s and the war years.[4]

In 1944 the Union decided to enquire into the ideas of religious faith that were actually current. It commissioned the Mass Observation unit to study attitudes to belief in a London suburb. From five hundred interviews and supplementary material, some of it from other M.O. surveys, a report was prepared, published as *Puzzled People: A Study in Popular Attitudes to Religion, Ethics, Progress and Politics in a London Borough* (1947). Alarmingly the report revealed a widespread ignorant respectfulness for religion. Most respondents thought there was, or probably was, a God of some kind, but 'ostensibly many people's religion today is one that in most cases they have "worked out for themselves". In fact, this means that in most cases it is based on a narrower acquaintance with its sources than before. It is not a new religion, but an incomplete version of the old, commanding less faith, covering a less wide field.' Mass Observation found an inarticulate need for, or interest in, faith, or 'leadership', which it concluded to be ominous, as established leadership appeared remote from ordinary people: 'If it does not re-establish contact soon, unattached loyalties and desires may well find a focus in some new leadership, uncritically accepted because it succeeds in establishing contact with immediate, long-felt needs.' People seemed all too ready for 'dynamic leadership'.

One person who was alarmed by the report was Harold J. Blackham, who contributed a preface to *Puzzled People*. Having, we saw in Chapter 4, worked in the Ethical Church he may have seen enough of 'dynamic leadership' in Coit. It was not that he was out of sympathy with the religious leaning of the Ethical Union. In 1945 he wrote five leaflets for it, under the series heading of 'The Way to a Common Faith', one on the ethical movement as 'a religion of rational beliefs', and one on how to orchestrate an ethical meeting which would have been fairly familiar to an attender at the Ethical Church. On the other hand, Blackham was sceptical of solutions which could affect only a minority – that is, work in isolated ethical societies. He favoured what had long ago attracted the thoughtful ethicist (like J. A. Hobson), a kind of sociology. Intellectuals should not imagine they could 'convert the masses'; rather they should try to develop what Blackham called 'situational therapy', resembling what had been done in the Cambridgeshire Village Colleges, or, in London, in the Peckham Health Centre. He wanted to have local circumstances studied in detail, so there could be 'a collective effort to unify, idealise, complete, experience, and express human life in the world'. To this end study tours were organised, to Suffolk (1947), Hereford (1948), the Black Country (1949) and South Wales (1950). This was the humanist's effort to find a 'centre'.

Blackham was able to develop to develop his thinking in a journal financed by the relatively prosperous Ethical Union, *The Plain View* which he edited from 1945. For the first time since the best days of Coit's

Ethical World (some of which will be described in the next section of this chapter) ethicists had a discursive, theoretical journal, this one quarterly rather than weekly, free of parochial matter, which was channelled into *News and Notes* (issued from 1941, re-named *Humanist News* in 1964). (A minor function of *The Plain View* was to be an outlet for the findings of another Union-related project, the Ethics and Economics trust, founded in the 1930s by the equalitarian treasurer, R. A. Price author of *Public Freeholds* (1935): he was a meticulous business man whose puritan disposition had been tempered first by membership of the Fabian Society and then by the necessitous reorganisation of an estate agency which had been run by his rather disorganised father.)

Despite Blackham's sympathy for the religious side of ethicism he was glad to see the Ethical Union join with the Rationalist Press Association in 1963 to form a British Humanist Association, a 'front office' to receive enquiries about both bodies. In 1965 both were affected by the new Charities Act as South Place was in 1967: they lost charitable status. In 1967 the Ethical Union was dissolved to become the British Humanist Association, the connection with ethicism only maintained by Blackham's association with it. It became essentially a body for the simple humanism described (without derogation) in Chapter 2 on South Place in the 1970s. A rather larger conception was expressed in Blackham's classic survey, *Humanism* (1968).

With humanism, and Blackham's *Humanism*, we leave ethicism and this brief survey of the corporate views of ethicists as registered in their Union proceedings. Ethicists were not at their best in generalisation, especially when formulas of belief were produced by means of their immaculate committee procedures. Gustav Spiller recognised this when he remarked in his admirable *Documentary History* that the 'repeated reformulations indicate both [the movement's] earnest desire of a satisfactory epitomising of the ethical faith and the difficulty of realising such an end'. But if in some things they were better off in the inexplicit, there were places in which ethicists could be thoroughly articulate. And times: because the ethicist point of view was most vividly expressed in the heyday of the movement, the turn of the century. To the moment of ethics at the front we now turn.[5]

Ethics to the front

The best public voice of ethicism was in Stanton Coit's Saturday penny paper, the *Ethical World*, which was founded in 1898 and later published under different names. In May 1898 the leading article, called 'Ethics to the Front', began like this: 'For the first time since the Ethical Movement started in England (twelve years ago) it is prepared to assert itself upon one of the great issues of the day, [in this case, education] for the Ethical Movement is pre-eminently educational in character.' The *Ethical World* was prepared to assert itself on numerous other matters of social policy and provides the best guide to the attitude to current events of the less introverted ethicists, so long as a certain caution is exercised. Many of the contributors to the paper lived by their pens and were engaged in propaganda and political activity which did not issue directly from the ethical movement. They found the paper a useful outlet. It was one of the small, but well-placed, stepping stones in the careers of some later celebrities (like Hobson or Ramsay MacDonald), who were involved with ethical societies and with other groups as well. The *Ethical World* does not show what was only thought by ethicists, but almost all its contributors were conscious that an ethical point of view should be established.

It was in the early years that an ethical point of view, of people and issues, was sought most alertly. After 1905 the paper became more like a parish magazine, retailing news and rhetoric. Early on the paper took on board all the issues that came to hand. Quite apart from the main essays and leading articles, there was continuous comment in short pieces or in 'The Passing Hour' section of rag-bag items. The following list is a cursory section: the Dreyfus affair and the Wagner season at Covent Garden in 1898; attitudes to temperance and gambling (both handled by Harry Snell, using his Nottingham experience), and to immortality; eugenics, and the Midwives' Registration Bill; the nature of the city, and the constitution of New Zealand (much admired by ethicists); advertising, and the Press; the Webbs, sociology, socialism, and liberalism; Irish political convicts, and lead poisoning; the Tsar's proposals for international arbitration; the organisation of the army, under which heading brutal Prussian training methods were mentioned in the context of R. B. Haldane's interest in Germany – and there was elsewhere a prescient remark from Hobson about guerilla warfare: 'It is not yet ascertained how far a certain individualism and spontaneity of fight among citizen-soldiers, animated by the strongest passion which can move men, and skilled in the independent use of arms, may enable them to baffle numbers.' The *Ethical World* frequently considered various wrongs of hierarchy which damaged, for instance, children (were they the property of their parents?), governesses, shop assistants. The paper must have been one of the first places in which the nomenclature of gender was discussed. In July 1901 a petition to the Scottish courts was reported, in which a woman sought to be allowed to sit for the law agents' examination which was open to 'persons' but not to women. Everyone knew that

148

women were persons in the home, so why could they not be persons for the Board of Examiners of law agents? Indeed, 'no woman can be a person within her home unless she is a person everywhere else in the community'. The range of comment shows that the *Ethical World* was militant in the comprehensiveness of its analysis. The writers thought that there were no matters which could not be brought to the bar of ethics, the organic relationship of one matter being shown to another. The paper therefore had a certain unity of mood. It also possessed some unities of theme, because, despite its variety, there were three binding subjects: women, empire and education. We shall consider the mood of the *Ethical World*, then its attitudes to women and to empire, reserving education for the next section of this chapter, on ethics in the class-room.

The mood of the *Ethical World* swung from indignant to rueful and bitter. When the Queen died in January 1901 the paper eschewed (in that third week of the official twentieth century) sycophantic mourning for the 'high, impeccable aristocrat who, in the eyes of the ignorant, redeemed the directorate of "Britain Unlimited" '. A thousand 'fungoid growths' flourished 'in the shadow thrown by the carefully manipulated limelight in which she moved'. This statement is aeons away from the worried expressions of concern tabled by the Ethical Union (even in the controversial report of 1909). Its author, G. H. Perris, was an extremist, but his attitude was characteristic of the early *Ethical World*: his view of 'Great Britain Inc.' and of the media (before this word had been used of the organs of communication) could have come from other contributors. The pioneering 1880s, when a 'going' was felt in the air, were over. At the turn of the century there was a 'national sluggishness in which the policy of Quintus Fabius Maximus is the wise one', although the paper was sceptical of the Fabians, not least for their attitude (or lack of it) to empire. Free-thought may have been more widely permissable than it had been: the obituarist of Grant Allen noticed that his death was greeted with respect, while obloquy had been heaped upon Charles Bradlaugh when he died only seven years before. But free-thinkers at the turn of the century seemed to lack leadership (a Coit-run paper would not award credit for this to J. M. Robertson); while for the mass, 'the newspaper is the kinetoscope of a "palace of varieties" in which millions waste their leisure hours'. In a leading article of June 1898 Ramsay MacDonald called for contemporary 'giants of righteousness', complaining that there was more beer drinking than democratic passion in the working-men's clubs. The spiritual as well as the political qualities of the old dissent appeared to have evaporated. More than once MacDonald appealed to ethicists to revive puritanism and learn from 'the old austere heroism in worship, the simple Covenanter's psalm, the silent Quaker's meeting'.

To his personal cost he discovered how little contemporary nonconformity could be relied upon: when he stood as an Independent Labour candidate in the London County Council election in South Hackney the local Congregationalists and Primitive Methodists who owned the only suitable meeting halls would not rent to him because 'Liberal and Conservative are part of our church life; Labour is not.' 'Today', wrote Coit, 'Labour must loathe the spirit, character, and outlook of Nonconformity as Christ loathed the Pharisee.'[6]

The *Ethical World* had its own 'giants of righteousness'. A selective roster of those to whom obituary tributes were paid in 1898 includes:

Thomas Ashton, Unitarian cotton factor of Manchester: major founder of Owen's College, and sustained the Hyde Mechanics' Institute and Technical School;

Sir James Stansfeld, also Unitarian, and an abolitionist, famous for his work (successful in 1886) for the repeal of the sexist Contagious Diseases (Women) Acts. Stansfeld's sister married

George Dixon, whose opposition to theological instruction in municipal schools (conducted through the National Education League of which he was co-founder) was a model for the education policy of the *Ethical World*. Chamberlain took his seat in Birmingham when Dixon retired from it in 1876, but after ten years of work for the Birmingham School Board, Dixon returned to Parliament to combat Conservative education policy;

Sir George Grey, former governor of Southern Australia, of New Zealand, and of Cape Colony: in 1877 he became Prime Minister of New Zealand, having been leader of the radical party. F. J. Gould wrote his obituary and stressed Grey's interest in Maori language and culture, as author of *Polynesian Mythology and Ancient Traditional History of the New Zealand Race (English and Maori)* (1855);

Martha Merrington, less illustrious, but significant as the first woman to sit on a Board of Poor Law Guardians, in 1875, for the Kensington Board.

Most illustrious among the dead of 1898 was W. E. Gladstone, about whom Ramsay MacDonald contributed a two-part eulogy in the May and June issues. In July he contributed an article called 'The Protestant Succession' in which one of his positions can be related to his conception of Gladstone, that is, his forceful rejection of other-worldliness. The ethicist, he argues, is unlike the theist, who thinks that 'earthly clothing matters naught', because he believes that conduct is 'the only medium through which religious conviction can be expressed' and that 'the body is more than raiment'. To the body MacDonald makes a startling reference in his first essay on Gladstone:

No man ever lived more fully in the light of the conviction that we all had to render account of the deeds done in the body; no man placed in the uncertain eddy of political life ever swirled in the current with a more fixed belief that his inconsistencies of thought, word, and deed were merged in the all-comprehending and mysterious consistency of the Unchangeable.

150

This view finds inconsistency permissable as 'an aspect of the genius of his personality', which could take the form of a 'Celtic romantic conscience [which] gripped him every now and again like a hand of mail', but the personality was authentic, as authentic as 'the body', and more so than idea or reason. Despite his liking for theological quiddity, Gladstone's convictions were substantial, more reliable than 'those dogmatic philosophies – such as Benthamism – which appeal to the generosity and aggressive assertiveness of youth'. If Gladstone was unstable, he was also flexible, and in this anti-theoretic personality the Celt MacDonald found a living emblem of Matthew Arnold's 'culture', which he had clearly in mind in a leading article of June 1898:

Taste, aesthetic and ethical, is of even more importance in life than opinion – at least so we should state if we were compelled to place the two in an unnatural opposition. But, opposition or no opposition, that part of the Ethical Movement which is in the middle of the stream of historical continuity must lay special stress on tone, that spiritual amalgam to which gold adheres and over which dross passes. It is this which we imply when we turn with apologetic fondness to the word 'culture', because that word, notwithstanding all its unpleasant associations, has the merits of carrying us beyond the formal operations of the reason and bringing to us the imperative affinities of the intelligence. The supreme problem for our Movement is, therefore, related to its aims as a culture movement . . .

Our distinctive claim to being historically fit – the heirs of the ages – is that around us, on every hand, we see the failure of old methods, the despair of old propagandas, the decay of old bulwarks.

The 'decaying bulwarks' were those of a Liberalism which had lost touch with radicalism. The Conservatives returned in triumph in 1895. Fifteen months before the first issue of the *Ethical World* the Earl of Rosebery resigned leadership of the Liberal Opposition, leaving the way clear for the man deemed to be the moral successor to Gladstone, Sir William Harcourt. But Harcourt's authority waned as the party inclined to the old Rosebery view of a foreign policy formulated in response to Chamberlain at the Colonial Office. In December 1898, as the *Ethical World* approached its first anniversary, Harcourt resigned, leaving the Opposition front bench to the imperialists. The paper saw his act as an invigorating east wind that could brace the meeting of the National Liberal Federation in Birmingham in mid-December, which 'if far from the ideal of ethical democracy . . . is probably the largest elective political assembly in these islands', and in whose sessions was to be heard the 'robust common sense of the northern shires' in support of the Harcourt line, from Jowett, Hollowell, Russell and Leveson-Gower, to itemise some minor heroes of the *Ethical World* who had to be reckoned with 'if Liberalism is to continue as the alternative to Toryism in our party system'. Very soon John

Morley announced that he would follow Harcourt in withdrawing active support from the Opposition's policies, an act which established his status as a 'giant of righteousness' for the *Ethical World*. Morley served to keep the ethicists in line with their avowed traditions: in November 1898 Ramsay MacDonald reminded them that they could do no better than re-read Morley on the foreign policy of Cobden. In April 1901 Coit reassured free-thinking readers that there was no basis in the rumours that Morley had reneged on his positivist and rationalist views – it had been whispered that he had prayed for Gladstone during the last illness of the Grand Old Man. Coit quoted a passage from *On Compromise* (1874) on the responsibilities of atheist or agnostic parents to do better than merely let their offspring make up their own minds: 'However desirable it may be that the young should know all sorts of erroneous beliefs and opinions as products of the past, it can hardly be in any degree desirable that they should take them for truths.' The old liberal avoided the weak liberalism even of the late twentieth century. On the media the paper approved of Morley's idea that classes should be established for instruction in how to read the newspapers, so that people could 'discriminate the essential from the sensational, and the mere multitude of happenings from actions that reveal souls and tendencies'. In February 1900 H. W. Massingham welcomed the lead given to the anti-imperialists by Morley's contribution to the Commons debate on the first day of the new parliamentary session, and in June 1901 W. S. Sanders applauded Morley's speeches to his constituents on South Africa, though he wished they had been delivered before the election of the previous October when the nation was on the boil with spurious patriotism. Nevertheless, 'at least one member of the Liberal party is saying what he thinks of the war'. Morley was largely retired from active politics, but there could still be a price to pay for speaking against the war, as was discovered by a lesser hero of the *Ethical World*, Leonard Courtney. Beatrice Webb noted that his Liberal Party regarded him as a 'quixotic crank', but 'what hurts him most, oddly enough, is the social boycott'. Morley's boldness made him for the ethicists '*the* ethical politician of our day'.[7]

Of the three major problems handled by the *Ethical World* the first was that of the treatment of women.

During its first year the paper did not show great interest in the women's movement. It published articles on the impending Midwives' Registration Bill from its parliamentary sponsor, which were followed by an angry presentation of an alternative by a doctor. Dora Montefiore complained that when the London County Council appointed female shop-work inspectors, it paid them less than men. Early in 1899 she criticised the Home Work Bill, eliciting a reply from Margaret MacDonald.

Ramsay MacDonald contributed a general piece, lamenting that women would continue to be pushed around until they had concerted aid from the best-off sisters. In March 1899 an article by such a sister appeared. Zona Vallance was secretary of the Union of Ethical Societies and of the Moral Instruction League (of which more in the next section of this chapter). She was to take charge of women's issues in the *Ethical World* until her death at the age of forty-three in December 1904.

As the daughter of an east London doctor Zona Vallance could speak with authority on working women's households. When the midwives' Bill eventually came much emended to the vote in the summer of 1902 she was able to comment scathingly on the practicability of compulsorily registering many women who helped at confinements, doing so from the motive of 'a common attachment' rather than for monetary gain. Well-meaningly the Bill wanted checks on the expertise of midwives, but left male doctors unchecked, who were just as capable of spreading infection: 'Who would dream of restricting doctors in their earning area and subjecting them to the supervision of a local committee wholly or partly composed of women?'

Zona Vallance witnessed a depressing period in the growth of feminism – the word which was first used in 1895 (usually derogatorily). When the suffrage campaigns began in the mid-1860s there were one million male voters; at the turn of the century the number had increased sevenfold without the addition of a single woman. The position had, indeed, deteriorated in some respects. Zona Vallance and her friends argued that the Municipal Corporations Act, a successor to the 1832 Reform Bill, actually removed municipal power from women, which appeared to be restored in London in 1888 when women were included in the electorate, only to be removed after appeal – from a defeated male candidate. Zona Vallance kept up a commentary on Parliament, the courts, and on women's societies. She was not preaching to the converted in the *Ethical World*, in which she had to justify female suffrage from the beginnings. She had to speak out against scepticism among the progressives, and indifference, shown on the occasion when a S.D.F. speaker finished his question-time with an assured tail-piece: 'Oh, I nearly forgot, there is a petition on the table in favour of the Women's Suffrage Bill. I have nothing to say about it, except that it will increase the vote of the propertied classes.' Supposed shrewdness of this kind frequently had a measure of banal chauvinism stirred into it. A dry comment from Zona Vallance on 'sex slavery' and the hypothesis of the withdrawal of conjugal rights by wives, drew a snarling accusation from E. Belfort Bax that the *Ethical World* feminist had at last shown her cloven hoof: the advocates of 'womanhood' really only offered, he expostulated, 'a thinly disguised expression for male slavery'.

Zona Vallance put her most interesting thought into her efforts to persuade a more considerable type of opponent, the socialist of good-will who simply could not understand the relevance of the woman question to analysis of capitalism, the socialist who – she thought – was so blinded by the obvious need to do away with the poverty and ignorance created by the economic system that he had 'become immersed in mere bread-and-butter calculations'. In her view such socialists did not understand the origin of individualism which was 'in the aggressive and aristocratic construction of the family which upholds this entire class edifice, and creates the need for aggressive economics. Yet, even from the narrow-graded point of view [of bread-and-butter calculation], there is not man on earth so poor as the poorest woman; for by social consent no man can be robbed of so much.' Zona Vallance had a theory to confute the 'narrow-graded point of view', whose beginnings can be seen in her first contribution to the *Ethical World*, 'Men, Women and Justice' (March 1899) in which a passage from Ruskin's *Fors Clavigera* distinguishing two types of justice is considered. On one side there is the blindfolded figure with the scales which, according to Ruskin, metes out reward and punishment mechanistically. On the other side there is Giotto's *Justice* in the Chapel of the Arena, a female figure personifying Christian judgment, one which 'feels with sensitive human hands the measures of culpability or merit'. Zona Vallance related Ruskin's idea about Giotto's figure to a conception of the mother which was at the root of her feminism. However, in writing about the mother-figure she expressed herself with a marked lack of the unction in which Ruskin slithered on this theme – not surprisingly as Coit had been her mentor, who said that from Ruskin's social ideal 'one shrinks as from the likeness of a beautiful corpse'. Zona Vallance thought likewise, seeing Ruskin as 'a wizard', dangerous to the moral development of women. In her theory the concepts of justice, woman and mother are merged. She believed that social reorganisation hung on the development of 'an unresting motherhood', a motherhood reconceived in such a way that it neither forced women to play the mother rôle normally expected of them, nor to abandon that rôle for the sake of an aspiration to become 'mere copies of the present and past egoistic men'. In one review she criticises a female Catholic writer on psychology for whom a web of tradition 'spun round her soul' had

forbidden her mind to create the full round whole of what motherhood may be one day to the State. She seeks the return of a cycle; but if progress be sometimes circular, it is also spiral. The self-effacement, the abandonment of motherhood, has hitherto been seen only as emotionalism ... but once permit women free and ample access to all the facts and doings of manifold life, then the ecstasy of belonging to something greater and larger than the self, this capacity to make things grow . . . will wed with reason and knowledge, and become a great motor power, and a natural starting point for the new social reconstruction.

It was not hard for the progressive companions of Zona Vallance to retort that the oppression of women was irrevocably located in both the idea and the actualities of motherhood. It was as easy for others to say that bread-and-butter socialism at least aimed to destroy the victimisation of *persons*, not women, and even less mothers, and it was as easy for the socialist to add (if *sotto voce*) that a paean for motherhood gave no reason for diversion from the urgent business of the day, the elimination of victimisation of male persons. Zona Vallance was well aware of these arguments: she knew what the Ruskinian sentimentalisation of motherhood was like; and she was not a Positivist. She made much of the mother-figure because of the place it occupied for her in an evolutionist's myth of origin which replaced the Christian myth of patriarchy. Under theology-based systems of ethics woman was passive, unenquiring and obedient, until sinful. Under a post-Darwinian system woman was, in a quite literal sense, capable of being held responsible for the 'ethical movement' of mankind. The human race alone possessed a complex moral consciousness and sense of history because of the uniquely prolonged nursing period undergone by human beings, in which the mother dominates. 'A steadily-increasing development of an altruistic nursing propensity in mothers must have been there', wrote Zona Vallance in the fullest presentation of her ideas, in two speeches published shortly after her death in the *Ethical World* (December 1904). Her view is mythical or explanatory. It is not meant to decree a retreat into solo responsibility for child-care in twentieth-century woman. On the contrary, Zona Vallance thought that husband and wife should act as partners, a collaboration between genders which contested the Christian single gender model of paired authority, that between Father and Son. Her model for the conduct of the collaboration she found in the nurturing role of the mythical mother, from which the modern wife *and* husband should alike learn. The family should be run by partners who have 'the power to serve', rather than be dominated by a master who has 'the power to fight'. That power to fight belonged to the individualistic tradition of capitalism, which in the far from distant past had appropriated labour from the family, damaged the rôle of the mother and dissolved partnership in production (including partnership in the production of children) which was possible in the pre-capitalist era, when status regulated human inequalities rather than contract exacerbated them. Of capitalism and the family Zona Vallance wrote:

In the eyes of the men who gradually changed this industrial system, their own right to rise in the competition with other men necessitated unrestricted ownership for men of all they could profit by, including the wife's labour. It was during the slow rise of capitalist and machine industry and this break-up of family industries that the status disability of coverture was actually extended over women. Previously there had been wives in England free to trade and own as *femmes soles* [*sic*]. On the other hand, this same revolution saw abolished all the rights of status, such as dower, in favour of man's absolute power to dispose of land and money. The status of a wife came to mean a bare right to the necessities from her husband, which she could only enforce if some tradesman would give her credit, or through the Poor Law. As to the widow, the husband attained, and still possesses, absolute right to leave her penniless after a life of home labour, either by choice or by his extravagance or folly, unless she acquires property apart from their partnership.

In ethicist circles there was no lack of respect for women, sometimes in a Comtean sense, which implied the consignment of women definitively into the home. In expounding her myth of the mother-figure, with its lesson for capitalist and socialist alike, Zona Vallance did not follow Comte. She recognised that many of the famous female virtues had been acquired *faute de mieux*, and had their roots in 'the sex-division of functions'. Women should now come out into public government because of what they had learned in family seclusion. 'For the human problem is no longer mere accumulation of the goods of life and secure intercommunication: it is healthy, equitable distribution of what co-operation of both sexes and all classes of men has won.' The women's movement, as conceived by Zona Vallance, was necessary not only for redress, but for the material it provided for a critique and theory of capitalism.[8]

Zona Vallance did not shrink from economic theory in her pieces on the woman problem, nor did the contributors on empire, which was inevitably a prominent subject given Coit's preoccupation with nationhood. Many ethicists shared his interest, their views ranging from straightforwardly moral, voicing distress at an evident decline of standards of conduct in public life, to the theoretical. Their political awareness was aroused after the 'Jameson Raid' on Johannesburg in 1895, igniting the Boer question, and from knowledge of German and Russian threats to British interests in east Africa. The ethicist position on empire is well described by Bernard Porter in *Critics of Empire: British Radical Attitudes to Colonialism in Africa, 1895–1914* (1968). Here we shall briefly note some of the peaks of concern among the *Ethical World* contributors for 'this constant craze for expansion, which at the present time is visibly embroiling us in Africa and Asia'.

And, of course, in South Africa. But in the early months of the *Ethical World* the issue of expansion was most disturbingly seen across the Atlan tic, because 'America has apparently decided to break anchor and leave her ancient moorings. She sets up in the imperial business with a stock in-trade consisting of Cuba, Porto Rico, Hawaii, the Ladrones, and the Philippines, all these islands largely populated by dark and uncivilized and turbulent races.' In July 1898 Ramsay MacDonald wrote that if America was in the process of modifying the Monroe Doctrine with a mission to promote international righteousness it was not necessarily transporting the best of its civilisation into the dark regions. America was industrially developed but politically barbaric: its democracy had become a 'byword for corrupt dealing and jerrymandering'. Its machine politicians acquired support by a process of ethical parody, a delicate play upon the aspirations of the electorate:

It is the corruption of the Christmas dinner, of paying the doctor's bill, of stan-ding bail for the wayward son, of passing votes of sympathy for the bereaved widow and orphans, of sending wreaths of white tender flowers for coffin lids.

MacDonald was one of the few ethicists with a gift for writing fiction, ex-ercised above in the care for detail in this description of the tarnished art of civic benevolence. It was an Orwellian talent which on occasion he used to deal with a characteristically Orwellian theme, the shooting-an-elephant syndrome, the behavioural implications of imperialism on resi-dent administrators. Comment upon such implications was part of an analysis by social class of British expansion. J. A. Hobson attacked Kipling's 'White Man's Burden' as 'the most audacious perversion of the truth that has ever tainted a fine poetic form' before he visited South Africa. MacDonald attacked the personality distortions created by the ideals of 'chapman adventure', and attacked them both for their effect in the imperialist arena of the territories, but also back in Britain. Expan-sion was a menace on the doorstep, a threat to British democratic institu-tions, 'which were increasingly enpeopled from the ranks of returned petty clerks to governor-generals . . . whose sense of human liberty and equality has been irreparably destroyed by false contact with Oriental and tropical peoples'. The tainting of officialdom (itself no more than an inconvenience, at first) was, argued MacDonald, only a symptom of 'the process which takes place in the public mind'.

Half-way between the 'pepper' and the mental twist of our retired Oriental of-ficial and the sickly moral Imperialism of Dr. Lyman Abbott and the staff of the New York *Outlook* is the state of mind of the average Englishman in South Africa, and the average American in a Southern Negro state.

The white man sinks to the level of 'the uncivilized Ishmael'. In the *Ethical World* there was more backing to this kind of opinion than moral fastidiousness. The theory behind it came from J. A. Hobson, who, in turn, owed a debt to the French sociologist, Gustave Le Bon. One of Hobson's specialities was the snipping down of cliché of which one such was the seemingly innocuous expansionist idea that an advanced nation may assist in the development of the backward one. This was contradicted, thought Hobson, by history, by evolutionary theory, and by Le Bon who, in *Les Lois psychologiques de l' evolution des peuples* (1891), found that national qualities were 'ultimate determinants', going deeper than concept or art. Years later, as Bernard Porter demonstrates, this idea was put by Le Bon to very different purposes from the liberal democratic ones which Hobson believed it could assist. For Hobson culture was, and had to be maintained as, multiform, in both 'progressive' and 'backward' nations. So if the opening up of Asia and Africa for industrial purposes involved a 'serious attempt to impose the deeper essentials of European civilization upon those countries, it can scarcely be denied that the gravest dangers are involved'. This statement comes near the conclusion of the series of essays published in the *Ethical World* between March and November 1898 which appeared in book form as *The Social Problem* (1901). In 1899 Hobson was in South Africa, for which he departed just after the declaration of war, returning to London in early December where he became a leading agitator in the 'Stop the War' campaign. During 1900 two conflicts of belief emerged among ethicists, originating in attitudes to the war, then spreading outwards. The conflict defines drives among those who put 'ethics to the front', and concerns two figures besides Hobson and MacDonald. One was the Idealist philosopher, D. G. Ritchie, a former Toynbeeite who was angered to see the pro-Boers attack Milner, another Balliol man. The second was Eduard Bernstein, the revisionist Marxist and German social democrat exiled in London.

The basic *Ethical World* demand on empire was for 'democratisation', requiring (1) no new acquisition of territory, (2) conservation of existing native organisations (because progress should come 'from within', organically), (3) prohibition of forced labour, (4) abolition of charterism, (5) establishment of free, self-governing native populations as soon as possible, (6) resistance to militaristic tendencies. If not imperialistic the editorial attitude was, thought Coit, *anti*-imperialistic, but it was interpreted to be so by D. G. Ritchie who wrote in to the paper from his chair of logic and metaphysics at St. Andrew's University in January 1900. His article, 'Another View of the South African War', was a reply to pro-Boer pieces by a South African Unitarian minister, Ramsden Balmforth, by G. H. Perris, the most violent of the ethical pacifists and by Hobson who began his campaign against the war with ammunition from another book by Le Bon, *La Psychologie des foules* (1895), which he used to interpret the herd-mentality of British jingoism. Ritchie's view was a subtle version of the British government view: according to him (and it) the war derived from a question of sovereignty, which had been usurped by the Boers, and the conflict resembled the strife between north and south in the American civil war – with the notable similarity (so it was argued) that while the British found much with which they were in rapport in the south (as rapport was felt, especially by non-conformists, with the Boers), the cause of empire was still, like that of the Federal government, 'the cause of true democracy, civilization, and of progress'. Ritchie gave credence to accounts of conditions in South Africa relayed by missionaries, reports whose contents and sources Hobson distrusted. But the main difference between his position and that of the returned correspondent for the *Manchester Guardian* was its static nature. Ritchie saw a conflict of interest; Hobson saw a conflict which had been devised, created or engineered by 'self-seeking politicians for definite economic purposes'. It was not defects of 'franchise, taxation, nor suzerainty' for the Outlanders which, he found, were the real cause of conflict, nor was there actual hostility in relations between Boer and Briton. Rather the issue was the desire for political domination expressed, typically, not by the 'hard living men, familiar with the dangers of frontier life, but by the shopkeeping and professional classes'. The conflict lay in the 'mass-mind', whose opinions were not spontaneous, but created by the mining companies' control of the media of information and opinion, having purchased 'nearly all the influential British newspapers in Cape Colony and the Transvaal . . . the *Cape Times* and the *Cape Argus*, the *Kimberley Advertiser*, the *Bulawayo Chronicle, Rhodesia Herald, Johannesburg Star*, and *Transvaal Leader*'. Ritchie scoffed at Hobson's conspiracy theory and at his belief that capitalism was the major factor at work, reducing what he saw as a matter of principle (a static matter) to one of vulgar economics. But, right or wrong, Hobson's economics was not reductive, with its aspirations to sociology, the science which was needed to detect organic movements, and which was *necessarily* socialist, as he explained in an editorial about the theory of social democracy. The metaphysical and economic basis assigned to it by Marx

> *may* be as groundless as it appears to most philosophers and economists; its materialistic interpretation *may* be repellent; its conception of the social ideal *may* be too rigidly mechanical. *But its critical and emotional significance is unmistakable.* It has seized some of the salient features of modern society . . . [notably] the impossibility of individual independence, self-support, in a modern industrial society, where the most intricate co-operation is essential to the life of man, [which] imposes upon society a character and a function never clearly recognized before the advent of Socialism. (My italics.)

Hobson's analysis of the South African situation lay not so much in the detection of capitalist cupidity, but in the discovery of a chain of events (in which the purchase of a controlling interest in newspapers was one of the links) which provided negative illustration of 'the living organic conception of society as affording continuous support to all its members'. It was his method, his sociology, which enabled him to see clearly that the 'gritty and unpleasant bedrock of known and admitted fact' showed that 'the chartered magnates of finance' did not deserve to be regarded as representatives of a higher civilisation which was potentially friend to the native.

When Hobson replied to Ritchie (February 1900) he was not yet quite the full-scale theorist of *Imperialism: A Study* (1902). In early 1900 his concept of expansion had only been sketched in some pieces of journalism, notably an essay in *The Contemporary Review* of January 1900, as well as in the *Ethical World*. It was to become more widely known in February when *The War in South Africa* was published, putting in permanent form his reports as foreign correspondent. When this book came out Ritchie renewed his attack, but from a different angle, on political rather than on constitutional (or factual) grounds.

The War in South Africa was noticed in the *Ethical World* (March 1900) under the heading of 'Mr. Hobson's Book and the Coming Settlement', consisting of a complimentary note from the aged Herbert Spencer and an attack from Ritchie. So, drily observed the latter, Hobson was rejecting federation to ensure that 'the next time there is any trouble with the natives, Boer and Briton will be fighting side by side, and the natives will not lose by the controlling influence of British sentiment'. What was this attitude but a socialist version of the old tune of *laissez-faire*, or mere sentimental anarchism? It was hardly worthy of responsible social democracy of the kind represented by Eduard Bernstein. An editorial note dissociated the paper from Ritchie's position, citing as the real anarchists the mining companies and the London jingo patriots. When, a few days later, Lord Salisbury declared that the independence of the two Boer republics must be destroyed, the paper lamented 'the policy of smash' – 'We are to make a desert and call it peace . . . Ah! the folly of it!' There were several replies to Ritchie, but Hobson himself left the ideological question on one side. 'Sentimental anarchism' was only discussed when Eduard Bernstein himself intervened in an essay *reconciling* socialism with imperialism. 'The mere fact that imperialism is connected with capitalism can of itself be no reason for Democrats to fight it root and branch.' Marx had thought that care should be taken to discern new social forms, in this instance centralised federations, brought into being not by militarism, but only by 'the mere forces of social necessity as conditioned by modern modes of life, modern trade relations and modern traffic'. Like Ritchie, he pointed to the example of Switzerland in which federal units (the cantons) had increasingly lost their self-sufficiency and acquired the character of counties in a centralised state. (Ritchie had claimed that such federation could never be spontaneous, progress 'coming from within', as the organicist socialists would have it: even in supposedly serene Switzerland this had not been the case because it was only by pressure from France that the cantons Vaud and Ticino had achieved parity with the German cantons. If force had created the modern Switzerland, then the possibility of its beneficial use in South Africa could hardly be rejected.) Bernstein argued against the type of socialist who had too much in common with the anarchist's absolute enmity for the state. The ethicists reply came to him from G. H. Perris, who rejected completely an equation of a desirable modern state with imperialism. 'Imperialism is as far removed from free federal union as concubinage is from monogamy.' For a model of federated organisation there is no need to go to the example of imperialism, but to its antithesis, internationalism, 'the system of co-operative commonwealths, evolving organically in pacific inter-relation . . . As Imperialism is the extension of class monopoly, so Internationalism is the extension of community, true patriotism.' Bernstein rejoined that inter-relationship was only possible 'between people who have evolved some national life of their own'. For those short of 'a certain state of civilization' a protective or preventive imperialism is necessary, unlike 'that kind of Imperialism we all loathe', but still recognised that 'it is impossible for me to have the same international feeling towards an Arab tribesman, a South American cattle driver, and a citizen of a modern civilized state'. MacDonald had already joined the debate, and at this point replied in a fashion which vividly illustrated the ethicist position. Of course, he agreed, Bernstein's interventionist 'democratic internationalism' was legitimate, but to what purpose did he align it with imperialism, a word which 'gave a guidance of its own'? He recognised Bernstein's tactics − the enlistment of support from those who would never be wooed by 'internationalism', leading them gently away from 'imperialism' (which they broadly and emotionally approved) ultimately 'to get control of their reason'. But this mode of propaganda, the political 'psychology of opportunism', was futile because such a word as 'imperialism' could not be wrenched away from its common associations. If Bernstein was an internationalist choosing to make treaty with imperialists or even calling himself an enlightened imperialist, then his supposed internationalism was discredited: 'Its "democratic internationalism" becomes monarchic or military nationalism, its "humane relation" and its "just and liberal treatment" becomes a species of despotism (benevolent, if you will) which the natives do not understand,

and which crushes out all chance of progress on truly native lines.' Bernstein's social democracy contradicted Hobson's idea of a 'multi-form' society. It contradicted that ethnological concern which characterised ethicism, as much in the pages of the *Ethical World* as in the meetings at South Place.[9]

Ethics in the class-room

When Coit brought 'ethics to the front' in his editorial in May 1898 the great issue of the day with which he was concerned was education – 'for the Ethical Movement is pre-eminently educational in character'. In this section we shall see how the ethical clerisy campaigned for changes in education.

In his autobiography F. J. Gould describes how 'the Education Act of 1870 . . . stirred our countryside, and country parsons shook their heads dubiously'. We saw in Chapter 1 that Gould himself taught in a tiny church school in Chenies which dispensed an education to country people far from the problems of the cities in which bodies such as the British and Foreign School Society strained to lever the proletariat from its torpor. By 1870 it was clear that such bodies could only scratch the surface of the problem of mass education. Registers only carried the names of two-fifths of the six- to ten-year-olds and a third of the children up to the age of twelve. Forster's Elementary Education Act devised School Boards empowered to have schools funded from the rates (local taxes), and to receive government grants. The religious bodies, responsible for their so-called voluntary schools, were given six months' grace in which to build schools which would be eligible for the same grants. Thus was born the dual system, and the history of popular education from 1870 thorough the period of the ethical movement is that of a contest between School Board and voluntary school authorities, a contest which turned in its most momentous form to one between state and church. The church complained at the burden of maintaining its schools to the level required by the government. At the turn of the century the Conservatives revised the Act and made all schools eligible for state grants. Balfour's Education Act of 1902 abolished the School Boards, putting all schools under the control of the newly devised county councils, putting Anglicanism 'on the rates', as it appeared to non-conformists, agnostics, atheists, and ethicists. Opposition to this Act united the Liberal Party which came to victory in 1906, but it was then not able to make any significant change to the settlement of 1902, in spite of Bills from Birrell, McKenna and Runciman. The issues which were important to ethicists emerged somewhat earlier than this: they dramatically affected the career of F. J. Gould.

In 1885 the Conservatives came back to power and appointed a Royal Commission under Viscount Cross to examine the workings of Forster's Act. The commissioners included several men who disliked the Act, notably Cardinal Manning. They had unrestricted terms of reference. Naturally they spent much of their time investigating what happened in daily practice to two of the most controversial paragraphs of the Act, the seventh and the fourteenth. Paragraph Seven said that children should be admitted to school irrespective of their religious affiliations (or lack of them) and not be compelled to attend lessons in religious instruction. Those lessons should be placed at the beginning or end of the school day, so that children could be 'withdrawn'. This became popularly known as the Conscience Clause. Paragraph Fourteen stated that 'no religious catechism or formulary which is distinctive of any particular denomination shall be taught in the school'. This was called the Cowper-Temple Clause after the mover of the amendment which effected its inclusion. The Cross Commission was concerned with godlessness in school which may have been fostered by the implementation of these paragraphs. It asked whether religion had declined since 1870 among school-managers, teachers and children, and whether pressure to teach the secular curriculum (on the examination of which grants were paid to the schools, under the system known as 'payment by results') had elbowed piety away. It was also exercised by the problem of the non-believing or 'infidel' teacher.

Some witnesses had a rough ride. The non-conformist city of Birmingham first responded to the Act by excluding all religious instruction from its Board schools, and later required brief Bible readings without commentary. It was represented to the Commission by Dr. Crosskey, chairman of the School Management Committee. He stepped unafraid across the coals of fire laid in his path by Cardinal Manning. The cardinal enquired whether a religious man, like Dr. Arnold, could teach morality without reference to the deity? 'I think', answered Crosskey, 'that to bring in the name of the Deity would be a mistake in teaching in schools. I think the children would become so accustomed to it that it would become mechanical and formal, and that the very name of our Creator would lose its power.' As for the infidel in the class-room, 'I would make no enquiries', at which Crosskey was harried into a query as to whether he would allow a godless governess in his home. He eloquently maintained the non-conformist view that religious teaching was best done by religious bodies.

The Conservative members of the Commission were better pleased by the answers of the chairman of the great London School Board. The Reverend J. R. Diggle described the daily lessons of the forty-five minute

Bible period set by his Board and administered by the Board's inspectors. By the age of fourteen (at Standard VII) pupils should have by heart the Commandments, the Lord's Prayer, two dozen verses of Matthew and John, Ephesians 4:25–32 and 6:1–18, Isaiah 53, 1 Corinthians, and the twenty-third Psalm. At this standard pupils revised the life of Christ, and the lives of Abraham, Moses, Samuel, Saul, David and Daniel, and Acts was introduced for the first time. Some of the examination questions for Standard VII were as follows:

– Write St. Paul's description of Charity. Give the meaning of the word 'Charity' as he uses it.
– On which clause in the Lord's Prayer did Christ lay special stress? What parable did he give to teach the same lesson?
– What worthy points are to be noticed in the character of King Saul?
– How are children taught in the Bible to behave: – (a) at home? (b) at school? (c) with their school companions.

Diggle was thoroughly questioned about infidel teachers. Lord Cross asked him how he would deal with an atheist, or one who thought that 'all religions are just as true or just as untrue the one as the other'. Diggle replied that he would wish to dismiss such a teacher, but that 'no case of that kind has ever come before the Board'. But one case shortly did come before the Board and before Diggle himself. A few months after he gave evidence Diggle was faced with an infidel in the person of F. J. Gould, self-confessed 'raging and tearing radical'. We noted his demotion in Chapter 1: though not dismissed for secular activities he was sent to a rough school in Limehouse and forbidden to teach the Bible as a 'human document'. 'I was an alien, unable to utter a Bible shibboleth.'

The Gould case illustrates the predicament which drove young teachers towards the support of the ethical societies. There were other problems, for it was not only aggressive radicals like Gould who suffered. J. Allanson Picton, who championed Gould, pointed out in *The Bible in School: A Question of Ethics* (1902) that even the believing teacher who was theologically up-to-date could be professionally victimised. He cited a debate which took place in March 1901 at the National Council of Free Churches at which Dr. Munro Gibson stated that in Sunday school there should be no attempt to gloss over controversial matters. If a child asked if the serpent in Genesis was real, then the teacher must say that there are different opinions. A teacher could not express himself so freely in a Board school. Further, teachers' problems were compounded by the extraordinary nature of the passages set for special study by some Boards. Picton gave examples: 'Under Wanstead Board, the higher standards were to study Joshua and Judges. It would be hard to find in all literature two books more full of bloodshed, murder, massacre and savagery of even more repulsive forms . . . How can any educated man or woman read these sanguinary legends with their innocent pupils without hastening to assure the children that these are no words of God?'[10]

Gould himself was relatively fortunate. In February 1896 he gave up Board School teaching, having been invited by Coit to do full-time work for the ethical movement. Within the societies there were moves towards disentangling moral education from Bible and theology. In May 1897 the first congress of the Union of Ethical Societies called for a conference to discuss lobbying candidates for the London School Board elections on their attitudes to moral education. The Union sent representatives, along with delegates from the S.D.F., the National Secular Society and several trade unions, to a meeting in Holborn Town Hall on 19 July 1897, at which Frederic Harrison made a plea for 'non-theological moral instruction in place of the present religious teaching'. In December a public meeting expressed the same conviction. From this the Moral Instruction League was generated, which held its first meeting on 26 January 1898.

The foundation of the Moral Instruction League coincided with the first issue of the *Ethical World*, in which its aims were announced:

That *in all State-aided schools the best possible moral teaching should be given*: that on psychological and educational principles the moral training should be separated from the theological elements; and that the *moral training should receive illumination and rational exposition in a systematic course of non-theological instruction, which should take the place of the present religious teaching*. (Italics in original.)

The demand in the last sentence was modified in April 1902 to one for moral instruction *as well as* Bible lessons. The League compromised because of the debate that raged in the intervening years about state schools, the Board schools, which were terminally attacked by the Education Act of 1902. When the work of the Boards was to be done by the county councils there would be less public accountability. The M.I.L. sensibly changed its policy because the change in organisation would have made its original task impossibly large. It could not even hope for the elimination of theological moral teaching once state and church schools were administered under the same authorities. So it abandoned its uncompromising secular stand, turning away from attempts at direct political intervention, which characterised its first years, to work of theory and example. This work should be seen in the context of other forms of agitation, on behalf of the School Boards in particular, and democracy in general, which appeared threatened by Conservative policy.

When the M.I.L. demanded moral instruction in state schools it was thinking of the elementary education which the Boards provided for children up to the age of eleven, the school-leaving age set in 1893. The

Boards came under threat because they had ambitions to take their education further on into children's lives. Children were staying on at school, even up to fifteen and beyond. Some Boards, of which Sheffield in Yorkshire was the first, provided separate schools for children at the post-elementary level, a trend noted with displeasure by the Cross Commission, because the Boards were moving into areas that put them in competition with forms of education from which the working class was traditionally excluded, and also in competition with those voluntary schools whose church administrators groaned under the burden of fund-seeking and maintaining standards to the Board of Education requirements. When the Conservatives were returned in 1895 the Archbishop of Canterbury petitioned the Prime Minister for help with his schools and for some wing-clipping of the Boards. This was attempted in an aborted Bill of 1896, which was followed by fiscal measures to repress the School Boards' ambitions, to quench the flow of funds to them which had been allowed by somewhat free interpretation of their founding terms of reference. The government determined to effect wholesale reorganisation in the Education Bill of 1902, which was implacably opposed by the labour movement in its various forms. To this opposition the Moral Instruction League was aligned. It therefore saw itself as working for both secular education and democracy. A defence of the Boards was an implicit defence of popular control over schooling. Through such popular control there seemed a chance of influencing pedagogic policy. So the moral instructionists' posture was that of a broad-based political stance. The stance was succinctly stated in February 1901 in the *Ethical World* by the chairman of the Bradford School Board:

The attack on the School Boards is really an attack on popular control in matters educational. It is not primarily a dispute as to delimitation between elementary and secondary schools; it is not merely, though it is that also, an explosion of professional jealousy and priestly hatred of higher developments in Board-school instruction; it is not even, in its deeper meanings, a mere effort to rail off secondary education from poor children, or to hand over immense sums of money to non-elected managers of secondary schools. It does, indeed, mean all these things . . . Let it be known throughout the land that this attack on Board-schools is a denial of the right and competence of the democracy of England to administer what is called 'secondary education'.

School Boards were elected bodies, with franchise for those entitled to vote for local councillors. Each voter had the same number of votes as the number of candidates offering themselves for election, which could be either distributed or given to a single candidate. When the government produced its Bill in 1902 the Boards were to be replaced by education committees of the new county authorities, and on them it was possible for co-opted members to out-number the elected members. Critics believed that at worst this meant continued control by squire and parson and at best control by dubious experts – who could be churchly experts.

When it started in 1898 the Moral Instruction League was able to proceed by means of these democratic processes whose survival was feared for. It lobbied the Boards and interrogated candidates at election time. In 1900 it asked two questions of London School Board candidates: do you favour replacement of theological by secular instruction? Failing that, do you wish schools to provide an alternative to Bible teaching? For this to be done demand would have to be demonstrated by a substantial number of parents, showing will to withdraw their children from the Bible classes. On this occasion of the thirty-seven members elected to the Board, ten answered the second question in the affirmative, some, perhaps, guessing that not enough parents would make their wishes known for it to be necessary to provide alternative classes. But the M.I.L. did its best to see that there would be enough. One of its first tasks was to convert parents to a knowledge of their rights under the Conscience Clause to withdraw their children. In Kensington and Highgate canvassers went from door to door, explaining the law and leaving behind 'A Plan for Moral Instruction' drawn up by Gould. They found many parents willing to sign a withdrawal form to be delivered to school. The canvassers gathered many signatures for a moral instruction petition to go to the London School Board, from which the M.I.L. received a cautiously favourable response. After a petition presented in 1901 this Board agreed to provide secular training for children taken out of Bible class, 'having regard to the possibilities of school organisation'. At local level the snag was in getting children definitively withdrawn: while the M.I.L. could persuade parents that they did not approve of theological teaching, the same parents could rather easily have their minds changed by a forceful head-teacher who believed in the present system (or disbelieved in rocking the boat). Head-teachers were sceptical of a sheaf of requests arriving by the same delivery and accused the M.I.L. of bullying parents. From the spring of 1901 the League realised that political action of this kind could have only limited effectiveness, given anyway the few canvassers it had at its disposal. Moreover, Coit was a driving force in the League, but he was moving towards a position which implied cooperation with the churches.

The Moral Instruction League had two major workers. Henry Harrold Johnson (1870–1940) was before he joined it a Unitarian minister in Birmingham. He was a London graduate, had studied at the Sorbonne and at Leipzig University, and received theological training at Manchester College (as Manchester New College was called when it removed from

167

Bloomsbury to Oxford). From 1902 to 1913 he was organising secretary of the M.I.L., principally responsible for its propaganda and for gathering information about the prevalence and development of non-theological moral instruction in Britain. The second pillar of the League was F. J. Gould who in 1899 fell out with Coit's autocratic ways and moved from London to a secretarial post with the Leicester Secular Society. There he scored a singular success in the School Board election of 1900. The streets blazed with yellow posters, proclaiming Gould's commitment to having children taught not about 'the details of British battles and trifling incidents in the lives of kings, but the history of mankind, and of all the wonderful works of the human race in the past'. He was elected, becoming the M.I.L.'s first School Board representative. He persuaded his Board to establish a 'Leicester Syllabus'. He helped the M.I.L. frame 'A Graduated Syllabus of Moral Instruction for Elementary Schools' to help teachers, who should have a 'broad and organic view of life', appeal 'to the scholar's feelings and also to affect his will'. The Syllabus consisted of a sequence of abstract nouns whose meaning was to be communicated at each Standard, such as 'PATIENCE: (a) Forbearance, (b) Contentedness, (c) Forgiveness'. Exactly how the concepts were communicated was amply illustrated by Gould's own published specimen lessons in the *Ethical World* and in book form. He travelled widely to publicise the policy of the League. After the Act of 1902 he stood as a Leicester councillor, so that he could get a place on the new education committee. He was successful in different wards in 1904 and 1908 – in which year he was converted to Positivism and started a Leicester Positivist Society, which had a life of two years. From 1910 to 1915 he was the League's paid instructor in moral instruction.

From 1902 the M.I.L. demonstrated what moral instruction could be like to the Board of Education and to the new county authorities. Some of these provided secular moral instruction in forms that had originated long before the Act and the League. Ethical lessons had been given in Burton-on-Trent since 1878, in Birmingham since 1883, in Huddersfield since 1889. By 1908 many more could be added to the list, thanks to the efforts of the League and to the consciousness-raising effected by two pieces of research with M.I.L. members at the centre of them. The International Union of Ethical Societies made a comprehensive report (assembled and edited by Gustav Spiller), as did another committee, chaired by M. E. Sadler, with ethicists, including J. H. Muirhead, as members.[11]

After 1908 the M.I.L. declined in authority. Some members were disappointed in and then alienated by a volte-face on the part of Harrold Johnson, who changed his mind about the independence of moral instruction from religion. The M.I.L. withdrew even further from practical intervention in the politics of education, announcing in 1910 that it saw its future role as that of an educationalist body, 'pure and simple'. And it changed its name to Moral Education League. These changes distressed many ethicists, including Spiller. His record of the ethical movement is scrupulously fair, but he is unable to avoid a wry note in describing the policy of the Moral Education League, whose very name 'took the definiteness and challenge out of the title and apparently out of the League'. 'Instruction' was on the way out. Further changes of name and policy followed. The League became, successively, the Civic and Moral Education League (1916) and the Civic Education League (1919). The war brought it financial hard times. Gould had to be released, but was able to continue to work as before in the employ of the 'Gould Committee', formed by his admirers, on which sat Nellie Freeman (of the South London E.S.) and C. A. Watts, leading free-thinker of the Rationalist Press Association and friend of Gould's early days in London. In 1924 the League merged into a Civics Teaching Department at Le Play House, home of the Sociological Society and centre for research in the tradition of Frédéric Le Play whose monographs of detailed urban observation had inspired Charles Booth's *Life and Labour of the People of London* in the last decades of the nineteenth century.

The Moral Instruction League performed an important function in stimulating thought about modernisation of the school curriculum. It took advantage of the changes in school administration, intermeshed with questions of the rôle of the church and the responsibility of the state, to start a debate on what moral values should be taught, and how. One of the best things the League had to offer was the work of F. J. Gould, his schemes, his lesson plans, his demonstrations.

Initially the League was concerned with instruction and Gould was very much an instructionist (which was consonant with his Positivism). Rather tragically this placed him in a unique position, insulating him from many teachers who could have learned from his inventiveness and vitality, but who would regard him with suspicion because of his remoteness from some of the received ideas of educational theory. Gould was, for example, distinctly unenthusiastic about 'self-realisation', or the cult of creativity. For him creativity was associated with 'incidental' teaching in which the child is left alone to make discoveries of his or her own. Gould believed that moral education should be direct, not acquired in passing from a teacher who only on occasion exploits academic material to impart an ethical lesson, or does the same by drawing a moral from some class-room incident. Then again Gould was actually hostile to using works of fiction to teach morality, something seemingly strange in one who loved telling stories and collecting them. But it was not so much the story-teller as 'the ingenious novelist who has consciously manufactured his ethical cases, and produced mock heroisms at will' with which he was antagonistic. These attitudes were in Gould consistent and rational. For him 'self-realisation' and creativity meant following the Froebelian system, which he thought was splendid for children below the age of seven, but, because it was value-free, inadequate for ones older than that. It encouraged the dramatic faculty (of equal use to egotist, hypocrite, and decent person). It set great store by appreciation of music, which had no connection whatever with moral purity. Its faith in beauty could end up in merely refined and selfish enjoyment. Further, moral teaching which arises in passing and spontaneously 'wants the universal touch'. If it arises in the course of administering discipline, the offender is effectively put on trial in a school court, not the proper use of a classroom. 'Such activity has no connection', thought Gould, with 'instruction as it was etymologically to be understood (from "*instruo*, I build, pile up continuously, and . . . set in order").' As for distrusting 'fiction', by this Gould meant 'Goldsmith, Scott, Dickens, Louisa Alcott, Harriet Beecher Stowe, and the rest', whose ethics he thought to be factitious compared to what could be learned from biblical or Talmudic narratives or from ballad-singers, and story-tellers of the Middle Ages, and allegorists such as Comenius or Bunyan; their wisdom is 'a collective product embodying the thought of a community, and of a succession of reciters from generation to generation'. Their work was *true*, belonging to history which, as a Positivist, Gould wished to see at the centre of the school curriculum.

Gould's plans for the curriculum were original. He did not believe that subjects should be slotted into particular hours. If there were to be 'psychological chambers' then they should relate to the key subject, the story of civilisation. Gould produced a scheme for this correlation in three parts, each designed for an age band, from eight years to ten, eleven to twelve, and upwards from thirteen. Each stage is divided into parts, named *Environment, Action* (social and political), *Thought and Expression* (wonder, art, science), and *Ethics* (moral interpretation of environment, action and thought). Within the scheme was a repository of teaching material, which was Positivist in so far as Gould made no secret of the fact that he wanted to demonstrate chronological progress and 'the moral unity underlying diverse achievements', referring in this instance to the evolution of religion and education, which was to be taught through the lives of reformers, social workers and politicians. But aside from the Positivist end, the scheme is remarkable for its multiplicity of interest, and for the ingenuity Gould used to choose his examples. If he sounds utility when he bans stories about the wicked (duellist, thief, 'Apache') from the class-room, he is exciting in his choice of instances of good (such as 'Grinling Gibbons, whose Dutch genius adorned so many mansions with exquisite oak-carvings'). His enthusiasm for knowledge and 'positive' achievement is infectious. It shines out from the records of his demonstration lessons. Gilbert Murray attended one of Gould's lessons, on 'Self', expecting to be bored. He found that the presentation of the 'quiet elderly-looking man' was conversational, but not Socratic. Gould did not like to interrogate children and 'the unintelligent notion that education is solely or mainly a "drawing-out" of hidden stores of knowledge and insight': he thought this approach was 'responsible for a great deal of needless suffering to childhood'. In the demonstration lesson, attempting to 'invest the idea of Self with honour and dignity', he told a series of stories and, after just a little questioning, tried to lead the class to certain words ('self-respect', 'self-control', 'self-reliance' and 'self-sacrifice') which he wrote up on the blackboard. That done he said to the class,

The Self which we began by respecting, and controlling and relying upon, is now suffering; it is denied; it is sacrificed; and how noble was the denial; and how noble was the sacrifice! This Self is wonderful. What splendid secrets there are in it. How wonderful to see these secrets *unfold* to the light.

Gilbert Murray reported that the last phrase was spoken slowly, 'with perhaps a significant gesture of the hands to indicate unfolding'. Gould then proceeded to the core of his subject, the 'unfolding self'.

To late twentieth-century ears the climax of the demonstration may not sound attractive. Some may agree with the teacher who said Gould would better teach 'Service' by telling children to kick banana skins into the gutter. But Gould just exempted himself from being a Positivist Mr. Chadband by his power of story choosing and telling. The 'Self' lesson began with Samuel Johnson throwing away a pair of shoes given him by an anonymous Oxford benefactor; then came a tale from W. H. Hudson's *A Shepherd's Life* (1910) about how to deal with a drunk man, followed by an anecdote from a Leicester school manager and one about a Moslem student 'from a book of addresses by a Vedantic teacher, Swamy Ram Tirath'. The lesson concluded with an episode from the life of Helen Keller.

Throughout Gould wanted to show what had actually happened. The optimism of Positivism is easily denigrated, but the undirected use of imaginative writing with children is also not invulnerable: it can generate worse theoretical cant because the source of its authority is less easily verifiable. Positivism has the advantage of a reality principle in its appeal to actual history. Gould made another kind of appeal, to the world outside school, in which he found another source of authority. He believed that parents should come to the class-room: 'The college-trained mistress should be regarded rather as a valuable professional aid to the mother than as an official autocrat over somebody's else's child.' And in an 'idealised' sense every teacher should be a politician, involved in local affairs, able to 'hold periodical conference with the more enlightened civic administrators, business-men, and social workers of their district, in order to preserve a healthy relation between the school and the city or county'.[12]

At the turn of the century the Moral Instruction League had its moment. An incident and a conversation illustrate the general problems it had to face.

In July 1899 the M.I.L. took a petition to the School Management Committee of the London School Board, presenting the usual request for an alternative form of moral instruction in schools. The petition was signed by 512 parents, representing 1,086 children. It was handed in by Stanton Coit and received by Graham Wallas, then chairman of the committee. In 1902 Wallas had a lengthy conversation with Beatrice Webb, showing his insight into the barriers set against educational reform in the ethical and religious sphere, the barriers which ultimately frustrated the M.I.L., Gould and others. Wallas thought that the worst enemy of secular moral education was not the Church but the agnostic who still fears materialism. The superstitious agnostic was to some extent responsible for the passing of the Education Act of 1902, putting 'religion on the rates'. Beatrice Webb was impressed by Wallas's thinking on the subject:

He and I had a long discussion – walking on Marley Common – as to our respective positions with regard to denominational religion. He recognizes but deplores the growing tolerance of it, if not sympathy with religious teaching, on the part of the confessed agnostics. He distinguished with some subtlety between the old broad Church party, who wishes to broaden the creed of the Church to one they could emphatically accept, and those religious-minded agnostics who accept Church teaching, not because they believe its assertions to be true, but lest worse befall the child's mind in the form of a crude materialistic philosophy. 'I cannot see, [said Wallas] 'the spirit of genuine reform, if there is no portion of the Church's teaching which you object to more than any other: if you cease to discriminate between what you accept and what you reject, denying all and accepting all, with the same breath, denying the dogmas as statements of fact, accepting them as interpreting a spirit that pleases you. Dean Stanley and the broad churchmen were in a quite different position: they denied the Athanasian Creed and wished it ousted, they believed the Apostles' Creed and fervently and sincerely desired it to be taught.'[13]

Beatrice Webb regarded herself as 'a religious-minded agnostic'. She pondered what Wallas said.

For my own children, and those of other people, I deliberately believed the lie of materialism to be far more pernicious and more utterly false than the untruths which seem to me to constitute the Christian formula of religion. Moreover, we are face to face with the fact that the vast majority of the English people are, as far as they think at all, convinced Christians. By insisting on secular education, I should not only be helping to spread what seems to me a bad kind of falsehood, but I should be denying to others the right to have their children taught the creed they hold to be positively true. I see no way out of the dilemma, but the largest variety possible of denominational schools, so that there may be the utmost possible choice for parents and children.

The dilemma was widely felt, it not widely expressed so precisely. The Moral Instruction League was wise to trim the exclusively secularist doctrine from its programme of 1902. But in so doing it took a step towards the liberalism to which Beatrice Webb gave assent on this issue, so making it the less likely that an ethicist mode of secular instruction be established. The fear of 'crude materialistic philosophy was too great'.

Epilogue

In the early summer of 1980 the ethical movement was scrutinised within history as enacted, though not by a historian. The High Court of Chancery heard the claims of South Place to be charitable (on grounds that it was religious), and judgment was delivered by Mr. Justice Dillon. On the face of it it may appear perverse to regard the examination of one, always exceptional, society as a study of the movement, when no other societies were considered, and when there was even disagreement among members of South Place about the view of their society presented to the court. Nonetheless, in the course of five days a picture (or model) emerged of what an ethical society might be or might have been: the major features in the movement itself were, actually, adumbrated, even though each feature may not have been allocated to the correct period or group. Three issues stood out, by which we may characterise the ethical movement: *worship, humanism, Platonism.*

Symbolic public action – worship or celebration (principally) – were endemic to the movement. Naturally this occupied much attention in Chancery: two subsidiary ideas are worth teasing out for the consideration they provoke of the movement and its place in British intellectual life. The first relates to oriental religion, the second to English literature.

In court South Place claimed that it worshipped, but that it was not theist nor recognised supernatural beings. Buddhist worship was invoked analogically, for also not depending on such beliefs, though it was, according to the judge, 'accepted by anyone as being religious'. However, Mr. Justice Dillon declined to explore this analogy, 'because I do not know enough about Buddhism'. The interesting thing is that the ethical movement did not know enough about Buddhism, or non-European religion in general, except in the Conway years at South Place. But that epoch passed, the orient disappearing behind the palings of church and dissent which though thoroughly contradicted to a large extent defined the shape of the horizon of the movement. Not quite trivially it could be remarked that a feature of the ethical movement was that it never would have commanded the interest of a Christopher Isherwood, when it almost might have been expected to do so.

174

The question of English literature arose tangentially during the hearing, when counsel for the society intoned *sotto voce* Shakespeare's 113th sonnet, to illustrate the contents of a South Place wedding service. Literature, like oriental religion, played a relatively small part in the movement, but here a contrary response is called for: why should it have played a significant part? Literary ideology in the period of the ethical societies contained disdain for the 'progressive'. Moreover, it is only with the hindsight of a period in which British literature, as an educational force, has been awarded iconic status that the appreciation of poetry and fiction should seem a necessary part of handling the problems (often immediately practical ones) which mattered to the ethicists. It is this period which may have bestowed a patina of eccentricity upon the ethicists. It has been argued that the profession of literature teaching in the United Kingdom displaces (even enfeebles) its intelligentsias. The ethicists may belong to the world we have lost in this process. It is a world which may return.

The two other words around which cluster the continuous concerns of the ethical movement are *humanism* and *Platonism*. They were related to one another in a manner highly characteristic of the movement in Court Number 37 in June 1980. Peter Cadogan, as a spokesman for South Place, stated that the present congregation still regarded itself as 'humanist', at which counsel for the Attorney-General asked, 'How do you treat humanism? Religiously or secularly?' 'Secularly', replied Cadogan. 'The present members do not believe in God?' 'They are agnostic.' 'What, then, is meant by religion?', asked Mr. Mummery reasonably. Cadogan explained that the present congregation – some members in court winced to hear themselves so called – looked back to William Johnson Fox who was in 'the apocalyptic Platonic tradition'. Here *humanism* and *Platonism* were brought together in a way that few members of South Place or any other ethical society would thoroughly endorse. On the other hand the religious understanding of humanism was the special field of the ethical movement. Conceivably such understanding was best worked for before the movement itself was established, before South Place Religious Society became South Place Ethical Society, in the Conway years in which scepticism (to a degree actually rare among late twentieth-century liberals) and interest in religion were brought to a level certainly never rivalled later by the ethical societies' federation, the Ethical Union, which we saw in Chapter Five to have become, before World War I, increasingly cautious in its attitude to religion. It is true that a combination of scepticism and interest was theoretically possible in the Coit group – or would have been had this group not been required by Coit to operate from a manfactured church;

but this criticism must be advanced with some tenderness. As for Platonism, it is likely that Cadogan was guilty of a little over-interpretation. But still it was right for Plato to be invoked in a public study of ethicism, because it was to Plato that parts of the movement faithfully returned. In the 1890s the London society of Idealists and the West London society of Coitians could not have been further apart. But Muirhead and Coit reunited under the auspices of Plato (and Hartmann) in the early 1930s.[1]

Peter Cadogan made his claim about the apocalyptic Platonic tradition in cross-examination. Mr. Justice Dillon was visibly puzzled by it and intervened with Wykehamist diffidence, to enquire whether Platonism was a wing of Unitarianism. The question could only have been asked in the context of the British ethical societies.

Bibliographical Notes

Introductory

At the head of the notes to Chapters 2, 3 and 4 references are given to sources and to major pieces of discursive writing by the ethicists considered therein. The ethical movement was one of ideas, so it is by their writings (albeit now obscure) that the ethicists should be known. Throughout the notes place of publication is London or New York, unless otherwise indicated. When a later edition of a book has been used, the year of the first edition is given in square brackets.

Most of the journals to which reference is made published issues with very few pages, so for the sake of economy page numbers for these references are not given. The following abbreviations have been used for journals published by South Place Ethical Society (or chapel in its early years): *SPM, South Place Magazine*; *ML, The Monthly List*; *MR, The Monthly Record*; *ER, The Ethical Record. The Ethical World*, originally edited by Stanton Coit, was known successively in a short period as *Democracy* and *Ethics* as well. It has been called the *Ethical World* throughout and designated *EW*.

For the ethical movement in general there are some important sources. Two volumes of essays illustrate a variety of its voices in its heyday, both edited by Coit, though only the second is attributed to him: *Ethics and Religion: A Collection of Essays* (Swan Sonnenschein, 1900), with essays by Seeley, Adler, Salter, Sidgwick, Bosanquet, Stephen, Von Gizýcki, Muirhead, Coit, and *Ethical Democracy: Essays in Social Dynamics* (Grant Richards, 1900), with essays by Ritchie, Perris, MacDonald, Hobson, Muirhead, Vallance, Gould, McMillan, Collin, Coit.

The best repositories of material are the library and archives of South Place Ethical Society, Conway Hall, Red Lion Square, London WC1 4RL, and the book collection and archives of the British Humanist Assocation, 13 Prince of Wales Terrace, London W8 5PG. The British Library has an invaluable collection of material relating to societies catalogued under its 'London' heading.

For histories of the movement there is the compilation by Gustav Spiller, *The Ethical Movement in Great Britain: A Documentary History* (Farleigh Press, n.d. [1934]), and two doctoral dissertations: C. B. Campbell, 'Humanism and the Culture of the Professions: A Study of the Rise of the British Humanist Movement, 1946–1963' (University of London, 1968) and Susan Budd, 'The British Humanist Movement, 1860–1966' (University of Oxford, 1968), which is considerably more detailed than her *Varieties of Unbelief: Atheists and Agnostics, 1850–1950* (Heinemann, 1978). A long essay by a leading humanist should be noted: H. J. Blackham, 'The Ethical Movement during Seventy Years', *The Plain*

View (Ethical Union, January 1946). For the history of thinkers relevant to the movement *The Dictionary of National Biography* (Oxford, Oxford University Press, 1882–1960) must be given prominence because the perspective of its original editor, Leslie Stephen, was that of an ethicist.

Some useful books deal with the ethical movement or its milieu in passing: Paul Bloomfield, *Uncommon People: A Study of England's Elite* (Hamish Hamilton, 1955); Noel Annan, 'The Intellectual Aristocracy' in J. H. Plumb (ed.), *Studies in Social History: A Tribute to G. M. Trevelyan* (Longmans, Green, 1955); William Sylvester Smith, *The London Heretics, 1870–1914* (Constable, 1967); Melvin Richter, *The Politics of Conscience: T. H. Green and His Age* (Weidenfeld and Nicolson, 1964); Bernard Porter, *Critics of Empire: British Radical Attitudes to Colonialism in Africa, 1895–1914* (Macmillan, 1968); Peter Clarke, *Liberals and Social Democrats* (Cambridge, Cambridge University Press, 1978).

For the American ethical culture movement there is H. B. Radest, *Toward Common Ground: The Story of the Ethical Societies in the United States* (Frederick Ungar, 1969).

Prologue

1 L. P. Jacks, *The Legends of Smokeover* [1921], fifth impression (Hodder and Stoughton, n.d.), pp. 67–8); T. S. Eliot, 'Second Thoughts on Humanism' [1929], *Selected Essays*, enlarged edition (Faber, 1951), p. 484, but it is not completely clear whether he means Britain or America; A. J. P. Taylor, *The Trouble Makers: Dissent over Foreign Policy, 1792–1939* [1957], The Ford Lectures (Panther, 1969), p. 42.

1. Ethical Epoch

1 Strachey: Michael Holroyd, *Lytton Strachey: A Critical Biography*, 2 vols. (Heinemann, 1967–8) vol. 1, pp. 180–1. The good and the real at Cambridge: Hugh Dalton, *Call Back Yesterday: Memoirs, 1887–1931* (Muller, 1953), p. 55.

2 G. E. Moore, *Ethics* [1912], Home University Library of Modern Knowledge (Williams and Norgate; Thornton Butterworth, 1975), quoted because it is 'the book I myself like better than *Principia Ethica* because it seems to me to be so much clearer and less full of confusions and invalid arguments', in P. A. Schlipp (ed.), *The Philosophy of G. E. Moore* (Evanston and Chicago, Northwestern University Press, 1942), p. 27. J. S. Mackenzie, *Manual of Ethics* [1883], 4th edn (Noble, 1926), p. 341.

3 T. H. Green, *Prolegomena to Ethics*, 3rd edn (Oxford, Clarendon Press, 1890), pp. 351, 355–6. Henry Sidgwick, 'The Aims and Methods of an Ethical Society' in Coit's collection, *Ethics and Religion*, pp. 139–40.

4 Mrs. Mary Ward: William B. Patterson, *Victorian Heretic: Mrs. Humphry Ward's 'Robert Elsmere'* (Leicester, Leicester University Press, 1976), p. 92; Janet Rose Trevelyan, *The Life of Mrs. Humphry Ward, by her Daughter* (Constable, 1923), pp. 88, 59. The account of Robert is based on Chapters 14, 20, 22, 24, 25, 27, 32, 37, 38, 40 and 49 of *Robert Elsmere*. 'School of Green': R. G. Collingwood, *An Autobiography* [1939], (Oxford University Press, 1970), p. 17. London heterodoxy: Moncure Conway, *Autobiography* (see heading to Chapter 2 notes), vol. 2, pp. 144–5 and his *Idols and Ideals: With an Essay on Christianity* (Holt, 1877); note also Deborah Wormell, *Sir John Seeley and the Uses of History* (Cambridge, Cambridge University Press, 1980).

5 Arnold Toynbee, *Lectures on the Industrial Revolution in England: Popular Addresses, Notes and Other Fragments . . . With a Short Memoir by Benjamin Jowett* (Rivington, 1884), p. 318. Samuel Barnett: Beatrice Webb, *My Apprenticeship* (Longmans, Green, 1926), pp. 174–5. MacDonald's novel: Public Record Office, London, MacDonald Papers, 30/69 3A. MacDonald worked in a type of settlement in Bristol where he joined the Social Democratic Federation. He reported on American settlements in *EW* (12 February 1898): 'Republican surroundings preserve [them] from superior airs . . . they are civic centres.'

6 Gould: *The Life-Story of a Humanist* (Watts, 1923) and F. H. Hayward and E. M. White, *The Last Years of a Great Educationist: A record of the work and thought of F. J. Gould from 1923 to 1938* (Bungay, Suffolk, Clay, n.d. [1938]). Snell: his *Men, Movement, and Myself* (Dent, 1936). Gould is quoted from the Prologue and chapters 1–7 of *Life-Story*.

7 Gould: Prologue, chapters 1 to 7, *Life-Story*; Snell, chapters 2–9, *Men*. Both liberally quoted to illustrate their narrative techniques, as in the case of Mrs. Ward above.

8 J. W. Harvey, ed., *John Henry Muirhead: Reflections by a Journeyman in Philosophy on the Movement of Thought and Practice in his Time* (Allen and Unwin, 1942). The unpublished 'Where Goodness Dwells: An Essay on the Metaphysics of Value' is item 25 in the J. W. Harvey papers, Birmingham University Library. Hobson's austere autobiography is *Confessions of an Economic Heretic* (Allen and Unwin, 1938). Hobson's politics: David Caute, *The Fellow-Travellers: A Postscript to the Enlightenment* (Weidenfeld and Nicolson, 1973), p. 162. Early life of Muirhead and Hobson: *Reflections*, pp. 29–32, 60, *Confessions*, pp. 14–26.

9 Caird's reading from Green (section 261 in published *Prolegomena*): Muirhead, *Reflections*, p. 60. Mansel and Hamilton: Leslie Stephen's entries on them in *Dictionary of National Biography*, and Noel Annan, *Leslie Stephen: His Thought and Character in Relation to his Time* (MacGibbon and Kee, 1951), pp. 35, 152–4.

10 Extract of 'Where Goodness Dwells' is from Chapter 10, Section 3 ('Alleged Spinozism'), citing Browning's lines 182–90 of 'Bishop Blougram's Apology'. The ideal 'within' this world: see Bernard Bosanquet's fine prefatory essay, 'The Other World', to his translation, *The Introduction to Hegel's Philosophy of Fine Art* [1886], 2nd impression (Kegan Paul, 1905), pp. xvii–xxii.

11 Hobson and Mummery quoted from their *The Physiology of Industry: Being an Exposure of Certain Fallacies in Existing Theories of Economics* (Murray, 1889), pp. 154, 70, 11–12 and (on paradoxes) 126–7 Under-consumptionism: E. E. Nemmers, *Hobson and Underconsumptionism* (Amsterdam, North-Holland Publishing, 1956), p. 67. Waste: J. A. Hobson, *The Social Problem: Life and Work* (Nisbet, 1900), pp. 118–19 (sport and parasitism) and 125 (teaching, literature and social class). Philosophy and brewing at Birmingham University: Muirhead, *Reflections*, pp. 105–6. Mummery: Walter Unsworth, *Tiger in the Snow: The Life and Adventures of A. F. Mummery* (Gollancz, 1967).

12 Henry Sidgwick, *Practical Ethics: A Collection of Addresses and Essays* (Swan Sonnenschein, 1898), pp. 17–18, 56, 120, 138. See also Muirhead, *Reflections*, p. 82.

13 Sidgwick, *Practical Ethics*, pp. 11, 63 and *The Methods of Ethics* (Macmillan, 1874), pp. 67–8, 388.

14 Muirhead quoted from his *Elements of Ethics* (see introductory note to Chapter 3) pp. 82, 113, 121; period of its composition described in *Reflections*, p. 83.

15 *Natural Religion: By the Author of 'Ecce Homo'* (Macmillan, 1882) was based on papers in *Macmillan's Magazine* between 1875 and 1878. 'On the Constitution of the Church and State According to the Idea of Each' [1829], in John Colmer (ed.), *On the Constitution of the Church and State, The Collected Works of Samuel Taylor Coleridge* (London, Princeton, N.J., Routledge and Kegan Paul, Princeton University Press, 1976). For Seeley, see Wormell above and R. T. Shannon, 'J. R. Seeley and the Idea of a National Church' in Robert Robson (ed.), *Ideas and Institutions of Victorian Britain: Essays in Honour of George Kitson Clark* (Bell, 1967), and especially Sheldon Rothblatt, *The Revolution of the Dons: Cambridge and Society in Victorian England* (Faber, 1968).

16 *Church and State*, Chapter 3; language and society: S. T. Coleridge, *Biographia Literaria . . .*, edited by George Watson (Dent, 1956), p. 197.

17 *Church and State*, pp. 19, 42, 96–101.

18 J. R. Seeley, *Natural Religion*, pp. 141, 145, 181, 186, 208–9, 227–8 (with one paragraph division ignored). 'Ministry of journalism': Seeley, 'The Church as Teacher of Morality', *Lectures and Essays* (Macmillan, 1895), pp. 174–5, an essay which first appeared in W. L. Clay (ed.), *Essays on Church Policy* (Macmillan, 1868).

19 Felix Adler, *An Ethical Philosophy of Life, Presented in its Main Outlines* (Appleton, 1918), pp. 8–12. Some of the early lectures are in Adler's *Creed and Deed: A Series of Discourses* (Putnam, 1886). For his life and times: Horace L. Friess, *Felix Adler and Ethical Culture: Memories and Studies*, ed. by Fannia Weingartner (Columbia University Press, 1981) and Robert S. Guttchen, *Felix Adler* (Twayne, 1974). The significance of Lange and his history of materialism is shown by H. J. Blackham in his 'Ethical Movement' (see introductory bibliographical note), pp. 139–44.

2. South Place in Finsbury and Holborn

For W. J. Fox, see *Memorial Edition of Collected Works of W. J. Fox*, 12 vols. (Fox, Trübner, 1865–8); Conway: *Addresses and Reprints, 1850–1907* (Houghton, Mifflin, 1909), *Demonology and Devil-Lore* [1879], 2nd edn (Chatto and Windus, 1881), *The Earthward Pilgrimage* (Hotten, 1870), *The Life of Thomas Paine*, 2 vols. (Putnam, 1892): these are major and characteristic.

Prime source for South Place is its committee minutes, annual reports and journals, all preserved at Conway Hall, where there is also a videotape made by the society about itself for a BBC-TV 'Open Door' programme (27 January 1975). The British Library has some journals and ephemera. The early journals (*The Monthly Repository*, edited by Fox, and *South Place Pulpit*, by Barnett) say more about the editors than the society. The first true house-journal was *South Place Magazine* (April 1895 to September 1909), followed by *The Monthly List* of events, which became *The Monthly Record* in 1920, and as *The Ethical Record* survives to the present. For abbreviated titles of these, see general bibliographical headnote. Except for *ML* they printed summaries of many of the Sunday discourses; some discourses were transcribed or published by South Place where they are archived. For chamber music at South Place, see Rosemary Hughes, *The Musical Times* (February 1953).

Major secondary sources are: Moncure D. Conway, *Centenary History of South Place Ethical Society, based on four discourses given at the chapel in May and June, 1893, with an Appendix containing an address by Mr. Fox, in 1842, an original poem by Mrs. Adams* [i.e. Sarah Flower Adams] *and a discourse by Mr. Conway, 1893* (Williams and Norgate, 1904); Moncure Conway, *Autobiography: Memories and Experiences of Moncure D. Conway*, 2 vols. (Cassell, 1904); Richard Garnett, *The Life of W. J. Fox, Public Teacher and Social Reformer, 1786–1864*, completed after the author's death by Edward Garnett (Lane, 1910); John D'Entremont, *Moncure Conway, 1832–1907; American Abolitionist, Spiritual Architect of 'South Place', Author of the 'Life of Thomas Paine'*, 58th Conway Memorial Lecture (South Place Ethical Society, 1977); S. K. Ratcliffe, *The Story of South Place* (Watts, 1955), a brief, interesting, well-illustrated 'official' history. For the Fox period note a peripheral work, Francis E. Mineka, *The Dissidence of Dissent: 'The Monthly Repository', 1806–1838, under the Editorship of Robert Aspland, W. J. Fox, F. H. Horne, and Leigh Hunt; with a Chapter on Religious Periodicals, 1700–1825* (Chapel Hill, N. J., University of North Carolina, 1944).

1 Winchester: see William Vidler, *A Sketch of the Life of Elhanan Winchester, Preacher of the Universal Restoration, With a Review of his Writings* (T. Gillet, 1797). Relly: Walter Wilson, *The History and Antiquities of Dissenting Churches* ... (Button, Williams, Conder, 1808), vol. 1, pp. 358–9; 'Universalism at South Place', *ER* (June 1975).

2 Taylor, Wright and Aspland: *Dictionary of National Biography* entries; Scarlett, *Notes and Queries*, 6th Series, 9 (14 June 1884).

3 Fox: Garnett, *Life*, Chapter 2; Mineka, *Dissidence*, pp. 191, 256. His review of *Pauline: A Fragment of a Confession*, containing the praise of Channing, appeared in *Monthly Repository* in 1833, and is reprinted in *Memorial Edition*, vol. 6, pp. 213–25.

4 Sarah's letter: Conway, *Autobiography*, vol. 2, p. 24. Fox's domestic problems and chapel conflict: Garnett, *Life*, Chapter 5, and Martineau on 'fearless investigators', pp. 169–70.

5 Fox on education: Garnett, *Life*, pp. 300–5. Passage from 'On the Religious Ideas', *Memorial Edition*, vol. 8, p. 276.

6 Barnett: *South Place Pulpit* (May 1863), and Conway, *Centenary History*, p. 100.

7 Conway's appointment: *Autobiography*, vol. 2, pp. 35–45 and D'Entremont, *Moncure Conway*, pp. 17–19. Peter Taylor: *SPM* (February 1905).

8 Conway, *The Sacred Anthology (Oriental): A Book of Ethnical Scriptures* [1873], 5th edn (Trübner, 1889) and *Autobiography*, vol. 2, p. 299. On innocent piety: *Idols and Ideals: With an Essay on Christianity* (Trübner; Holt, 1877), pp. 9–10. Conway's obituary lament for Ellen Dana Conway: *SPM* (October 1897).

9 South Place Library and Institute: Annual Report, 1884, 1885. Conway as journalist and man of letters: Dennis Welland, *Mark Twain in England* (Chatto and Windus, 1978), pp. 54–6, 68–71 and by the same author, 'John Camden Hotten and Emerson's Uncollected Essays', *The Yearbook of English Studies* (1976),

Modern Humanities Research Association, pp. 155–75. Conway describes the cartoon in *Autobiography*, vol. 2, p. 357. It was published as a broadsheet under the name of 'Ion', first produced in the 1870s but revised by F. C. Gould in 1883. It is reproduced on the endpapers of W. S. Smith's *London Heretics* (see introductory bibliographical headnote).

10 Coit's appointment: Annual Report, 1886, 1887, and Spiller, *Ethical Movement*, pp. 24–33. It is not clear how well Conway knew Coit and whether he was invited to give the sample lectures at Conway's suggestion.

11 The clergyman wrote on Coit in *The Passing Day*, quoted in *EW* (25 March 1899), which published the lectures on *Robert Elsmere* and *Helbeck of Bannisdale* (13 and 20 August 1898). Coit's prickliness about being dined out is shown in a letter of 21 November 1891 to Conway from a member unknown, which also says that Coit was 'dreadfully hurt because Mr. Robertson (who has given us discourses on many occasions before Dr. Coit came) was invited to give some lectures at South Place after he had criticised Dr. Coit in the National Reformer [26 April 1891]'. This letter is in the Conway collection, Butler Library, Columbia University, a reference kindly supplied by John D'Entremont.

12 Information about members from *SPM* obituaries: Clarence H. Seyler (March 1906), W. J. Reynolds (November 1900), William Crowder (February 1902), Robert Hampson (April 1805); and from *MR*: Thomas Barralet (July 1923), Caroline Fletcher-Smith (March 1932). Coombe Hill School: F. G. Gould, 'An Educational Experiment', *EW* (19 March 1898), *SPM* (November 1905), and information supplied by Athene Seyler (Hannen). South Place rambles started in May 1887: *SPM* (April 1904).

13 J. M. Robertson and Hobson on Conway: *SPM* (December 1907). Conway on ethnology: *Autobiography*, vol. 2, pp. 302–13; Reynolds on hell-fire: *SPM* (November 1900).

14 Annie Besant quoted by Smith, *London Heretics*, pp. 18–19. Formulation of statement of belief: Annual Report, 1894, 1896. See H. J. Blackham, *ER*(July–August 1981) on the weakness of the conception of religious sentiment, interestingly citing William James.

15 Pro-Boer South Place: S. C. Cronwright-Schreiner, *The Land of Free Speech: Record of a Campaign of Peace in England and Scotland in 1900* (New Age Press, 1906), pp. 248–52. Contains a good photograph of the campaign's sponsor, Hobson.

16 Herbert Burrows: *ML* (September 1910, October 1922, January 1923).

17 J. M. Robertson: Archibald Robertson on his myth theory and Martin Page on his 'paradoxical genius' *MR* and *ER* (January 1957, September 1970). For a brief life by J. P. Gilmour (with bibliography and appreciations from Hobson, H. P. Bonner and Ernest Newman) see his introduction to Robertson's *A History of Freethought: Ancient and Modern, to the Period of the French Revolution* [1899], 4th edn reprinted (Dawson, 1969). See also John Gross, *The Rise and Fall of the Man of Letters: Aspects of English Literary life since 1900* (Weidenfeld and Nicolson, 1969). For his attitude to foreign policy, see parliamentary debates (4 August 1906, 22 July 1909). Robertson's critique of individual genius: *Montaigne and Shakespeare and Other Essays on Cognate*

Questions, 2nd edn (black, 1909), pp. 178, 289 and 'The Economics of Genius', *Essays in Sociology* (2 vols. Bonner, 1904), vol. 2, pp. 7–8.

18 'Make us a god' is number 204 in *Hymns of Modern Thought, Words and Music*, 2nd edn (South Place Ethical Society, 1912). The retention of hymns in their original forms was defended by A. S. Toms in a letter to *MR* (December 1925); he made other interesting contributions in *ML* (July, August 1913), *MR* (September, December 1927). The appearance of the chapel: photograph in William Kent, *London for Heretics* (Watts, 1932), and see C. Maurice Davies *Heterodox London or Phases of Free Thought in the Metropolis* [1874] (Kelley, 1969).

19 Plans for rebuilding: Annual Report, 1901, 1912; *ML* (July 1912, August 1919), *MR* (April 1923). Frank Overy: obituary, *MR* (September 1932) and Peter Cadogan, '1929–1979: Fifty Years at Conway Hall. Anniversary Lecture', *ER* (October 1979), containing also an overview of the transition to Conway Hall.

20 Ratcliffe: obituary, *MR* (October 1958). Delisle Burns: obituary by Ratcliffe, *MR* (May 1942 and see June 1942); his League of Nations address: *MR* (November 1924). Quotations from *The First Europe: A Study of the Establishment of Mediaeval Christendom, A.D. 400–800* [1947], 2nd impression (Allen and Unwin, 1949), pp. 55–6. Circumstances of its publication: letter from Margaret Delisle Burns to Jim Middleton (15 February 1942) Labour Party Library Middleton Papers, obituary file.

21 F. H. Mansford: obituary, *MR* (July 1946), *Journal of the Royal Institute of British Architects* (August 1946), *Middlesex Advertiser and County Gazette* (21 June 1946). Conway Hall: reviews in *The Architects' Journal* (25 September 1929).

22 Early days in Conway Hall: letters to the author from Percy Sowter (16 May 1982) and Edith Washbrook (4 May 1982). Archibald Robertson: his memories, *MR* (October 1961); obituary, *MR* (January 1962). The Marxist Robertson debated ethicism vigorously, notably in exchanges with H. J. Blackham in *The Plain View* in which see his 'Ethics in a Changing World' (April 1946) and Blackham (October 1946, January 1949), Robertson (April 1949, Summer 1949). John Lewis: interview, *ER* (May 1972), obituary, *ER* (April 1976).

23 Blackham: interview, *ER* (January 1972). On Huxley and Coit: letter to the author (11 February 1983). Huxley: Blackham on, *ER* (September 1975) and his *Religion Without Revelation*, 'What I Believe' series (Benn, 1927), p. 339.

24 Sorensen, Brockway: *ER* (January, February 1972).

25 Hawton: interview, see note 29. Hutton Hynd: biographical sketch, *MR* (September 1947). See his mournful criticism of 'simple humanism', *ER* (September–October 1967) in the Ethical Union as anti-religious radicalism masquerading as the sum of British humanism. Cadogan: interview, *ER* (June 1972). On his 'having to go', despite being forward-looking, letter to the author from Percy Sowter (see note 22).

26 Cadogan on the Red Lion Square incident: *ER* (July–August, September 1974). Lewis on Potsdam agreement: *ER* (November–December 1974). Lovecy: flysheet, 'An Appeal to Prevent Decline and Fall at Conway Hall' (21 September 1977). Banned anarchists: Annual Report (1893). Camden Council resolved on 17 November 1976 that it re-affirmed 'its fundamental belief in the freedom of speech within the law but its facilities shall not be let or licensed to organisations which . . . attempt to incite racial hatred . . .' requesting grant-aided bodies to do likewise. Bernard Levin: *The Times*, 20 February 1980.

27 Conduct of weddings: *ER* (April, May 1977).

28 Cadogan on the continuity of the society: *ER* (July–August 1978). Nicholas Walter: *ER* (September 1980). The South Place defence: see papers for special general meeting (16 April 1975), *ER* (July–August 1971), Lovecy's flysheet, 'Information concerning the South Place Ethical Society'. Cadogan's view of organised humanism: *ER* (February, March, April, May), with rebuttal from Blackham, *New Humanist* (September–October 1979) and Smoker, *ER* (June 1979). See also statement on his revision of contract to part-time status, *ER* (July–August 1979).

29 Simple humanism: interviews with Hawton and Smoker, *ER* (November–December 1972, February 1973).

30 Lovecy: on the society and religion, *ER* (February 1972) and his flysheet, 'A Plea for Constructive Thinking on Charity Law'.

31 The Chancery hearing (3–11 June 1980): *The Weekly Law Reports* (19 December 1980), 1573E–1577C (the judgment).

32 The Cadogan–Smoker dispute in its earliest stage: *ER* (November–December 1979). Blackham on 'rational religious sentiment': *ER* (July–August 1981), and note 'South Place: From Unitarianism to Ethical Humanism', *New Humanist* (Spring 1981).

3. Bloomsbury and the Strand: the London Ethical Society

The following works, among many, by associates of this philosophers' ethical society are important: F. H. Bradley, *Ethical Studies* 2nd edn, 'revised, with additional notes by the author' (Oxford, Clarendon Press, 1927); J. H. Muirhead, *The Elements of Ethics* [1892], University Extension Manuals, 2nd edn, 'revised and enlarged (new impression)' (Murray, 1906); J. H. Muirhead, *The Platonic Tradition in Anglo-Saxon Philosophy: Studies in the History of Idealism in England and America* (Allen and Unwin, 1931); Bernard Bosanquet, 'Life and Philosophy', *Contemporary British Philosophy; Personal Statements, First Series*, edited by J. H. Muirhead (Allen and Unwin, 1924); Edward Caird, 'Metaphysic' in his *Essays on Literature and philosophy*, 2 vols. (Glasgow, Maclehose, 1892), containing an excellent index; R. L. Nettleship (ed.), *The Works of Thomas Hill Green*, 3 vols. (Longman, 1885) and T. H. Green, *Prolegomena to Ethics* [1883] edited by A. C. Bradley, 3rd edn (Oxford, Clarendon Press, 1890).

The social and personal history in this chapter is based on memoirs, ephemera of the London Ethical Society and unpublished writings, informal and otherwise. The leading memoirs of J. H. Muirhead, *Reflections* (see note 8 to Chapter 1); of T. H. Green, see *Works* above; of Edward Caird in Sir Henry Jones and J. H. Muirhead, *The Life and Philosophy of Edward Caird, Ll.D., D.C.L.* (Glasgow, Maclehose and Jackson, 1921); and in Helen Bosanquet, *Bernard Bosanquet and his Friends: Letters illustrating the Sources and Development of his Philosophical Opinions* (Allen and Unwin, 1935). Annual Reports, syllabuses, flysheets and other L.E.S. material are in the British Library (catalogued under London societies) and Newcastle University Library, for which see *Bosanquet Papers:*

Handlist, 2nd edn. (Newcastle: University Library, 1973). This collection contains letters by Mrs. M. S. G. Husband, and her summary of the evidently lost society minute books, prepared for the use of Helen Bosanquet. The activities of the L.E.S. are described in more detail in I. D. MacKillop, 'The London School of Ethics and Social Philosophy: an adult education movement of the 1890s', *History of Education*, 7 (1978).

1 Interview in F. J. Gould, *Chats with Pioneers of Modern Thought*, reprinted from *The Literary Guide* (Watts, 1898), pp. 106–10; also contains interviews with Coit, Conway, W. C. Coupland, and Mrs. Gilliland Husband.

2 Jones: H. J. W. Hetherington, *The Life and Letters of Sir Henry Jones* (Hodder and Stoughton, 1924), p. 20. Caird's *Encyclopaedia Britannica* is in *Essays*: see especially the third section. Muirhead isolates two key works, 'perhaps the simplest and clearest statement of the central difficulty in Kant and in Caird's own metaphysics': Caird's *Hegel*, Philosophical Classics for English Readers (Edinburgh and London, Blackwood, 1883), Chapter 6, and Caird's reply to J. Hutchinson Stirling, dealing with contradictions in Kant, 'Professor Caird replies to Dr. Stirling' and 'Kant's Deductions of the Categories, with special relation to the views of Dr. Stirling', *The Journal of Speculative Philosophy*, 13 and 14 (St. Louis, Miss., October 1879, January 1880).

3 Muirhead on Spencer, Stephen and Clifford: *Elements*, pp. 136–59. He alludes to Clifford's 'On the Scientific Basis of Morals', *Essays and Lectures* (Macmillan, 1879), edited by Leslie Stephen and Frederick Pollock. Muirhead is quoted from the enlarged edition of *Elements* (see headnote to this chapter). In *Reflections* he criticises the callowness of this book, regretting when he wrote it that he had not fully absorbed Bradley's *Appearance and Reality* (1893), which he had known before its publication as it appeared in his 'Library of Philosophy'. Muirhead's mature view was that he had been uncritical of Hegel's equation of the real and the rational and that Bradley gave him greater understanding of feeling, as essential an element in experience as perceiving and thinking: *Reflections*, p. 100. Spencer's satire is in Chapter 1 of *The Man Versus the State*, 'The New Toryism'.

4 Bosanquet: *Contemporary British Philosophy*, p. 58 and letter from Muirhead (24 December 1922), Bosanquet Papers.

5 University Hall and Manchester New College: V. D. Davis, *A History of Manchester New College: from its Foundation to its Establishment in Oxford* (Allen and Unwin, 1932); Stephen Kay Jones, *Dr. Williams and His Library* (Cambridge, Friends of Dr. Williams' Library, 1948); Anonymous, *List of Professors, Lecturers and Principal Officers, and a Roll of Students of Manchester New College, London, 1866–1889; Manchester New College, Oxford, 1889–1893; Manchester College, Oxford, 1893–1899* (Oxford, Manchester College, 1899). Useful on Unitarianism: C. G. Bolam and others, *The English Presbyterians: from Elizabethan Puritanism to Modern Unitarianism* (Allen and Unwin, 1968).

6 Muirhead on M.N.C: *Reflections*, pp. 64–5, part of a beautifully written, generously critical account. R. H. Lotze, on whom C. B. Upton worked, was important for L.E.S. sympathisers; on him: John Passmore, *A Hundred Years of Philosophy*, 2nd edn (Duckworth, 1966), pp. 46–50 and P. G. Kuntz introducing George Santayana, *Lotze's System of Philosophical Idealism* [1890] (Bloomington, Ind., Indiana University Press, 1971). James Ward admired Lotze, as did

R. B. Haldane: Eric Ashby and Marjorie Anderson, *Portrait of Haldane at Work on Education* (Macmillan, 1974), pp. 7–9. Haldane and Andrew Seth (A. S. Pringle-Pattison) prepared and edited the seminal work, prefaced by Caird, of British Idealism, *Essays in Philosophical Criticism* (Longmans, 1883); Muirhead called Haldane's contribution to it 'the first clear statement of the view of the relation of philosophy to science in general and of the categories of the particular sciences to one another', *Platonic Tradition*, p. 179.

7 Croom Robertson: 'Philosophy in London', *Mind: A Quarterly Review of Psychology and Philosophy*, 1 (1876), pp. 531–44, following previous articles on the state of the university discipline in Oxford, Cambridge and Dublin, and Alexander Bain and T. Whittaker (eds.), *The Philosophical Remains of George Croom Robertson, With a Memoir* (Williams and Norgate, 1894). University College: Anonymous, *Notes and Materials for the History of University College, London: Faculties of Arts and Sciences* (University College, 1898), prefaced by W. P. Ker.

8 Early L.E.S.: Spiller, *Ethical Movement*, pp. 1–4; Muirhead, *Reflections*, 74–6; manuscript notes by Mrs. Husband in Bosanquet Papers.

9 James Bonar: his diary (evidently lost) says that he attended two pilot meetings on 19 May and 8 June 1886, so he probably helped Muirhead with the initial manifesto (Spiller, *Ethical Movement*, p. 2); his career: *Dictionary of National Biography*. Chubb: Stanley Pierson, *British Socialists: The Journey from Fantasy to Politics* (Cambridge, Mass., Harvard University Press, 1979), pp. 7–12, quoting his letters to Davidson. The initial meetings of Fabians and New Lifers, and settlement in London of north British intellectuals: Willard Wolfe, *From Radicalism to Socialism: Men and Ideas in the Formation of Fabian Socialist Doctrine, 1881–1889* (New Haven and London, Yale University Press, 1975), pp. 157–9.

10 Bosanquet: 'Individualism and Socialism', delivered to the Fabian Society (21 February 1890), appearing in his *The Civilisation of Christendom and Other Essays* [1893] (Swan Sonnenschein, 1899). Shaw: Sydney Caine, *The History of the Foundation of the London School of Economics and Political Science* (University of London, 1963), p. 197. Muirhead on public opinion: *Reflections*, p. 87.

11 Bryant: 'An Old North Londoner' (Edith A. Jackson), *Mrs. Sophia Bryant, D.Sc., Litt.D.*, (Glasgow and London, McCorquodale, 1922), M. Vivian Hughes, *A London Girl of the Eighties* (Oxford University Press, 1936), with photograph, Sara A. Burstall, *Frances Mary Buss: An Educational Pioneer* (S.P.C.K., 1938) and Josephine Kamm, *How Different from Us: A Biography of Miss Buss and Miss Beale* (Bodley Head, 1958). Wicksteed: C. H. Herford, *Philip Henry Wicksteed: His Life and Work* (London and Toronto, Dent, 1931).

12 Location of classes: Mortimer Rowe, *The Story of Essex Hall* (Lindsey, 1959), p. 47. University Extension: Richard G. Moulton, *The University Extension Movement* (Bemrose, n.d. [1887]) and the detailed records in *The University Extension Journal*, first appearing in 1890; archival records appear to be lost. De Glehn: letter to Bosanquet (7 February 1895), Bosanquet Papers. 'Continuing education': Benjamin Jowett, *The Republic of Plato: Translated into English*, 3rd edn (Oxford, Clarendon Press, 1888), pp. ccx–ccxi. Henry Balfour Gardiner's gruff annotations are in the author's copy of *Prolegomena* (see headnote). Mrs. Husband's admiration for Bosanquet's course: letter to R. C. Bosanquet (25 August 1925). The romance of Idealism: Muirhead, *Platonic Tradition*, p. 171; Jones and Muirhead, *Life and Philosophy of Caird*, p. 33.

13 Muirhead working for philosophy: *Reflections*, pp. 90–3 on his apprenticeship in Bloomsbury. Plans for reform of London University: Ashby and Anderson, *Portrait of Haldane*, pp. 27–8, 32–40. L.S.E.S.P.: Mrs. Husband's notes in Bosanquet Papers, including 'Memorandum on the Work of the London School of Ethics and Social Philosophy, June 1899'. Richard Wollheim on psychology quoted from his *F. H. Bradley*, 2nd edn (Harmondsworth, Penguin, 1969), pp. 130–1. Psychology at University College: H. Hale Bellot, *University College, London, 1826–1926* (University of London, 1929), p. 388. Bain: James Sully, *My Life and Friends: A Psychologists's Memories* (Fisher Unwin, 1918), pp. 244–5. The disclaimer of competition by the L.S.E.S.P. is a typescript memorandum in Bosanquet Papers dated November 1899. 'Finding one's millionaire': Muirhead (ed.), *Bernard Bosanquet*, p. 93; the last meeting, Third Annual Report (1899–1900). Muirhead, *Reflections*, p. 89, closes his account of the school by saying that it was finally directed by E. J. Urwick and taken over by the London School of Economics and Political Science, where Urwick became the first Professor of Social Philosophy. In fact, Urwick became director of a School of Sociology, which was absorbed into the L.S.E., but it was not a direct extension of the L.S.E.S.P., despite Bosanquet saying 'We – that is really the Charity Organisation Society – invented and started the thing (of course it doesn't fly the C.O.S. flag)': it was for training social-workers and grew out of economics classes begun by the Women's University Settlement. See Bosanquet, *Bernard Bosanquet*, pp. 54–5 and Marjorie J. Smith, *Professional Education for Social Work in Britain: An Historical Account* [1953, as pamphlet] (Allen and Unwin, 1965). Urwick: H. J. Cody's introduction to H. A. Innis (ed.), *Essays in Political Economy in Honour of E. J. Urwick* (Toronto, University of Toronto, 1938).

14 Legacy of L.S.E.S.P.: Muirhead, *Elements of Ethics*, pp. 145–6 and *Reflections*, p. 97; F. A. Mumby and Frances H. S. Stallybrass, *From Swan Sonnenschein to George Allen and Unwin Ltd* (Allen and Unwin, 1955), pp. 35–9. The Institute: 'The British Institute of Philosophic Studies', brochure containing essay on the value of studying philosophy and *Manchester Guardian* article (2 April 1925) reproduced.

4. Bayswater: Stanton Coit's Ethical Church

Necessary works of Coit are: *National Idealism and a State Church: A Constructive Essay in Religion* (Williams and Norgate, 1907), *National Idealism and the Book of Common Prayer: An Essay in Re-interpretation and Revision* (Williams and Norgate, 1908), *The Soul of America: A Constructive Essay in the Sociology of Religion* (Macmillan, 1914), *Neighbourhood Guilds: An Instrument of Social Reform* (Swan Sonnenschein, 1891).

Coit's life: F. W. Chapman, *The Coit Family or the Descendents of John Coit who appears among the settlers of Salem, Mass., in 1638, at Gloucester in 1644 and at New London, Conn., in 1650* (Hartford, Conn., Lockwood and Brainard, 1874); R. S. Fletcher and M. O. Young, *Amherst College Biographical Record of the Graduates and Non-Graduates: Centennial Edition, 1821–1921* (Amherst, Mass., Amherst College, 1939); H. J. Blackham, *Stanton Coit, 1857–1944: Selections from his Writings with a Prefatory Memoir* (Favil, n.d. [1948]) and Blackham in *South*

Place Magazine (December 1948); George O'Dell, *News and Notes* (September 1957). Coit began an autobiography of which a typescript fragment survives, 'My Ventures on the Highway of Truth', in keeping of the Coit (Flemming) family with whose permission it is quoted. As shown in this chapter, Coit is portrayed in novels by R. O. Prowse and on the stage in Israel Zangwill, *The Next Religion* (Heinemann, 1912) and in St. John E. C. Hankin, 'The Charity Which Begins at Home', *Three Plays with Happy Endings* (French, 1907).

For the Ethical Church, note especially Jean Wagner, *La Religion de l'Idéal Morale: Etude sur les sociétés de culture morale en Angleterre* (Lausanne, 1914) and *A Souvenir of the Ethical Church, with Thirty-Six Illustrations* (Ethical Church, 1917). The remains of Coit's library are at South Place and the British Humanist Association (B.H.A.) which also possesses some personalia and newspaper cuttings collected by Coit.

1 Early life: 'Ventures'. Coit on Kant: *EW* (9 April 1898); on supernaturalism: *National Idealism and a State Church*, pp. 155–6. Spiritualism: Emma Hardinge (Britten), *Modern American Spiritualism: A Twenty Years' Record of the Communion between Earth and the World of Spirits*, 3rd edn (New York, privately printed, 1870).

2 Emerson: 'Address delivered before the Senior Class in Divinity College, Cambridge, Sunday Evening, July 15, 1838' and 'Worship'.

3 Settlements: R. A. Woods and A. J. Kennedy, *The Settlement Horizon* [1922] (Arno, 1970), *The Christian Union* (New York, 5 January 1888). Conway's letter of support: Spiller, *Ethical Movement*, pp. 25–7. Leighton Hall mural: Henry Holiday, *Reminiscences of My Life* (Heinemann, 1913), pp. 452–3, 460; for later history of these designs, Executive Minutes of the Labour Party, 11 December 1913, 9 February 1914, and *The Daily Citizen* (14 November 1913). Leighton Hall produced the short-lived *Moscheles Review*, later *The Neighbourhood Guild Review*.

4 L.E.S./W.L.E.S. coalition: Spiller, *Ethical Movement*, pp. 63–6, Muirhead, *Reflections*, pp. 75, 89. Hegel: Gould, *Chats*, p. 79.

5 Mrs. Coit: obituary by Harry Snell, *The Literary Guide* (December 1932).

6 Ethical Propagandists: *EW* (19 March 1901); Quilter, quoted from *EW* (31 December 1898). Collin: *Ethical Democracy*, pp. 293–4. Fechheimer's later career at Cambridge University Day Training College: Ian Anstruther, *Oscar Browning: A Biography* (Murray, 1983), pp. 156–8.

7 Coit letters: MacDonald Papers, Public Record Office, London 5/9 (1 December 1899), 5/10 (16 April 1900). Proposal of democratic convention and new party, notably *EW* of 1900: Coit (6 January, 14 July), Barnes (17 February), MacDonald (10 March, 17 February), both unsigned but Coit indicates MacDonald's authorship (16 April), Massingham (7 April), J. F. Green (28 July), S. G. Hobson (4 August, 29 September). Socialism and ethical movement (19 October 1901, 1 March, 15 February 1902), Coit's resignation (8 March 1902). Union of Ethical Societies, Battersea, socialism: congress minutes (5 July 1896, 27 February 1902). Coit's newspaper cuttings have items about his American campaign in winter of 1900.

8 Coit at Wakefield: Labour Representation Committee (L.R.C.), 11/488, 10/230 and 10/99, Labour Party Library, London.

9 Wakefield campaign, see notably the *Echo*; it and other local papers: J. W.

Walker, *Wakefield: Its History and People* [1934], 2nd edn, 2 vols. (Wakefield, privately printed, 1939), vol. 2, p. 565. Coit's slogans: his 1906 and 1910 election addresses.

10 O'Dell alleges the Pankhurst connection in a cutting from *The Standard* in Coit's collection at the B.H.A.; Coit and East Birmingham: Labour Party General Correspondence (L.P.G.C.), Labour Party Library, 12/11, 21/429–32.

11 Evolution of Ethical Church: its committee minutes, including those when it was West London Ethical Society, and minutes of council and congresses of Union of Ethical Societies, and the papers at B.H.A. of Coit, Prowse, and O'Dell. Bosanquet on conflict between those of like mind: *Civilisation of Christendom*, p. 314; Budd on '*only* a religion' uniting left-wing groups: *Varieties*, p. 280. Alex F. Dawn: letter to the author (9 October 1977).

12 'Ten Commandments . . .', 'England as Organic Unit': *EW* (3 October, 26 November 1904); and *National Idealism and the Book of Common Prayer*, p. 4.

13 Five-point programme: *EW* (31 December 1904). The use of 'Ten Words' and 'Universal Litany' only agreed by close vote on 27 March and 3 April 1911. The suggested forms in *National Idealism and the Book of Common Prayer* were elaborated in Coit, *Two Responsive Services in the Form and Spirit of the Litany and the Ten Commandments for Use in Families, Schools, and Churches* (W.L.E.S., 1911). Coit claimed he valued his creed more than the church at E.C. committee meeting (5 October 1934).

14 Stages of purchase of chapel: W.L.E.S. minutes of 1909.

15 R. O. Prowse: *The Prophet's Wife* (Gollancz, 1929), pp. 205, 210–11 and *James Hurd* (Heinemann, 1913) pp. 328–45. Details of E.C. activities: Wagner, *La Religion*, pp. 56–66. When the church ceased altar and stained glass were given to Trinity College of Music, and the Crane painting to the Tate Gallery; other artefacts were dispersed in the B.H.A., many subsequently lost. Coit's 'normality': *Social Worship*, p. xxxi and Budd, *Varieties*, pp. 242–3.

16 Coit's Durkheim (trans. Swain): marked '2nd reading begun Aug 22, '23, finished Aug 25, '23. 3rd reading begun Aug 25, '23, finished August 25, '23' (*sic*: Alex Dawn recalls that he was a fast reader). Quotations and annotations from pp. 416–18. Coit wrote on the back endpaper: 'Durkheim's theory of social psychology is an excellent correction to Freud, Adler, Le Bon', with reference to p. 17. He owned the French (1912) edition, but read it with less passion, though its endpaper is inscribed 'Persist!' With the E.C. or Durkheim? The responses: *National Idealism and the Book of Common Prayer*, pp. 218–39. T. S. Eliot: 'Introduction' to Tennyson, Hayward (ed.), *Selected Prose* (Harmondsworth, Penguin, 1955), p. 183. Coit on James: *National Idealism and a State Church*, pp. 3–23.

17 Humanism: F. H. Bradley, 'On Truth and Practice', *Mind*, 31 (1904), pp. 309–35; Spiller: *EW* (19 November, 3 December 1904). 'The younger Oxford': Prowse, *James Hurd*, pp. 176–7.

18 The advertisement: *The Literary Guide* (December 1932). Coit read Hook, 'A Critique of Ethical Realism', *International Journal of Ethics*, 40 (January 1930), pp. 179–210: see especially pp. 185, 191. Coit collected reviews; notably see: Howard O. Eaton, 'The Unity of Axiological Ethics', *International Journal of Ethics*, 43 (October 1932); C. E. M. Joad, 'A World of Value', *New Statesman and Nation* (7 April 1932); J. L. Stocks, *Philosophy*, 7 (October 1932); J. E. Turner,

The Hibbert Journal, 31 (October 1932); J. S. Mackenzie, *Mind*, 42 (April 1933). Note especially F. L. Cross, 'Nicolai Hartmann', *Church Quarterly Review* (January, July 1932). Muirhead's struggle: *Platonic Tradition*, pp. 437–41, and on Hartmann's place in the sequence of Idealism, Nicolai Hartmann, *Ethics*, translated by Stanton Coit (Macmillan 1932), vol. 1, pp. 3–4; pp. 40–1 also quoted, with paragraphs run together.

19 Coit: L. L. Riley, 'Hitler's State Religion: An Interview with Dr. Stanton Coit', *The Churchman* (1 October 1933). Religious institutes: *Soul of America*, pp. 108–9. Virginia Coit: *The Ethical Church: A Lecture delivered by Mrs Virginia Coit Flemming to the Society for the Study of Religions* (Ethical Church, n.d. [1938]), final paragraph. Coit as Broad Churchman: Blackham, *Stanton Coit*, pp. 12–15, *ER* (December 1938). Vallance: *EW* (3, 10 January 1903). Explicitness: *Social Worship*, vol. 1, p. ix.

5. The Ethical Movement

1 Gould: *Life-Story*, pp. 75–7 (see note 6 to Chapter 1).

2 The ethical societies: Spiller, *Ethical Movement*, minute books of individual societies and of the Ethical Union (at the British Humanist Association, mostly un-catalogued), ethicist periodicals (especially *South Place Magazine*, *The Ethical Societies Chronicle*). Meetings on 20 March 1901 taken from *EW* weekly listing. The total figure of forty-two ethical societies calculated not by totting up: it is Coit's figure in *National Idealism and a State Church*, p. 82. He was in the best position to know the number of societies – and there were ethicists enough to contradict exaggeration. Ethical Religion Society: *EW* (19 March, 2 April 1898), and see W. R. Washington Sullivan, *Morality as a Religion: An Exposition of Some First Principles* (Swan Sonnenschein, 1898). Coit and Labour Churches: *EW* (25 May 1901). 'Belsize this or that': Ivor Brown, *The Way of My World* (Collins, 1954), pp. 46–7.

3 Snell: his *'Fifty Years of Religious Progress' and 'The Ethical Movement'* (Ethical Union, 1926), two essays in pamphlet form, p. 5. Painful experiences in church: Walter Gregory (East London society) and Mrs. Seaton-Tiedmann (member of Council of Ethical Societies for twenty-five years and vice-chairman from 1924) in *Ethical Societies Chronicle* (May 1931, March 1925). As for the speech accents of ethicists, two leaders were idiosyncratic: Hobson's staccato was often noted and one hearer compared Coit's speech to that of an Orkney Islander, with its 'clearness and precision'. He said that his mid-West accent was modified by contact with the L.E.S. Scotsman: Frank Hall in *Tributes to Stanton Coit* (Ethical Church, 1944). Harrison: his *Autobiographic Memoirs* (Macmillan, 1911), vol. 2, pp. 260–4, quoting himself from *The Pall Mall Gazette* (29 November 1883).

4 Union policies: Council and annual congress minute books.

5 Blackham: *Puzzled People* . . . (Gollancz, 1945), pp. 8–9, and see p. 158. Blackham's position well expressed in *The Plain View* (January 1945), especially in references to review in *The Times Literary Supplement* (29 July 1944) which he found ominously favouring a return to Christianity. See also note 22 to Chapter 2 above. Ethics and Economics trust: *Plain View* (July 1946). Spiller on ethicist generalisations: *Ethical Movement*, p. 102.

6 Turn of century pessimism compared to sense of 'going' twenty years before: C. F. G. Masterman, *The Heart of the Empire: Discussions of Problems of Modern City Life in England. With an Essay on Imperialism* (Fisher Unwin, 1902), p. 2. Perris: *EW* (26 January 1901); 'Fabius Maximus', newspapers, democratic passion, marginality of Labour politics (3, 24 September, 18 June, 26 February 1898).

7 Heroes of righteousness: *EW* of 1898 (18 June); Ashton (5 February), Stansfeld (26 February), Grey (1 October), Merrington (1 January). MacDonald on Gladstone and culture: *EW* (28 May, 4, 18 June, 2 July 1898). Liberalism: *EW* (24 December 1898). Morley: *EW* (3 February, 16 June 1900). Courtney: Beatrice Webb, *Our Partnership* (Longmans, 1948), p. 199 (diary entry for 19 July 1900).

8 Vallance: the major statement in her posthumous essays, 'The Ethical Movement and Women': *EW* (24, 31 December 1904). Her first contribution, 'Men, Women, and Justice': *EW* (18 March 1899). Midwives' Registration Bill and Act; L.C.C. elections; chauvinist S.D.F. speaker; Ruskin: *EW* (11, 18 June, 30 July 1898, 5 April 1902; 23 February 1901; 15 September, 27 October 1900; 5 May, 9 June 1900). Vallance praises Coit on women; reviews Catholic psychologist (Laura Marholme): *EW* (17 November 1900; 9 December 1899). MacDonald on women's rights; letter from E. C. W. Elmy on suffrage: *EW* (11 February 1899, 6 October 1900).

9 Imperialism in *EW* of 1898: craze for expansion (12 February); American expansion; MacDonald on America and empire (12 November; 9 July). MacDonald series on 'Ethics and Empire' (5, 12, 19 November); Hobson on ' "Expansion" in the Light of Sociology' (19 November), and on 'The White Man's Burden' (18 February 1899). *EW* policy on imperialism, 'The Passing Hour' (19 May 1900). More important Hobson *EW* contributions (9 December, 18 March 1899, 10, 24 February 1900). Ritchie's first critique of Hobson–*EW* attitudes (13 January). The main contributions to the subsequent debate in *EW* of 1900: Ritchie's second attack and *EW* defends Hobson, 'The Passing Hour' (10 March); the policy 'of smash', 'The Passing Hour', and letters, of which the most significant are from 'A Student of International Law' and 'A Woman Fabian', scorning her Society's imperial policy (17 March). Hobson replies to Ritchie who has rejoinder (24, 31 March); Bernstein intervenes (12, 26 May), with editorials (12, 19 May), and article by MacDonald (2 June).

10 Gould: *Life-Story* (see note 6 to Chapter 1), pp. 8, 38–41, 46–8. Gould is in this section freely quoted and paraphrased as was Mrs. Mary Ward in Chapter 1 to show habits of mind (in this case those of a masterly story-teller), Gould published prolifically: apart from usual collections, the one in the London University Institute of Education Library (donated by the ethicist L.C.C. school inspector, F. H. Hayward) should be examined. Cross Commission: *Elementary Education Acts: Second Report of the Royal Commission appointed to enquire into the Working of the Elementary Education Acts (England and Wales)* (Cmnd 5056, 1887); for Diggle (examined 9 February 1887), p. 540, and Crosskey (30 March, 5 April 1887), pp. 932–4, 968. London curriculum quoted from this Commission's *Final Report* (Cmnd 5485, 1888), p. 497–500. Problems of secularism: James Allanson Picton, *The Bible in School: A Question of Ethics* (Watts, 1902), p. 40 in the useful chapter on 'New Religious Disabilities', and see *Record of the First*

Moral Education Congress . . . September 25–29th, 1908 (1908). The most detailed study of the debate on secularism is Benjamin Sacks, *The Religious Question in the State Schools of England and Wales, 1902–1914: A Nation's Quest for Human Dignity* (Albuquerque, University of New Mexico, 1961).

11 School Board propaganda: Spiller, *Ethical Movement*, pp. 124–30. Problems of 'withdrawal' from state schools: 'Moral Instruction in State Schools', *EW* (18 May 1901). Harrold Johnson: *Unitarian Year Book* (1940). The *Syllabus* appeared in *EW* (12 April 1902). On 'The Passing of the League': Spiller, *Ethical Movement*, pp. 152–5.

12 Murray: White and Hayward, *Last Years* (see note 6 to Chapter 1 above), pp. 62–4, which contains an excellent Chapter 1 on Gould's 'Relation with Rationalists and Ethicists'. Gould: *Moral Instruction: Its Theory and Practice* (Longmans, 1913), pp. ix, 18–19, 27–8, 43–4, 181–7.

13 Petition: *EW* (1 July 1899). Wallas: Webb, *Our Partnership* (see note 7 above), pp. 241–2 (diary entry of 5 June 1902).

Epilogue

1 Mr. Justice Dillon: *The Weekly Law Reports* (19 December 1980), 1573G–H: although saying he knew nothing of Buddhism, he pointed out he had received an affidavit from the celebrated judge and English Buddhist, Mr. Christmas Humphreys, which did not accept the suggestion that Buddhism denies a supreme being. The claim that the British sanctification of literary studies was debilitating: Tom Nairn, 'The English Literary Intelligentsia' in (ed.) Emma Tennant, *Bananas* (1977).

General index

Index

Index of ethicists